SUE THE BASTARDS!

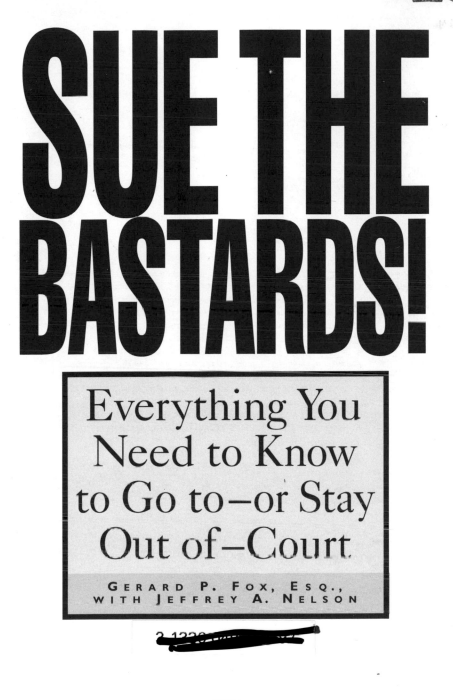

Everything You Need to Know to Go to—or Stay Out of—Court

GERARD P. FOX, ESQ.,
WITH JEFFREY A. NELSON

CB

CONTEMPORARY BOOKS

Library of Congress Cataloging-in-Publication Data

Fox, Gerard P.
    Sue the bastards! : everything you need to know to go to—or stay
out of—court / by Gerard P. Fox with Jeffrey A. Nelson ; illustrations by
Ariel McNichol.
        p.   cm.
    ISBN 0-8092-2874-2
    1. Law—United States—Popular works.   2. Trial practice—United
States—Popular works.   I. Nelson, Jeffrey A., 1956–   .   II. Title.
KF387.F69   1999
347.73'7—dc21   98-51655
                                                                    CIP

This book is not a substitute for hiring a lawyer; it is intended as a supplement to hiring legal counsel. Use this book to educate yourself about some common pitfalls of the litigation process, to assist in making your own evaluations about your case, and to help in working with your chosen attorney. The authors have endeavored to provide useful and accurate information. However, laws and procedures frequently change, are subject to different interpretations, and vary from one jurisdiction to the next. Therefore, the authors present the information in this book as is, without any warranty of any kind, express or implied, and are not liable for its accuracy nor for any loss or damage caused by your reliance on this information. It is your responsibility to make sure that the facts and general advice contained in this book are applicable to your situation.

Note: Throughout the book, for simplicity and brevity, the authors have used the personal pronouns *he, his, him,* and *himself* to refer to both males and females.

Cover design by Scott Rattray
Interior design by Impressions Book and Journal Services, Inc.
Interior illustrations by Ariel McNichol
Interior illustration concepts by Sabrina Nelson

Published by Contemporary Books
A division of NTC/Contemporary Publishing Group, Inc.
4255 West Touhy Avenue, Lincolnwood (Chicago), Illinois 60646-1975 U.S.A.
Copyright © 1999 by Gerard P. Fox and Jeffrey A. Nelson
All rights reserved. No part of this book may be reproduced, stored in a retrieval system, or transmitted in any form or by any means, electronic, mechanical, photocopying, recording, or otherwise, without the prior written permission of NTC/Contemporary Publishing Group, Inc.
Printed in the United States of America
International Standard Book Number: 0-8092-2874-2
99   00   01   02   03   04   BG   18   17   16   15   14   13   12   11   10   9   8   7   6   5   4   3   2

To my wife and partner, Claudia,
who has steadfastly served as my motivation and inspiration.
—Gerard Fox

To my loving parents, Jim and Mary-Armour;
to my cherished wife, Sabrina;
and to my three little angels, Randa, Nina, and Willie;
may you never need this book.
—Jeff Nelson

Contents

Preface   xi

1   Sue the Bastards—or Turn the Other Cheek?   1
The "Litigation Reaction"   2
A Lawsuit Is a Business Venture   3
Evaluating Your Potential Investment   3
Leap Before You Look?   4
Cool Down!   5
What Can You Gain? What Can You Lose?   5
Seek Advice from Trusted Advisers   6
Avoid Bad Legal Advice from Friends   7
How Much Will Your Case Cost?   8
Take Inventory of Your Exposure   11
Let It Go if You Can   12
Cutting Your Losses   13
Preparing Yourself for Battle   14

2   How Much Will It Cost?   17
"Fees" Versus "Costs"   18
Fee Arrangements   19
Contingency Does Not Always Mean "Free"   24
Too Strong a Case for Contingency?   26
The Contingency Lawyer: Who's in Charge?   27
Cost Estimates   28
Your Cost-Benefit Analysis   29

3   Hiring Perry Mason   33
How Do I Find a Lawyer?   34
Interview More than One Attorney   35

Do You Want to Retain Mr. Big?   36
How Corporations Hire Lawyers   36
You Deserve the Same Treatment   37
A Lawyer Should Impress, but You Don't Have to Fall in Love   39
Avoid the Conveyor Belt   39
Attorneys Who Specialize   42
The Perfect Attorney   43

4   **Preparation and the Demand Letter**   **45**
Preparation Saves You Money   45
Should You Send a Demand Letter?   47
Don't Buy a Worthless Demand Letter   49
What May Work; What Never Will   50
Defense Mentality   51
To Demand or . . . ?   52
Handle with Care   53

5   **Nuts and Bolts: Before Filing**   **55**
Plaintiff, Defendant, and Parties   55
Your Claims or Defenses   56
What Relief Is at Issue?   60
Burden of Proof   61
Statute of Limitations   62
If You're a Corporation or a Partnership   64
Insurance Coverage   65
Selling the Rights to Your Lawsuit   66
Jurisdiction   67
Venue   68
Judge, Jury, or Administrative Proceeding   69
Choice of Law and Venue Provisions   71
State Versus Federal Court   72

6   **Nuts and Bolts: Damages**   **75**
What Are Your Damages?   76
Forms of Monetary Damages   77
Be Reasonable in Your Request   80
Attorney's Fees   81
Damages from the Defendant's Perspective   82
Damages and Discovery: Opening Pandora's Box?   82

7   **Nuts and Bolts: The Complaint   87**

What's in the Complaint?   88
Getting It Right the First Time   89
The Complaint as Public Document   91
Step by Step Through the Complaint   92
Amending Your Complaint   99
How Quickly Should You File?   100
Is Your Lawyer Stalling?   101
Why You Must Understand the Legal Jargon   104
Inviting Trouble   106
The Summons   107
Serving Your Complaint   109

8   **Nuts and Bolts: The Defendant's Turn   113**

Strategy: What's in Your Best Interest?   114
Filing the Answer   116
Procedural Technicalities   117
Countersuits   121

9   **Nuts and Bolts: Written Discovery   123**

What Is Discovery?   124
What Is Discoverable?   125
Forms of Discovery   125
Service   141
Discovery Referees   141
Confidentiality Agreements   142
Subpoenas and Motions to Quash   145
Attorney-Client Privilege   146

10   **Nuts and Bolts: Written Discovery and Discovery Motions   149**

When the Other Side Doesn't Comply   150
Discovery as Harassment   152
When They Hit Below the Belt   154
A Preemptive Strike to Avoid Discovery Fights   155

11   **Nuts and Bolts: Depositions   159**

Deposition Basics   160
Loose Lips Sink Ships   161

Check Your Ego at the Door   162
Nothing but the Truth   162
Prepare for Your Deposition   175
Reading the Transcript   176

12   Witnesses   177
Getting to Know Your Witnesses   178
More than Just the Facts, Mac   179
Biased Witnesses   181
Contacting Your Witnesses   182
Naming Your Witnesses   184
Think from Your Witness's Perspective   185
Getting Witness Statements   187
Out-of-State or "Unavailable" Witnesses   188
Having Your Lawyer Represent a Witness   189

13   Motion for Summary Judgment or Adjudication   193
What the Summary Judgment Motion Means   194
Timing for Filing a Summary Judgment Motion   195
The Defendant's Strategy   196
The Plaintiff's Strategy   199
Motion for Summary Adjudication   201
Final Thoughts   203

14   Experts and Expert Exams   205
What Does an Expert Do?   206
Experts Versus Consultants   207
Do You Need an Expert?   208
Bench Versus Jury Trial   209
Designating Your Expert   209
Qualifying Your Expert   210
Budgeting for an Expert   210
Who Talks to Experts?   212
Experts Help Rich Defendants Most   213
What Makes a Good Expert?   214
Common Mistakes and Problems   215
Expert Reports   216

Cross-Examining the Expert: Things to Keep in Mind 217
When an Expert Examines You 218

15 Alternative Dispute Resolution 223
The Mediation Process 224
Why You Might Want to Mediate 226
Why You Might Not Want to Mediate 228
The Arbitration Process 231
Creative Settlements 232
Where to Find Mediators and Arbitrators 233

16 Trial Preparation 235
Exhibits 236
Witness Preparation 238
Preparing for Cross-Examination 240
The Longest Day 243
See the Sausage Being Made 244
Trial Prep Costs 245

17 The Trial 247
The Courtroom as Theater 248
Chronology of a Trial 249
A Jury or a Bench Trial? 251
Selecting Your Jury 252
Jury Costs 254
Pretrial Motions 255
Decisions About Witnesses 256
The Verdict Form 259
Conducting Yourself at Trial 260
Who's in Charge of Your Case? 261
What if You Win? 263

18 The Appeals Process 265
Your Right to an Appeal 266
Basis for Appeal 266
Motion for a New Trial 268
Filing a Notice of Appeal 268

Stay of Judgment 269
Designating the Record 270
Exchange of Briefs 271
Oral Arguments and Ruling 272
Why You May Need an Appellate Specialist 273
How Much Will It Cost? 274
The Easiest Way to Blow a Winnable Case 275
"Appealing" an Arbitration Decision 276
Appealing Decisions of Administrative Agencies 277
You May Only Appeal "Final" Decisions 277

19 Your Legal Bills   279
How the Law Firm Generates Your Bill 280
Examining Your Legal Bills 281
Learning the Law 284
Learning Your Business 285
The Importance of the Estimate 286
Ask Questions and Keep a Loose Leash 287
Phone Calls with You and Opposing Counsel 289
Staffing 290
Billing for Costs 293
Review of Backup 298
The Client Must Be Honest, Too 299

20 You and Your Lawyer: A Special Relationship   301
Active Periods 302
Being a Good Client 303
Walk a Fine Line 304
Don't Throw Your Good Sense out the Window 305
Avoid Litigation Burnout 306

Appendix A: Cost-Benefit Analysis 309

Appendix B: Examples of Retainer Agreements 317

Glossary 325

Index 331

Preface

Fools and obstinate men make lawyers rich.

—Henry George Bohn,
19th-century English publisher

Litigation was originally conceived as a hearing or trial between two adversaries before a judge or jury of their peers. In fact, this trial, in which both sides placed their evidence before the finder of fact, used to be the main event in a litigation. All that was required was some moxie, money, and a lawyer with charisma and charm.

Today, the process of litigation involves much more than the ultimate trial on the merits. The filing of a lawsuit places in motion a process that certain lawyers don't fully understand and that often spins out of control. Many litigants go emotionally or financially bankrupt before their lawsuit is resolved. In short, litigation has become more a process than an event—and a challenging, frustrating, and potentially expensive process at that.

The goal of this book is to counsel people who are contemplating filing a suit or are defending a suit for the first time. This book will instruct you on how to evaluate whether to file a suit (or how to work with a lawyer to defend a claim that is filed); how to find competent, cost-effective legal counsel; and how to follow your case to a successful conclusion without going bankrupt or crazy.

I will overview the litigation process from the decisions that go into filing a lawsuit, to filing a complaint, through the discovery process, and ultimately the trial. I will discuss how to work with your attorney and manage your case, and will help you construct a realistic budget for your case. I will also review alternative means of dispute resolution, such as arbitration and mediation.

If you have picked up this book, I'm assuming you are faced with a problem that goes beyond the day-to-day challenges of your personal life or business, the type of problem that involves the assertion of "claims" and "defenses." My goal is to help you manage this legal problem so that you minimize your out-of-pocket costs and maximize your return on investment. If you're already halfway into your case and are starting to pull your hair out, read this book, and maybe you won't need a toupee by the time it's over. Your best bet, though, is to read this book *before* you reach that point.

The first and most important mistake to avoid in litigation is the expectation that you can just hand your case over to a lawyer, who will then treat it as though it were as important to him as it is to you. Too many litigants go into a lawsuit believing that their lawyer will simply take over and take all necessary steps to ensure that everything goes as the client would want it to go. These people expect that a lawyer will correctly evaluate their case, make the right moves at the right time, and essentially tell them when to show up, where to collect the check, and what kind of champagne to pop open at the end. It seldom, if ever, happens that way.

You wouldn't just give a broker a pile of money and say, "Handle it and call me when I'm a millionaire." If a doctor told you that you needed surgery, you wouldn't just lie down on an operating table and tell the doctor, "Handle it and wake me when I'm cured." If you're like most people, you would try to educate yourself first. Perhaps you would find experts to talk to. You'd probably also read, explore alternatives, and try to learn from the experience of others who faced similar situations. People will do this when their health and money are involved, but many fail to go through the same kind of research before launching into a lawsuit—something that can certainly affect your finances *and* health!

The problem with this thinking becomes painfully apparent when your legal costs cut into your vacation money or life savings, or when you come out in the red, even after winning your case. Or worse, after losing your case, you realize you should have stayed on top of it more.

Lawyers are always more ready to get a man into troubles than out of them.

—Oliver Goldsmith, 18th-century English writer

This book is not about how you can be your own lawyer. It's about how to work with a lawyer and understand what a lawyer does. To effectively manage your lawsuit, you need to educate and prepare yourself for what may lie ahead—so you can be certain your lawyer is preparing properly and protecting your interests.

Lawsuits are sometimes the only way to ensure a fair resolution of a problem. They can serve a valuable function in helping secure justice. But they do come with a cost, whether you're paying your lawyer on a contingency or hourly basis, and sometimes a very heavy one. Figure out what that cost will be. Weigh it carefully and make an informed decision.

If you decide to proceed with a lawsuit, become knowledgeable about litigation before you begin. As with anything in life, mistakes will be made in your case, and you won't win every battle. The key is to reduce the mistakes and losses, and to avoid a fatal blow. If you can do that, you've put yourself in the strongest position to fight the good fight, to get the other side to settle, or—if necessary—to present your facts before a jury—and get justice.

1

"I want my lawyer."

Sue the Bastards— or Turn the Other Cheek?

Go not for every grief to the physician,
nor for every quarrel to the lawyer,
nor for every thirst to the pot.

—George Herbert, 17th-century English poet

The other day as I was picking up my two-year-old son, Jacob, from day care, I saw another child push him and grab his toy. Jacob exploded: "Mine!" He was hurt and angry at having his space violated and his property snatched. Like many two-year-olds, his first response was to scream, push the other kid back, and get even.

As a litigator, I am very familiar with reactions like my son's. I see this behavior almost every time a new client marches into my office. The people who walk through my door have one thing in common: they're seething. They feel that something terrible has happened to them, and not just some kind of ordinary life occurrence but

1

something so upsetting that they feel some important part of their life is out of sync. Until they resolve the emotions of this issue, their lives won't get back on track. They want satisfaction, and too often their emotions have completely overcome their reason. All they want to hear is how they can annihilate some bad guys in court, and a lawyer can easily feed the fire of their indignation, get a retainer agreement signed, and charge ahead.

In this state of mind, you have preordained your own fate. You've come to the office of a litigator. The litigator makes money by helping people sue other people. Your emotions are running away with you; you're just waiting to hear how you can get even. What's going to happen? Very often, the litigator is going to sell you a lawsuit!

If you buy a lawsuit in this state of mind, you may later come down with a serious case of buyer's remorse.

The "Litigation Reaction"

For lack of a better term, I have come to call the state of mind I first see in many potential clients the "litigation reaction." It's the same passion that made my two-year-old want to get even, and it often triggers lawsuits.

Perhaps you've been wrongfully terminated or sexually harassed at work, were physically injured or defamed, or want more alimony or a larger inheritance. Maybe a supplier breached a contract, your neighbor built a fence on your side of the property, your landlord refuses to make a repair, or a tenant refuses to pay his rent. All of these situations are very emotional, and lawsuits are usually born of an emotional reaction. If you're like many of the people I've observed, you're going to spend little or no time weighing the potentially colossal consequences of engaging in litigation.

What if you woke up with a sore elbow and went to see a specialist, who advised you to get surgery on your elbow? What would you do? Most people would carefully consider this diagnosis, perhaps get a second opinion, and check their health insurance coverage. They might talk with someone who had gone through similar surgery, discuss alternatives, or investigate unconventional approaches to dealing with the problem. They'd carefully consider a variety of approaches and potential outcomes, taking time to ascertain that they're making the best decision.

People will do this with regard to their physical health, but just about every person who comes through my door with a legal problem is ready to file suit immediately and begin a process that can often have bigger emotional, financial, and even physical long-term effects than major surgery. Unlike surgery, a lawsuit doesn't generally unfold in just a day or two; it can involve a commitment of several years. Ultimately, it might even require a longer rehabilitation process than major surgery.

A Lawsuit Is a Business Venture

The problem is that lawsuits often have too much to do with "Damn it! I'm pissed off!" and too little with "What exactly am I getting into? Is filing a suit a good investment of my time and money?" Too often people don't realize that ultimately a lawsuit is a business decision. And as with any other business decision, you have to take time to think it through carefully. I am still amazed when I observe the lack of thought that goes into many people's desire to file a lawsuit.

Repeatedly I observe plaintiffs several months into a lawsuit suddenly realize that the lawsuit itself—the emotional and/or financial toll of ongoing litigation—feels much worse than what they originally filed suit over. If these people had not been so irate at the start, and had they been able to take a dispassionate view of their situation and an informed view of what litigation entails, perhaps they would have understood that a lawsuit was not the right solution to their problem.

Evaluating Your Potential Investment

Before deciding to file a lawsuit, you must estimate how much your lawsuit will cost (financially, emotionally, professionally) and how much personal exposure you have. Even if you're prosecuting your case on a contingency basis (which, as I'll discuss later, doesn't mean "free"), you have exposure.

At the same time, you must develop a concrete and realistic idea of how strong your claim or claims are and what damages you can likely recover. The key will be to weigh how much time, money, and emotional commitment you'll probably be making to file and carry your lawsuit through to its conclusion—a trial—against what you might recover in your situation. The goal of this cost-benefit analysis is to weigh the potential upside against the potential downside. Do this *before* you file your lawsuit, *before* you set into motion a series of actions that will take on a life of their own.

How do you educate yourself? I'll get into specifics in Chapter 2, but in essence you do it by reading the rest of this book, speaking with your counsel, and getting a good sense of what may lie ahead if you file suit. By educating yourself and identifying what can happen in your litigation, you'll position yourself to make an intelligent cost-benefit analysis. Only then can you decide whether you want to invest a chunk of your life in a lawsuit.

Leap Before You Look?

A motion picture producer was very upset with her employer, an independent production company. She was so mad (red flag number 1) that she couldn't see any way of dealing with the production company other than to sue. She reasoned that filing a lawsuit was the quickest way to get what she was owed because, damn it, she was right and could prove it! She was certain that as soon as she filed suit, an immediate settlement would be forthcoming (red flag number 2).

This woman suffered from the same affliction that I see in just about everyone who comes to my office. I call it the it's-a-breeze disease. It causes thinking that goes like this: "I'm going to file my complaint, and poof, they'll crumble. They're going to get served with this lawsuit, and then, bang, they'll settle!" It rarely happens that way.

As it turned out, the producer filed suit and didn't get a settlement, but, bang, she was countersued! Although warned this might happen, she hadn't considered it.

As time wore on the lawsuit was going well, but there were great consequences to my client. She became more and more stressed, and was less able to focus on other aspects of her life.

As she become more frustrated, she instructed my firm to become more and more aggressive. However, with every new tactic employed came a larger and larger legal bill.

Only after months of time-consuming, stressful, and expensive litigation did this client finally—out of sheer desperation—open her mind to a more objective analysis of her situation and form an alternative dispute resolution.

Cool Down!

Filing a lawsuit will take a toll on your budget, your family, and your life—often for two or three years, sometimes longer. All too frequently, people don't consider this but are overtaken by the immediate reaction to push back when their rights have been violated, just as my son pushed back in day care. Never view a lawsuit as an adult way to "push back." It isn't just a five-minute skirmish at the bus stop. The process can be long and involved, expensive, and fraught with all sorts of hidden repercussions; it should never be launched in haste.

If you're considering litigation, first give yourself a cooling-off period. You may not decide to be passive or to turn the other cheek, but you need to give yourself a time-out. Try to put the emotional part of the problem aside and get the perspective you need to evaluate matters objectively.

What Can You Gain? What Can You Lose?

Get a notepad and draw a line down the center of the page, dividing it into two halves. At the top of the left half, write, **Pro;** on the right side write, **Con.** Under **Pro,** write down every reason you can think of for suing—the benefits you hope to obtain. These usually include money, but they could also include obtaining a court order against someone (e.g., to stop using your material or to remove their fence from your property). Benefits might also include emotional satisfaction, such as the vindication of getting a public verdict against someone or preventing someone from "getting away with it."

Under the list of benefits, write what you think is the best-case scenario for suing. Go ahead and fantasize a bit. At this point, you will not know what your damages or potential recovery might be, but you'll refine your list as you proceed in this book. Following your best-case scenario, list the major facts that you believe support your right to get the benefits you envision: "He slandered me" or "She's using my trademark without permission."

Under **Con,** list the potential negatives as you now see them, including, say, the expense of suing, the time it could take, the emotional stress and strain of being in a lawsuit, and any concerns that the defendant could come up with some adverse evidence against you. Think about the facts or issues that might be of concern in your particular case. If there's some nagging question about the facts of your situation, write it on the **Con** side.

Finally, do a cost-benefit analysis by comparing the size and likelihood of the pros and cons. This basic cost-benefit analysis will be fleshed out throughout this book. A cost-benefit analysis of whether or not to sue is the most crucial exercise that you must do *before* you make the decision to sue. The rest of this book is about how to assess what expense, emotional stress, and pitfalls lay ahead in your particular situation if you decide to bring suit. You have to determine to your best ability what you might be stepping into. Remember, a lawsuit should never be viewed as revenge; it's a large investment of time, energy, and money.

> "Two farmers each claimed to own a certain cow. While one pulled on its head and the other pulled on its tail, the cow was milked by a lawyer."
>
> **—Jewish parable**

Seek Advice from Trusted Advisers

In developing your cost-benefit analysis, you're trying to take a dispassionate look at your situation. Take counsel from people you trust. You should consult as many key people in your life as you can about your situation. By "key people" I don't mean acquaintances around the water cooler or friends you like to gossip with. Talk to wise people who play important roles in your life: your spouse; business partner; accountant; minister, rabbi, or priest; a counselor. Tell them you're considering filing a lawsuit and consider their input. You're not trying to get them to rubber-stamp your urge to sue but to provide some perspective.

You need to bounce your ideas off other people because you often can't make such an important decision on your own. You are the one who's been wronged, whose rights have been violated, whose foot has been stepped on. Thus, it will be difficult for you to take the most balanced look at the situation by yourself.

If friends, family, and trusted advisers are counseling you to slow down, to explore alternatives to a lawsuit, that's a good indication that you should think long and hard about what you're considering undertaking.

Avoid Bad Legal Advice from Friends

Some people—even some lawyers—will listen to you pour out your story and tell you, "To hell with those bastards! Sue 'em!" People constantly end up in my office because some lawyer-friend they ran into at a cocktail party has led them to think their case will be a walk in the park. It doesn't occur to these people that their lawyer-friend handles real estate deals or contracts for the phone company or divorces, but never a case like theirs.

A real analysis of your case from a legal perspective doesn't involve a five-minute conversation over drinks. It's an involved process of analyzing a claim and the proof that needs to be gathered, the potential defenses or countersuit the other side could raise, what court your case would be filed in, how much it's going to cost, and the fact that you, your life, your family, your budget, and your everyday existence are on the line.

What if you said, "Hey, I have a chance to fight Mike Tyson," and your friend said, "What the heck, get in the ring and take your shot!" Would you go into the ring? You're the one taking the punches, not your friend, and it's always a great deal easier said than done.

Remember, too, that when your rights have been violated, your friends are going to be very sympathetic. To begin with, they already know you, believe you, and want you to win. (A jury won't start off with the same bias.) Then, your friends probably haven't heard the other side of the story—and there's always another side. (Even if it's "pure fabrication," there is another side.) Finally, the issue you're thinking of suing over isn't life and death for your friends. They're not really involved, so it doesn't cost them anything to be supportive and say, "Go get the bad guys!"

How Much Will Your Case Cost?

Suing is going to cost you time and money, even if you represent yourself. For example, if you file a simple action in small-claims court, you have to go down to the court, get forms, fill them out, return, and file them. You might miss a day of work, and you pay a filing fee, perhaps parking costs, and additional costs to have the other party served using the court-required process. You have to spend time gathering, thinking about, and preparing your proof, and you'll probably take another day off work for the trial.

The trial itself can be a very stressful, difficult experience. And if you win and get a judgment against the other party, that doesn't mean your opponent will pull out his wallet and pay you right then and there. You may have to collect on the judgment yourself. You may have to go back to court to fill out even more forms and have them served. Maybe you'll have to hire a firm that collects on judgments, or you might have to pay a sheriff to collect your money. You might even have to take something called a Debtor's Exam, and that can be expensive and time-consuming, too. All of this can certainly amount to more time and money than you would spend going out for dinner and a movie or buying a bag of groceries, so unless you're wealthy and don't care, you'd better think through your decision to sue and estimate the total costs.

How do you figure out the potential cost of your case? By asking the lawyer you're thinking of hiring? You certainly should discuss costs with a potential lawyer, so long as you keep one thing in mind: **Do not simply rely on an attorney to advise you whether you should sue and how much your lawsuit would cost.**

Yes, this is an attorney speaking. Why can't you rely on an attorney's initial estimates and evaluations? Well, for a few reasons, most notably the attorney's perspective.

A baker is in the business of baking goods and, in the end, selling those baked goods. A litigator is in the business of litigating. Now, while it would be unfair to say that all or even most litigators are looking to sell you a lawsuit, litigating is in fact how they earn a living. Like anyone, lawyers must pay their rent and put food on the table. They're also trained to look at a dispute from an adversarial perspective, so when you walk in their door, their initial reaction to your situation may be to encourage you to sue. You're there to evaluate whether you want to hire them, so they want to show you that they are willing to defend your rights and to kick the stuffing out of the other side. They'll try to impress you with their machismo, intellect, and commitment to you.

Don't assume that the first lawyer you consult with will be entirely objective about whether you should litigate your problem, as opposed to settling or not filing suit at all.

I have had clients referred to me by a transactional attorney, or their manager or accountant, and they are just seething. Sometimes the person who referred one of these angry people was too afraid to suggest that the best course of action was probably to cool off and leave the issue in the past. Instead, I get the referral. Of course, when a prospective client comes in to see me, I don't want to seem like a wimp, either. After all, the sign outside my office doesn't say "mediator"; it says "litigator." I'm going to show prospective clients that I identify with their angst and am willing to be forceful and stand up for their rights. That's what I focus on in the first meeting: "Thank you for coming here. I have the expertise. I will be aggressive in asserting your rights."

The potential client, on the other hand, is frequently trying to market his claim to me. He's trying to persuade me that he'll be a good client. He wants me to be intrigued by his case, to be interested in him.

What's being withheld here? Well, on the litigator's side, he doesn't really know enough about you or your situation to be able to give you much useful advice yet. While you might actually be able to win a million dollars, the best advice for you may be that, due to considerations in your marriage or business life or the college tuition payments you've committed to, you'd be better off to settle the matter for $200,000. Or maybe the best advice would be to try to forget about it; it's going to be too expensive and complex to prove in court. There could be several personal factors a lawyer will have no way of knowing about early on, but that absolutely should be factored into your decision to sue. The lawyer won't be familiar enough with your financial situation or other important considerations in your life. Even if he were, some lawyers may not *want* to tell you to stop and think. Remember, in England lawyers are called "solicitors." Some will try to solicit your business—to sell you a lawsuit. You can't assume that in your first meeting a litigator is going to lead you through the carefully balanced analysis you should be making, and that he can truly advise you what's best for you in your particular situation.

What's the client holding back? Often, clients are reluctant to discuss financial limitations. Maybe the lawyer estimates that litigating the case will cost $75,000, and the client says, "Oᴋ, I can handle that." The client is really thinking that he's going to have to get a second job and work weekends, borrow money from his parents, use his credit card, and pray he'll be able to survive. Clients who are under financial pressure and don't pay their bills promptly almost never disclose that in the first meeting. Nor do they mention the bits of bad evidence against them.

In sum, potential clients, like most lawyers, treat the initial meeting as if it's a first date; they're cautious about what they disclose.

Before your first meeting, go through your cooldown period, research any attorney you're considering hiring, and put together your cost-benefit analysis. Do your homework before you set foot in the door. You're not seeing a litigator just so at the end of the meeting you can say, "Sold! You're hired!" If the attorney makes a good impression, your next step might be to decide to have him spend some time investigating and looking into the law, studying your case, and then have a second meeting to decide how to more formally approach the issue.

This process is important whether you're a potential plaintiff or a defendant who's just been sued. Take a detached look at what's best for you. Should you settle? Should you try to postpone, or use discovery as an asset? Should you try to secure insurance coverage or offer mediation or arbitration to the other side? If you're a plaintiff, you need to consider whether to proceed at all, whether to make a demand or come out with your guns blazing.

Get to know a prospective lawyer and decide whether you are compatible with him from a financial standpoint and from the standpoint of personalities and goals. Figure out what's in the best interest of you, the client. Generally, there are a lot of options. The best answer may not be a lawsuit.

> A lawyer with a briefcase can steal more than a hundred men with guns.
> **—Don Corleone in Mario Puzo's *The Godfather***

When an attorney makes an initial estimate early on, remember that it's going to take more than just twenty minutes to work up a budget of any accuracy or usefulness. You'll need to take into account myriad factors that can affect the litigation, many of which are the subject of the rest of this book. Some also have to do with who the defendant would be and how that person might respond to your suit. An attorney probably can't take all this into account in one meeting, but it can have a significant impact on the potential cost of your case. (In Chapter 2 we'll explore asking an attorney to prepare a budget based on detailed input and give you an itemized breakdown of potential costs. This can be very useful, but some attorneys may charge to do it.)

Take Inventory of Your Exposure

Although I hate to liken litigation to a street fight, it's often like that. Let's say a kid trips you every time you get on the school bus. You have options. You can go to another bus stop; you can find a friend who will try to mediate things for you; you can punch him. If you're going to brawl, be ready to receive some blows in return. (In my experience defendants are far more emotional than plaintiffs. They're usually thinking, "How dare he sue me! I'll teach him!" They'll look for every piece of garbage they can possibly throw at you. They would have you jailed if they could.)

Take a close, objective look at yourself. Sure, you're angry, and you perceive that you're 100 percent in the right and they're 100 percent in the wrong, but that doesn't mean a jury will agree. Cases are decided by third parties: judges and juries. The members of a jury collectively try to come to what they believe to be a fair resolution. Juries have their own biases and prejudices, so you can't simply assume that a judge or jury will affirm your side of the argument.

Part of your lawyer's job will be to provide an objective overview of how a judge or jury might see your case. Lawyers who are busy with other cases and overly eager to get your business may not do that. So you need to take inventory of yourself and ask yourself the following questions:

- Why am I suing?
- What, precisely, do I hope to gain?
- How can I cool down, step back, and gain perspective? Who can I talk to help me see things objectively?
- What goes into a lawsuit? Can I afford it?
- Could I get sued back? If I did, could I afford that? Will my fee arrangement be different with my attorney if that happens?
- Can I find a contingency attorney who would agree as part of the agreement to defend me if I were countersued?
- Can I handle the pressure of a lawsuit?
- Could I handle the pressure of being a defendant as well as a plaintiff?

Let It Go if You Can

We lawyers know well, and may cite high authority for it if required, that life would be intolerable if every man insisted on his legal rights to the full.

—Sir Frederick Pollock, English judge, 1845–1937

One of your aspirations in life is to coach a Little League team. Finally, Big Chief Muckety Muck of your town's Little League Association promises in a passing way that you can be the coach. You're ecstatic! You go out and buy all sorts of hats and baseball gear, and you tell your kids you're going to be the Little League coach. Life just doesn't get any better.

But suddenly, after you've gotten your hopes up and spent a fair amount of money, Big Chief Muckety Muck tells you, "Sorry, I gave the coaching job to somebody else." And you say, "To hell with that bastard!

I'm going to sue him!" It feels good to say that, and it sounds good. You talk to your friends around the dining room table, and they say, "Yeah, that son of a bitch, he *promised* you that job! He *promised,* and now he's breaking his promise! Go sue him!"

Well, my friend, maybe you think you should sue him. But in this world of ours, there's a certain amount of injustice that you have to learn to put up with. Have you found yourself in a tangle with someone like Chief Muckety Muck over an issue like Little League? If so, do yourself a favor and let it go.

Cutting Your Losses

Let me give you an example of someone who, I believe, came out way ahead by doing her homework before jumping into litigation.

A woman who worked at a large and well-known corporation came to me very distressed. An executive in the company had sexually harassed her—teased, propositioned, and even groped her. She finally complained and was fired. She had carefully documented what had happened, and had two witnesses, who were both still at the company. She seemed to be in an excellent position in terms of proof. She was also a member of a minority group in a district where that group would likely be well represented in the jury pool. And she was a very strong, credible witness. In short, I felt the company had "stepped in it" in a big way, and this woman had a great lawsuit.

The company was denying this woman her severance pay, which was $60,000. When she first came to me, she was thinking, "I'm not going to let them get away with this. I want to sue!" After we discussed her case for a while, I suggested she take some time to cool off, and I stressed the importance of doing a cost-benefit analysis. I also told her I felt she had an excellent case and that I would be happy to represent her.

This woman was intelligent. She spoke with other lawyers, family members, and friends. She had insisted that I provide her with a detailed, realistic budget to file suit before she would retain me. She went through that budget objectively, and from her questions, I could see that she was diligently educating herself about litigation.

Ultimately, her focus changed. What was most important to her, she decided, was to make certain that she could move on in her career. She wanted to evaluate whatever course she took with this idea as a central concern. Her business objectives were meaningful to her, and she felt there would be several potential downsides to filing a lawsuit—and not just the financial cost. She was worried she might be blackballed by other prospective employers in her field. Additionally, she came from a culture where it was considered inappropriate to assert this kind of claim in a lawsuit, and that was another major consideration for her.

Ultimately, rather than filing suit, my client decided to make a reasonable demand for an amount lower than the full amount to which she was entitled. If the corporation would pay that amount, she would cut her losses, not file the lawsuit, and move on. She ultimately received the sum she demanded and shortly thereafter found an excellent job at another company.

Many people might suggest she made the wrong decision. She did have a strong case against a bigwig at a large, highly visible corporation. While the corporation would have fought hard, this woman probably could have won a big judgment or settlement in the end. But considering this individual's professional, personal, and cultural concerns, she made the best decision for herself. She was able to calm down emotionally and contemplate the big picture. As a lawyer, I couldn't have initially done that for her, because there's no way at the outset I could take into account her life, health, budget, culture, family, and all the other concerns she contemplated. That kind of analysis is something only you, as a prospective plaintiff, can do yourself.

> I was never ruined but twice: once when I lost a lawsuit, and once when I won one.
>
> **—Voltaire (1694–1778)**

Preparing Yourself for Battle

Whether you're an individual, family, or small business, the first step in considering a lawsuit is to prepare a budget for your litigation. This applies whether you're hiring an hourly attorney or contingency attorney. Work the lawsuit into your family or company budget so that it's part of your everyday life for the next two years and so you're not grasping for money to pay your legal bill every month.

Next, expect litigation to be stressful. When you're under stress, it's important to eat right, sleep right, and exercise. Even if you aren't already doing those things, they will be even more important, and you need to recognize that as early as possible.

Your litigation may involve emotional issues. Perhaps you're very angry about the situation and it's affecting your sleep or your relationship with your spouse, boyfriend, girlfriend, or kids. Even if your case does not involve damages for emotional distress (see Chapter 6), it may be a good idea to find a counselor to talk to, perhaps even one who's had experience with people in litigation. Almost anybody in a lawsuit should have an emotional outlet, because there are going to be difficult moments: experiencing financial strain, being deposed, or hearing the other side tell lies about you.

Next, you may need to hang a huge poster somewhere in your house inscribed with the word *Patience!* You must develop patience. A lawsuit does not unfold like a one-hour episode of *LA Law*. It's almost akin to the cancer patient who goes for chemotherapy for two or three years. You're going to be in and out of court for a two- to three-year period. There will be lulls, and then there will be periods where the case is on a fast track. You've got to develop the ability to put the case out of your life once in a while, to enjoy a ball game or a family brunch.

Set up a filing system in your home or office. Most lawsuits generate truckloads of documents; you'll want copies of everything. Your attorney will have his own copies, but you will sometimes want to refer to pleadings, motions, and even depositions yourself. Get organized early on to prevent a paper nightmare, and then you won't have to ask your attorney for copies of documents he may have already given to you.

Set up a protocol for communicating with your attorney. Maybe you both use E-mail; maybe it's the phone. Be sure to insist that you receive a copy of every letter and document that relates to your case, and read them. Keep aware of the schedule for your case as it evolves. You don't want out-of-town trips or your family vacation to interfere with the deposition schedule. Start thinking ahead, and plan your life the way you would if you were going to have a baby arriving in nine months.

Before you launch the litigation missile, ask yourself again, "Is there some other way to resolve this?" If you can find a way other than a lawsuit, use it. Yes, litigation is a way to stand up to someone who's wronged you, but it's not that simple. It takes part of your life or your business; it sucks up resources. It is a blunt sword, not by any stretch of the imagination precise, dependable, or mechanical. It can be grueling, unpredictable, and frustrating.

You wouldn't get in a car and start driving if you didn't know where you were going. Don't file a lawsuit without some sort of road map either. The rest of this book is about what happens in litigation. Once you've formulated a reasonable estimate of the value of your claims, you can evaluate your potential costs (the time, money, and stomach juices you'll expend) in light of the potential benefit of your goal. The time to start being smart in a lawsuit is before you've taken any big steps.

You may decide that if you file suit and it hasn't settled by a certain date, then you're going to withdraw your suit. But if you cannot say at the outset that you'll drop it in x months if your case hasn't settled, then you need to be prepared to go the distance. What does "going the distance" mean? The following chapters will explain.

2

"We're very cost conscious here at Serve'em, Sue'em & Try'em."

How Much Will It Cost?

In law, nothing is certain but the expense.

—Samuel Butler

Any way you cut it, pursuing justice is not cheap. Syndicated columnist Jane Bryant Quinn put it eloquently: "Lawyers are operators of the toll bridge across which anyone in search of justice must pass." The question you need to have answered before you step onto that bridge is: How costly is the toll?

First off, it's virtually impossible to know what your suit will really cost. Why? Because in litigation, as in war, you can never predict what the other side will do. The defendant could raise the white flag before a shot is fired, figure out a way to bring in an armada of costly obstacles (even after you've won and are trying to collect your judgment), or do anything in between. You make a game plan as a plaintiff, but the defendant may decide to take a bunch of depositions, file a bunch of motions, or pull a bunch of legal maneuvers to wear you down. That translates to more of your lawyer's time, and more costs.

If it is almost impossible to know exactly what your suit is going to cost, you may wonder about the purpose of trying to make an estimate. Well, you may not be able to predict the exact future of a case you file, but you *can* determine a range of scenarios for how much money you might be spending. This is a critical step in doing a cost-benefit analysis, and you must take that step before signing up with a lawyer.

You will do best if you consult with more than one lawyer and consider having a lawyer prepare a budget for you (for an hourly case). Before you sign your life away and pull the trigger on your lawsuit, you need to be fully informed.

> Doctors purge the body, preachers the conscience, lawyers the purse.
>
> **—German proverb**

"Fees" Versus "Costs"

On whatever basis you hire an attorney, it's very important to know the distinction between legal "fees" and legal "costs." Fees are the compensation the attorney receives for the time he and his associates or employees gave to your matter. An hourly firm charges an hourly fee; in a contingency arrangement, the firm's fee will be a percentage of any recovery.

Costs are the out-of-pocket expenses associated with the litigation. Costs can include such items as court charges to file a complaint, an answer, a motion, an opposition to a motion, or other court documents; charges for messengers to deliver documents to the court, a witness, or the other side of the lawsuit; charges for a court reporter to attend a deposition to record and transcribe everything that was said; charges for a witness's time to attend a deposition or trial and for his travel; costs to prepare exhibits for trial; costs for experts to conduct examinations, be deposed, and travel to and testify at trial; jury and court reporter fees at trial. For a typical personal injury case, it's easy to rack up $5,000, $15,000, or even as much as $30,000 in costs, if you have to take depositions, hire experts, and take the case to a jury trial. If you win at trial, it's possible to recoup a number of these types of costs, pursuant to certain statutes.

Costs can also refer to other amounts your attorney may charge on your case for nonsalary expenses, such as telephone charges, photo-copying, faxing, computer research fees, parking, mileage, and travel.

Fee Arrangements

There are essentially four ways you can retain a lawyer on most matters: flat fee, hourly fee, contingency fee, and modified contingency fee.

Flat-Fee Basis

A flat fee is a fee arrangement where you and the lawyer agree to a set price for the lawyer's complete services on your matter. In many states, lawyers drafting a will, assisting in filing bankruptcy, or handling a real estate transaction will quote you a flat fee for their total services. This is attractive because there will be no surprise charges; you know exactly what your matter will cost. It is very rare, however, to find a lawyer to prosecute or defend a lawsuit on a flat-fee basis. There are typically too many variables in litigation for a flat fee to be feasible.

Hourly Fee Basis

An hourly fee means that the lawyer and any associates or paralegals he puts on your case will work at set hourly rates, and you agree to pay for each hour or portion thereof that he or his staff works on your case. (This shouldn't include people who are supplied under overhead, though, such as a secretary, whose time you should not have to pay for, as discussed in Chapter 19.) Under an hourly fee agreement, you also agree to pay all of the costs associated with the litigation.

When you retain a lawyer on an hourly basis, he should inform you of his hourly rate and that of any of his employees who might work on your case. In most cases, you will also be required to pay a retainer at the time you hire the attorney. This amount is generally held by the attorney for the duration of the case and applied toward your final bill. It's the lawyer's "insurance" that he won't be stiffed should you fail to pay your bill.

Each month you will receive a detailed statement from the attor-ney, listing the time each employee spent on your case and specifically what that person did. You should also receive a detailed breakdown of any costs incurred during that period. Generally you will be expected to pay the fees and costs within thirty days. (For more details on billing, see Chapter 19.)

When you retain an hourly attorney, don't be afraid to negotiate any of the terms he's proposing. He may tell you his firm requires a $5,000 retainer. If that seems too steep, ask if he will accept $3,000, $2,000, or $1,000. Attorneys often make such accommodations, and some might take your case with no retainer at all. (Don't count on it, though.)

It's also possible to negotiate a reduction in the hourly rate of the attorney or other people who might be working on your case. Large companies often negotiate fee reductions based on the volume of work they will be bringing in. If you have what may become a large piece of litigation, or if some other aspect of your case makes it potentially very attractive to an attorney (celebrity cases or cases with a lot of potential for publicity for the firm), you may have the clout to negotiate reductions.

Fee Cap

After doing your cost-benefit analysis, you may conclude you would be comfortable spending only up to x dollars on your matter. You may realize that the potential cost of your case could be substantial, but if you are assured that the case would only cost you x dollars, it would be worth pursuing. If so, try to find an attorney who will agree to do your case for your maximum. The amount your attorney agrees will be the maximum he will charge you for working on your case is called a fee cap. Once you've paid that amount, the attorney will continue working on your case at no charge until you have a settlement or verdict (or whatever other conclusion you and the attorney agree to).

For example, let's say you've reviewed your case and have estimated the potential costs and your possible recovery. You've decided you would feel comfortable investing up to $20,000 in prosecuting your case, but you'd be uncomfortable spending more than that. Why not ask the lawyer to cap his fees at $20,000? See if you can get him to agree that once he has billed and you've paid a total of $20,000, he will finish the case at no further charge to you. Depending on how much that attorney charges per hour, how much work he envisions the case may entail, and how much risk he's willing to take, he just might go for it. If he won't, talk to another lawyer. There may be a good one who will agree to a fee cap.

Many lawyers, particularly sole practitioners, will accept the bird in the hand (with the possibility of doing some amount of work for free beyond that amount), versus watching your $20,000 worth of potential billing walk out the door. Naturally, for his own sake, the lawyer should inspect your case carefully before accepting such an arrangement, to see just how much work he might be getting himself into. The way he views your case after taking that hard look can be educational for you, whether or not you sign with that attorney.

If you negotiate a fee cap, it's important to specify whether the cap applies only to attorney's fees or to both fees and costs in the case. An attorney who agrees to cap his fees is most likely to ask you to continue paying the costs.

Contingency Fee Basis

Under a contingency fee arrangement, the attorney will charge you no legal fees unless and until your case settles or you win at trial and collect a judgment. At that time, the lawyer will receive an agreed-upon percentage of the recovery. What should that percentage be? It varies. Typically, an attorney asks for one-third of any recovery.

Nowadays, attorneys want to have escalation clauses in their agreements. These clauses provide for their percentage to increase at certain points, depending on how far your case goes before it is settled or resolved. A contingency fee attorney's percentage may start at 25 percent if recovery is obtained through negotiation, 30 percent after filing suit, and 35 percent (or higher) if it goes to trial. Depending on the kind of case and the reputation of the trial attorney, the fees may be even higher, up to 40 or even 50 percent for some top attorneys.

When a lawyer takes your case on contingency, he is in effect becoming your partner in the case. It's still your case and your lawyer cannot settle it without your permission, but now he's investing his time and (frequently) his money in your claim. He now has a financial stake in the outcome. He gets paid—or doesn't—based on how the dice roll in your case.

Not every case lends itself to contingency. Personal injury cases—cases where you were hurt in a car, job, medical, or other accident—

are the most common ones taken by contingency attorneys, but by no means the only type. If a lawyer believes you have a strong claim, with good proof and damages and a good chance of prevailing, he may be willing to take your case on contingency. (Just because a lawyer won't take your case on contingency doesn't mean he believes you have a weak claim or will lose at court. He may believe that your case represents more work than he wants or can afford to take on contingency. Or your case may not be the type he's had a lot of experience with, and he doesn't want to "go to school" on a new kind of case on a contingency basis.)

In addition to taking a percentage, most contingency agreements require that your lawyer's out-of-pocket costs be deducted from the settlement or judgment. This can become a sizable amount of money, depending how far the case has to be taken to resolve it. Here are some important cautions:

Make certain to define in writing what constitutes costs in this situation. It is reasonable for the attorney to expect to recoup out-of-pocket costs such as those commonly awarded to the winning side after trial in your state—generally items like expert fees, witness fees, costs of service, and filing fees. Recouping normal, everyday overhead costs, such as photocopying and phone charges, is another matter. A contingency agreement may call for you to reimburse the attorney for these office costs, or you may have to pay monthly office costs above and beyond the contingency fee. However, you should consider whether you really should have to pay charges for faxes and photocopying on your contingent case (particularly if these costs have a "profit" built in). You might be able to strike out such provisions. You may wish to incorporate into your retainer agreement a provision that the attorney must get your permission before spending over a certain sum of money on a given cost. Everything's negotiable, and you don't want to arrive at the end of your case with $30,000 in costs for a $30,000 win.

Also make certain you agree on the amount used to calculate the attorney's percentage. This amount—either the gross recovery or the net recovery after costs are deducted—is important. Let's say you settle for $50,000, and the attorney has already racked up $15,000 in costs. Deducting the $15,000 in costs from the $50,000 settlement leaves a net recovery of $35,000. If the attorney takes 40 percent of this amount, then he'll get $14,000, leaving $21,000 for you (or 60 percent). If, on the other hand, the attorney took his 40 percent off the gross sum, the calculation would work out like this: 40 percent of $50,000 equals $20,000 (for the attorney's fee), leaving $30,000. Out of the $30,000 left over, deduct the attorney's $15,000 in costs, leaving $15,000 for you. You get nearly 50 percent more if the costs are deducted *before* he takes his cut!

When your attorney bases his percentage on the net recovery, he's got added motivation to keep his costs down. The more costs he racks up, the less of a net recovery for him, as well as you. If you have a very appealing case, you should use this argument to ask an attorney to consider taking his percentage off the net recovery.

Modified Contingency Basis

The other way you can retain a lawyer is on what I call a modified contingency basis. This generally means some sort of combination of hourly and contingency fees.

Perhaps you want your lawyer to work on a contingency basis but can't find an attorney willing to take your case. Perhaps you've asked an hourly attorney if he will give you a fee cap, and he needs some additional incentive to agree to your terms. It's time to get creative.

I have worked with certain clients on a modified contingency basis. Here's a hypothetical example. Bob, already a plaintiff in a lawsuit, is referred to me by a colleague of mine. He is looking for a new attorney for his case. The defendant in this matter is represented by an insurance company, which is trying to run Bob off by making the litigation enormously expensive. Bob asks me to prepare an estimated budget for bringing his case to trial and trying it.

A few days after our initial meeting, Bob calls me and says there is no way he could ever pay the amount of money I estimated it would take to prosecute his claim, even in the best-case scenario I'd offered. He requests I cap my hourly fees at about half of the best-case scenario, and from that point forward work on a contingency basis. Once I billed the total he could pay, I would switch to a contingency basis on his case and collect $x\%$ of the settlement or judgment. He also asks if I will reduce my hourly rate and the rates of my associates by about 25 percent, so that the money he will have to spend in order to reach the cap will go further.

I like Bob and feel he has a good case. I do my own cost-benefit analysis of the situation and end up accepting his proposal with one condition. I can see investing my time on the case after the fee cap, but I know the costs at trial could be substantial and feel uncomfortable about getting stuck shelling out the huge costs associated with a trial a year down the road. So Bob and I agree that after we hit the fee cap, Bob will continue to pay all the costs of the case, and I will switch to a contingency.

There are as many possible modified contingency fee arrangements as there are lawyers, clients, and cases. Be creative and don't be afraid to haggle. If an attorney wants to work with you, wants you as a client, but can't take your case on a pure contingency basis, maybe he can do it on some modified basis. You need to look at how much your case might cost and how much it might bring in, and then try to arrive at a percentage you'd be willing to share with the attorney in exchange for capping his fees.

No matter how you choose to retain an attorney, remember that everything is negotiable. Don't rush, but shop around and try to find a good attorney who's open to handling your case in the manner you can live with over the long haul. No matter what, you must think in terms of the long haul.

Contingency Does Not Always Mean "Free"

Some contingency attorneys will take your case on 100 percent contingency. They'll not only work on contingency, but they'll also advance all costs on your case, and if you lose, they may eat the loss. This is a virtually risk-free arrangement for a plaintiff; it's what you'd like to get if you're looking for a contingency arrangement. But consider what happens when you have a contingency arrangement and lose. If you sue someone and lose, the defendant will be able to file a motion to recover his costs.

So even if your own attorney charges you nothing for his time and your own costs, if you lose, you could be looking at paying out five, ten, or possibly thirty thousand dollars of the defendant's costs. And don't kid yourself—this happens. I've seen personal injury cases where a contingency lawyer encourages someone to sue the supermarket where he tripped and fell, the supermarket takes a hard line and makes no settlement offer, the case goes to trial, the plaintiff loses—and the supermarket gets $15,000 in costs against the plaintiff. No contingency lawyer is going to agree to pay the other side's costs if you lose.

Too often people decide to sue on a personal injury case, thinking, "What the hell! What do I have to lose?" The answer is, if you have a weak claim or your case takes an unexpected turn for the worse, you can lose a lot. Your 100 percent contingency lawyer might tell you that he's taking all the risk in your case and you should therefore defer to his judgment on matters in the suit, but if something goes wrong and you end up losing, it can cost you a lot of money. Remember, there is no such thing as a free lunch and litigation is no exception.

Also, most contingency agreements require that you pay costs. So although lawyers may advertise, "No recovery, no fees!" that doesn't mean, "No recovery, no charges to you." You may even be asked to advance some costs on your case. Some contingency attorneys ask clients to put down a "cost retainer," just as hourly attorneys will ask for a fee retainer. (In fact, in many instances the law prevents an attorney from paying costs himself.)

If you're thinking of filing a case with a contingency attorney, estimate at the beginning how much costs you can expect to pay. Don't be like Joe Schmoe, who's earning $30,000 a year and runs to Johnny Contingency-Fee, who tells Joe his case is a "slam dunk" and will never go to trial. A year and a half later, the case hasn't settled and Joe Schmoe's already paid more money in costs than he ever expected—ten thousand dollars! Now he's on the verge of going to trial and is learning he may have to pay another ten grand in costs, including $3,000 for that expensive expert he didn't anticipate hiring. This is not a good place for Joe to be. He should have thought through his exposure more carefully ahead of time. Now he may have to drop his suit because he can't afford to go on.

Some contingency agreements have a provision where the attorney can ask you at any given point to reimburse all costs on the case to date, or advance anticipated costs. Under such agreements, your contingency attorney may come to you and say, "I want to take the depositions of these three witnesses. I need $1,500." You'll probably think, "$1,500?

Where am I going to get that kind of money?" Don't allow these clauses, to become a surprise. These clauses may require that you pay the necessary money on ten or thirty days' notice. If you can't pay, the lawyer may withdraw because he can't prosecute the case in a manner that he believes he needs to. No court is likely to force an attorney to keep representing a client who won't honor his retainer and pay necessary costs (except perhaps if it's on the eve of trial and the judge believes the client's interests would be severely jeopardized if his lawyer bowed out).

Too Strong a Case for Contingency?

If an insurance company has already offered you a sum before you hire an attorney, it's not uncommon for the attorney to agree to accept a percentage based on any amount recovered beyond the company's offer. For example, say you were in a car accident and the other person's insurance company offered you $15,000, but you felt you were entitled to more. When you hire a contingency fee lawyer, offer to give him a percentage of anything he can bring in above the $15,000 you've already been offered without his help.

Remember Joe Schmoe, who was told by Johnny Contingency-Fee that his case was a slam dunk? Well, what if that's true? What if Joe's claims *are* extremely strong and the attorney knows it? He's eager to sign up Joe on a contingency basis. "Hey! No cash down, no risk to you!"

Then what happens? Johnny Contingency-Fee sends off a letter, and suddenly Joe has an offer to settle his matter for $200,000. Wow! He'll take it! But wait—all the lawyer did was write a letter for Joe, and now he's getting one-third of $200,000? Joe has just spent $60,000 to have a letter written!

Watch out for this scenario. Just because you can't afford or don't want an hourly attorney doesn't mean you should immediately sign over 33 percent of your claim to a contingency lawyer. There are all sorts of interim steps you can consider to prevent yourself from being locked into giving away such a large percentage of your recovery. You might want to hire a lawyer to write a strong, detailed demand letter, and then see what happens. I have had clients hire me on an hourly basis for the first two or three letters and through any negotiations, but when and if the time comes to file an expensive complaint, they want to pay a contingency fee. Maybe they rack up $500 or $1,500 in letters and negotiations and then reach a good settlement. If the letters don't work, they may ask me to go on contingency.

The Contingency Lawyer: Who's in Charge?

A contingency fee arrangement can be a good deal for a client, but you may have to work with your attorney to make sure your case is handled appropriately. The reason is that some contingency firms are high-volume firms by necessity. They have to take on a lot of cases so that they secure enough cash flow to pay for the time and money invested in what turn out to be losers. As a result, some of these firms are set up to handle many cases at once. The key for you is to make sure your case does not get lost in the shuffle. If you want your lawyer to make your case a priority, then you need to stay involved and ask the type of questions suggested in this book.

Typically, a contingency fee lawyer will be in court on a regular basis. They may not return your phone calls on the spot. They are typically used to clients turning their cases over to them. The purpose of this book is to assure that you never "turn" your case over to just anybody—regardless of the fee arrangements. Be persistent.

If you sign with the wrong contingency firm they may want to do the minimum they feel they need to do (or have time to do), and your case may suffer as a result. With a good attorney, doing the minimum can actually turn out to be more efficient sometimes because it forces the attorney to pare your case down to its essence. A talented contingency attorney will be good at getting to the core. But a poor contingency attorney's tendency is to let too much work slide, and you may regret it later—if you even realize what's going on. This is why it's crucial for you to stay on top of your own case and be in a position to question, remind, and prod your attorney. If you can ask questions about work that should be done—and you do ask—and your attorney fails to do the work, you'll be able to change attorneys before it's too late.

Another hazard you may encounter with some contingency fee situations is that, even though by law only the client has the right to settle, in some instances the attorney may assume a controlling position. Because he feels like a partner in a joint venture, he may start advising you out of his own interests more than yours.

This can work a couple of different ways. Say you get an offer to settle your case for $100,000 and think, "$100,000 at the end of the day is good, and I'll be happy to walk away with that and pay my lawyer his cut." But the lawyer might tell you, "I know I can win a lot more money in a jury trial. Don't take this offer!" You may find yourself being pressured by your lawyer. Some attorneys may fail to inform you of the risk of turning down a decent settlement because they have decided to go for the gold. Remember the movie *The Verdict*, where Paul Newman's character rejects a $210,000 offer made to his clients (and doesn't even tell the clients about it at the time—a failure for which a real-life lawyer could be disciplined)? Newman's character thinks he's sitting on a huge case. He turns out to be right and hits the jackpot in the end. But that's a movie. In real life you don't want someone else's needs or desires deciding what's best for you; therefore, with some lawyers you may need to ask a lot of direct questions to make sure they're showing you the whole picture.

On the flip side, maybe you feel your case is worth a lot more than the $100,000 offer, but your attorney—out of his own considerations and interests and not necessarily yours—urges you to take the offer. What can you do about these kinds of situations? Put yourself in the best position to be able to ask questions, evaluate answers, and think for yourself.

Cost Estimates

If you retain an attorney on an hourly basis, you'll be expected to pay costs, and the same is true in many contingency fee arrangements. Even if your contingency fee attorney doesn't require you to advance costs, he will likely deduct them from any recovery.

As part of your cost-benefit analysis, try to estimate the costs associated with each task on your case. For example, if your attorney has to file a complaint, answer, motion, or other document with the court, there will generally be filing fees and messenger costs. If your lawyer takes a deposition, there will be costs associated with the court reporter who records it, as well as costs to obtain transcript copies.

Make sure to discuss these possible tasks with an attorney you're considering hiring, and be clear on what you might anticipate the costs being. Table 1 lists examples of typical costs; actual costs in your jurisdiction will vary.

Your Cost-Benefit Analysis

Before you decide whether or not to sue, get down to brass tacks. You might begin talking with lawyers at this stage, but you shouldn't retain one until you've run the potential numbers.

How do you do this? First, consider these questions:

- Are you going forward under a contingency or hourly deal, or do you hope to find some sort of modified contingency? Maybe you have no choice—you must find a contingency lawyer, or maybe no contingency lawyer is interested in your case.
- If you will have a contingency arrangement, will an attorney carry the costs on your case?
- Do you think that your case is so strong that you want to pay an hourly or flat fee for the first few letters and see what happens?
- Who is the defendant? What is his net worth? Is he "judgment proof" (without collectible assets)? Does he have insurance coverage to pay you to settle or if you win?
- If he has insurance coverage, are you prepared to confront an insurance company that could decide to mount an expensive defense to try to shake you?
- How many potential witnesses would need to be deposed for your case? (See Chapter 12 for how to decide.)
- What are your damages? How much money can you get if you win? What kinds of damage claims can you make and prove? Do you want to open up your life or business to a microscope from the other side? (Damages are discussed in Chapter 6.)

Table 1.   Typical Costs of Litigation.[1]

DESCRIPTION	COST
Civil complaint—filing fee	$235.00
Answer to complaint—filing fee	$232.00
Amend complaint—filing fee	$ 75.00
Motion—filing fee	$ 27.00
Summary judgment motion	$127.00
Jury fees (deposit)	$300.00
Witness fees:	
▪ Documents only, no appearance	$ 15.00
▪ Witness appearance	$ 35.00 + mileage per witness
▪ County employee, peace officers	$150.00 per witness
Process server (complaint, subpoena, file motion, etc.)	$ 25.00 to hundreds
Deposition fees	$800.00 or more per day
Attorney's parking and/or local travel costs (mileage)	$ 10 or more per hour
Attorney's transportation, meals, lodging, and other costs for out-of-town travel	$500 or more per day (average)
Fees to private investigators, photographers, graphic artists	$100 or more per hour (average)
Fees to experts for consultation and/or for appearance at deposition or trial	$200 or more per hour (average)
Mail, messenger, and other delivery charges	$ 50 or more
Long-distance telephone charges	Varies
Photocopying (in office)	$ .25 per page
Facsimiles	$ 1.00 per page
Computerized legal research (research conducted using computer databases)	Hundreds of dollars plus attorney's fees

[1] *Again, this chart refers to out-of-pocket costs and not attorney charges or fees for their time.*

- Is there a contract or statute that would permit you to be reimbursed for your legal costs and fees by the other side?
- Do you have insurance of your own that will cover the costs of the lawsuit, or is there potential coverage?
- How much have other people won at trial for the kind of complaint you're considering bringing?
- What's your exposure? What is the chance you'd lose? (There's *always* that chance.) Could you survive getting hit with a $2,000, $5,000, or $20,000 cost judgment? Do you believe, after careful analysis, that the potential upside justifies that risk?
- What is the chance the defendant will turn around and sue you? If so, what is your exposure?
- Are you willing to invest the time and emotional commitment your specific case may require? Are you willing to accept the potential impact on your family, career, friendships, religion, or whatever?
- Are you willing to see this affair to the bitter end or have you planned a point at which you'll just drop the case if it hasn't settled? (If you drop your suit, are you confident that the defendant won't then turn around and sue you for malicious prosecution?)

If you're like the average first-time litigant, you probably have no idea how to begin answering these questions. That's OK. Here's what to do:

1. Read the rest of this book and educate yourself about complaints, damages, motions, depositions, interrogatories, witnesses, legal bills, appeals, dirty tricks, and many other aspects of litigation.
2. At the end of the book, use the cost-benefit worksheet in Appendix A. It lists questions to answer and litigation categories, events, fees, and costs you'll have to consider. Fill out that form using knowledge you've gained from this book and from talking with friends, acquaintances, and attorneys.
3. Following the instructions in Appendix A, begin determining the range of potential financial, emotional, and spiritual costs associated with your unique matter. Observe what you could be in for on your case.

4. Next, list your potential damages. Come up with a range for how much you might make from your case.
5. Try to weigh the potential costs against your potential gain. If the gain is greater, you may want to go ahead with a lawsuit.

   If you've taken the time to cool off and educate yourself, you should be in a good position to evaluate your situation objectively.

"Confess! *You* backed into
my client's car!"

Hiring Perry Mason

> Lawyers use the law as shoemakers use leather: rubbing it,
> pressing it, and stretching it with their teeth, all to the end
> of making it fit for their purposes.
>
> **—Louis XII, king of France, 1462–1515**

You should be as picky about finding the right lawyer as you are in choosing your mate. And just as when playing the dating game, you may have to kiss a few frogs before finding your prince. You can learn some important lessons from how major corporations go about evaluating and selecting a law firm, just as you can learn from the mistakes of individuals who chose before taking a careful look. Some cases call for specialized attorneys, while others are best served by a strong, general litigator. Let's take a look at what to keep in mind when retaining legal counsel.

How Do I Find a Lawyer?

To find a lawyer, talk to people. It's really that simple. Do you know anyone who was involved in a lawsuit? What happened to those people? What did they learn? What did they think about their attorney?

If you don't know anyone who's been in litigation, go down to the courthouse and find someone who's embroiled in litigation right now. At any given time there are cases going on in most courthouses. While parties to a lawsuit are not likely to talk with you while it's transpiring, you might ask if they'd be willing to talk with you when it's over, since you're in a similar boat. They might tell you to buzz off, or they might say, "Sure, I'll talk with you. Give me a call next week."

You can also go to a public library and do a computer scan of articles from your local papers. Put in key words like *lawsuit, litigation, sue, plaintiff, defendant, trial, judge,* and *verdict.* Often, when cases go to trial, they're written up in the local paper. Can you find the plaintiff in a case similar to yours? Maybe. Even if you don't know the litigants, they might be willing to talk with you. Get them on the phone. Take them out to lunch. Let them walk you through the difficult part of a deposition being taken, the hidden costs no one told them about, or the lawyer who nearly blew their case. Hear them out.

People who've "been there" are among the greatest potential assets available to you. If you were about to have open-heart surgery, wouldn't you try to talk to someone who'd had it already? Such people can tell you in unedited, layperson's terms what happened to them, how they felt, how they recovered. They may have some valuable recommendations about what to do and what to avoid, and perhaps they'll share a few lessons they learned the hard way. They might be a big help in directing you toward a great doctor or away from a bad one.

There is a universe of people who have been in your particular situation. Your task is to find them in your city or town, or on the Internet, and talk with them. Unless you're coming up on the statute of limitations (see Chapter 5), you can probably afford to take a few weeks or a month to find and talk with people in a situation similar to yours.

Use your phone book, yellow pages, or (if you have Internet access) Web browser to find resources you might use to locate lawyers. Call your local or state bar association, which has attorney referral services. Get some names of people in your area. Call them up, and tell them you'd like to come in and discuss their representing you on your case. Most lawyers will give you a free consultation but some may want to charge you. Before you go in, ask if the consultation will be free. You don't want to pay for a consultation if you don't have to.

Interview More than One Attorney

Never see just one lawyer and then sign up with him, even if you think he's perfect for your case. Try to see two, three, or four lawyers. That way you'll see different styles and have different feels; each one of them is going to tell you a little something different about himself and about your case. They're going to contrast each other and may even contradict each other. One attorney might make a great suggestion that you can share with another attorney you end up going with. Every attorney's legal experience is different. Ignore pressure to "sign up today." If an attorney offers you an agreement to sign, ask if you can take it home with you and review it. Tell him you've really enjoyed meeting with him (if you have), and that you'll be getting back to him.

If there is one message I hope you take away from this book, it is this: do not put any aspect of your case on autopilot. That includes talking with attorneys. When you're interviewing attorneys, don't simply ask questions like "Do you think I have a good case?"; "How would you handle it?"; and "How much do you think it's worth?" Ask them where they live, how long they've been practicing law, when their last trial was, what kinds of things they enjoy doing, what types of cases do they prefer. Don't just talk about you; try to have the kind of interaction that will give you a good feel for the attorney as a person as well as a professional.

You want a combination of intelligence, experience, ability, devotion, and the availability to put in the needed time on your case. In the end, your choice of attorney is going to come down to a gut decision, but it has to be based on lots of information.

Do You Want to Retain Mr. Big?

One of the attorneys someone may refer you to is Mr. Big. "He's sensational! Did you see him on TV or read that article about him? He won that huge case! I'd try to get him if I were you!"

So you meet with Mr. Big, you're wowed, and you sign with him. A short way down the road, you realize that it's really Susie Small who's going to handle just about everything on your case, and you're never going to see Mr. Big again. He's very busy on some other huge case, and he can't return your call this week. You sat and poured your heart out to Mr. Big, and he told you how you could cream the other side. But then you were ushered down the hall to some other lawyer, who has only three, two, or maybe one year of experience out of law school—and who, by the way, may not know a whole lot about litigation yet. The point is to make sure the lawyer you hire will be the same lawyer who actually ends up handling your case.

How Corporations Hire Lawyers

Big companies generally have an in-house general counsel, a full-time lawyer who helps watch out for the company's business. He helps evaluate which law firm the corporation should go with, and then he oversees the corporation's legal work. When shopping for a law firm, the general counsel starts out by asking for the curriculum vitae (résumé) of every lawyer who is going to be assigned to work on the corporation's case. He may ask for a written commitment from the firm for each of the lawyers who would work on the corporation's business (so that the firm won't yank them off in the middle of the case and substitute someone who may be less experienced and/or may have to bill a lot of time just to come up to speed). He also gets in writing what each of those lawyers' hourly rates will be and asks for the opportunity to meet with those lawyers.

When the meeting takes place, the law firm makes a pitch to the general counsel, talking in glowing terms of how its people are going to work on the corporation's case. Usually the firm's lawyers tell the general counsel about where they grew up and went to school, their legal and personal background, and what they do at the firm. Finally, the firm's head honcho talks about how the team interacts and who's going to do what if they get the corporation's business.

That's what the corporation's general counsel gets up front, before he signs or pays anything. The law firm is more than eager to make the pitch, to introduce the team, to deliver the curricula vitae, to give the firm's statement, and to offer to make a commitment.

You Deserve the Same Treatment

If you are thinking of using a big law firm that is also used by corporations, why shouldn't you ask for and get exactly the same treatment? These firms often ask individuals to pay as much as the institutional clients, so why should they have any less of a presentation to help them make their decision? Realistically, a client like Nabisco or Chrysler is going to get white-glove treatment because a big corporation represents a huge amount of business. Even if you don't get the same dog and pony show, if you're going to be a paying client, you should expect or insist on *some* show.

Whatever type of firm you're considering, you should be able to walk in and meet the paralegal, the associate, the secretary, whomever. And someone should tell you, "This is how we would work, this is who you would call, here's what we can do for you, and let's all talk about how we would work together." You need to find out who would be handling your case on a day-to-day basis. There's nothing wrong with a paralegal or a junior associate doing certain tasks. But you should find this out right up front, and you should try to meet those people before making a decision. If no one can tell you who would be working on your case at that moment, someone should be able to give you an answer in a short time, before you retain the firm.

If a "team" is going to be working on your case, it's important to try to meet everyone before you sign up. If your case is complicated, the firm may not be able to tell you definitively who will be working on your matter. People do take vacations, leave firms, and so on. But you should know generally with whom you'll be working and what their level of competence and skill is. It would be nice to be told, "Jane Green is my paralegal and has been with me for six years, and Bobby Wexler is going to be my associate; he just graduated from Georgetown two years ago." Try to get as much information as possible before making your final decision. If you're going to be handed off to someone else, find out and meet that person now.

If you have a sophisticated case, you can afford to be a little choosy. You can immediately start crossing lawyers or firms off your list if they hesitate to make the necessary commitment. If they're not initially willing to grant you half an hour to bring a group of people together in a room and make a presentation for your business, you can be assured they're not going to be all that able to spend a great deal of time answering your important questions later. Such firms may be brusque and impatient, Try to go with the firm and lawyer that truly does have the time for you and your case.

If you're going to sign with a contingency fee law firm, this shouldn't mean surrendering your right to know who will be working on your case and how it will proceed. If you can't get this information up front, that reflects the kind of service you will (or won't) be getting from that firm down the road.

Law firms are like any other entity in the world: they have their shining stars, their less-shining stars, and the people who are on their way out the door. Now, what if your case happens to be handed off to a person who's on his way out the door? What if your lawyer has a drinking problem or is overburdened and overworked? What if he's about to leave and start a new law firm, so he barely has time for any of his old cases?

Another important question is whether your prospective attorney is experienced in your kind of case. The world of litigators breaks down into criminal and civil attorneys. I would never hire a criminal attorney to handle a civil matter, nor would I have a civil attorney handle a criminal matter, no matter who that attorney was.

Maybe you're told Mr. Big won't handle the preparation of your case, but he'll take over and handle it if it goes to trial. Often the Mr. Bigs of the trade are brought in at the last minute to do just that. But if Mr. Big didn't do all the discovery and is only working off a crash course the week before trial, he may not do the best job for you.

Don't just go with the flow. Just because everybody in town is saying a person is a great lawyer doesn't mean that he's going to be a great lawyer on your case. It doesn't even mean that he's truly a great lawyer. It might mean that people *think* he's a great lawyer, or that he was a great lawyer in the past, not necessarily any longer. And it doesn't mean that some young lawyer in his fourth or fifth year out of school won't do a better job, even though nobody knows who he is yet.

A Lawyer Should Impress, but You Don't Have to Fall in Love

When hiring a lawyer you want to be comfortable, but you don't have to look for a best friend. You need someone who can address your problem and with whom you can communicate. Remember that lawyers will try to sell you on themselves as soon as you come through the door; there'll be lots of schmoozing. And a good litigator should be charismatic and able to speak comfortably on his feet. When you first meet a litigator, he's probably going to overtake the conversation and sound very authoritative, especially because he's talking about something that he knows a lot about and you, presumably, know very little about. Your job is to take everything in, ask questions when appropriate, and then go home and think about what you've seen and heard. Just remember, you're not hiring a friend, but rather a professional.

Avoid the Conveyor Belt

Try to be prepared before meeting with your lawyer. Develop a list of questions based on what you've read, conversations with others, and the facts of your case. You want to interview him, which means you'll be the person in charge of that first meeting. Table 2 provides examples of questions to include on your list. If you wander in zombie-like, wondering, "What do I do?" then you may find yourself taking a trip on a conveyor belt to somewhere you don't want to be.

For a personal injury case with a contingency lawyer, the conveyor belt might proceed like this: The firm will look at the initial facts, do an initial readout, send you out to a doctor, get you examined, then at some point send out a demand letter. The letter is drafted by a junior-level

Table 2. Attorney Interview Questions

Where did you go to law school, and how long have you been practicing? Where have you worked since law school?

How many trials have you handled? What were the outcomes?

Have you had experience with my kind of case? What happened? Who was involved?

Have you had any past dealings with the defendant or the defendant's insurance carrier?

Do you have references I can contact?

If I go with you, will you be doing the work on my case? Will others be doing it or helping out? Can I meet them?

Are there attorneys who specialize in handling the kind of case I have?

What is your present caseload? Do you have time for my case?

How soon could you begin work on my case? How quickly could we file?

How long do you think it will take to get this case to trial?

What is the statute of limitations on my case?

What kinds of legal claims would be appropriate for my situation?

How much do you think my case is worth?

What's your opinion of mediation? In my case?

Do you think that my case will require an expert?

Can you prepare a budget for what my case might cost? Is there any charge for the budget?

Do you work on a contingency fee basis?

What costs do you charge for?

associate based on a brief conversation during an elevator ride with the attorney you originally met with. The attorney you thought you were getting on your case told the junior associate six important ideas to put in the letter. The junior associate gets four of them right. You don't see the letter before it gets sent out or otherwise have a chance to make comments or corrections.

After the insurance company's attorney gets the letter, the company might cough out a settlement offer. Maybe it's a really good settlement offer, or maybe you could get more money. Your law firm will decide whether it's a good offer or not, based on the firm's ideas of a "good" outcome, how busy they've become and whether they want to keep your case on their docket, or other factors—some which have nothing to do with you. Or maybe the firm has a history with this insurance carrier, and a friend on the other side asked for a favor: "Settle this case on lower terms, and I'll scratch your back on another one."

If your case doesn't settle, nothing will happen for a year. After you get frustrated, maybe the firm will take one deposition to pacify you. Someone will ask the insurance carrier for a bigger settlement. They'll say no, so the case will go to trial.

The senior attorney you originally met with won't have time to do the jury instructions himself and will give the assignment to the junior associate. The senior attorney will go in for the trial, since he's really good on his feet (just hope he studied up on your case enough). The case gets tried. If he loses, well, he did his best. If he connects with the jury and wins a lot of money, the other side will take an appeal. If the junior associate screwed up on the jury instructions, the case will get reversed and sent down for a retrial. And you'll only learn about the problems on your case after it's too late to do anything about them.

The point of this example is that the idea that you can blithely walk into a law firm and rely on an attorney to always look after your best interests is just not reality. Many will, but some may not. Even the best of them often get too busy.

It's exactly like going to a mechanic and knowing nothing about your car. A certain percentage of the time, you are going to get ripped off. Likewise, if your business has a complicated computer system and you don't know what you're doing, you're open to being defrauded by your consultant until you learn enough about your system to know what kind of work should be done.

If you were thinking of investing ten, twenty, or thirty thousand dollars in a business deal, you would probably spend at least twenty hours of your time talking to investment bankers, walking out to the job site, looking at the product, looking at the private placement offer, asking for advice, or otherwise learning about the field you are planning to invest in. Do the same if you're going to invest time and money in a lawsuit. If you don't, don't be surprised if the dose of reality you taste is bitterness and disappointment.

Attorneys Who Specialize

Within the world of civil lawyers, some are very specialized: they may do only personal injury cases, wrongful termination cases, securities litigation, product liability litigation, or copyright litigation, and so on. Other firms do a little of everything. Do you need a specialist for your case or a jack-of-all-trades?

There are pros and cons for each. Sometimes firms that do a little bit of everything have a fantastic trial lawyer who can try just about any case, and his just being associated with the case could help you settle early.

Certain kinds of cases, however, including certain employment termination cases, are largely decided by administrative agencies. Specific forms must be completed, and a labyrinth of rules and procedures govern these matters. The firms that specialize in these kinds of cases already have all the right forms and know exactly how to plug your facts into those forms. They've seen ten different possible fact patterns and know recent changes in legislation. They may even know the labor commissioner, and for a reasonable fee, they'll get you in and out, and you'll get paid.

If you take that kind of case to a general litigation shop that has handled maybe one or two of those claims over time, they'll probably have to spend twenty or more hours just trying to learn the labyrinth of rules or calling their friends for advice. And you may (or may not) be asked to pay for their learning curve. In that scenario, you'd probably be at the wrong place. You don't need the brilliant civil litigator, but a specialized, competent employment lawyer.

Medical malpractice is another area of the law that has its own set of rules and schedules for payment. A lawyer who works in that field knows the insurance companies, and they know him. He knows the judges who hear these cases, and he probably tries these cases in front of those judges routinely. This can be a distinct advantage.

In just a few instances, this could be a drawback. Familiarity can breed too much friendliness between the parties involved. When a community of lawyers are dealing with each other regularly—plaintiff's attorneys on the plaintiff's side, defense attorneys on the defendant's side—they can become buddies. Somewhere along the line, plaintiff's attorney John Smith and defense counsel Bill Jones go to the tavern together after a case, or treat each other to lunch, and they may start to compromise claims. The heck with the courts and the juries, we'll just start to mediate between ourselves. This is a great deal for them. It may not be such a great deal for you.

If you find yourself in a tight community of lawyers who are dealing with each other regularly, just keep an eye out and be wary that you don't find yourself in that chummy zone. This can be true in the legal area of any industry. In the entertainment industry there's a circle of entertainment lawyers, and if you're a performer and go to a lawyer who also represents studios, well, there's some give-and-take. If you think those kinds of conflicts of interest don't happen, then you're not thinking straight.

The Perfect Attorney

Although I've been exhorting you to demand the very best in service from any attorney you meet, and to reject any who doesn't impress you as being service oriented at the start, litigation in general can't always be that way, no matter what attorney you end up hiring. Have you ever had the experience of going to your doctor for some blood tests when you're sick and worried about your health? Someone takes your blood on a Monday and tells you the results won't be back until the following Monday. Maybe you're upset. Even though your health is so important to you, you still have to wait seven days. Litigation can be the same way. Even when you're thinking, "Hey, it's me! It's my case!" the legal profession isn't set up to stop on a dime for anybody. Litigation is a public bus, not a private plane. You've got to understand that, no matter what firm you go to.

Also, while your case may cause you to have many sleepless nights, your lawyer *can* sleep at night. He's got ten, fifteen, or forty other clients with the same problems. While he may genuinely sympathize with you, he's not going to have the same pain and anxiety you have about your matter. He's going to put you on a stack with dozens of other folders, and if he's a good lawyer, he'll do the best job he can. But you're not going to get every single minute you want out of him. It's just not going to happen. So you have to say to yourself, "This is not going to be perfect. It's going to be anxiety-producing, and I'm not going to be happy at some points, and I may be a little upset, but I've got to find the best situation for my bottom line. I've got to take responsibility for knowing what's happening on my case and making sure things happen right."

Preparation and the Demand Letter

Men have feelings but the law does not.

Napoléon I, emperor of France, 1769–1821

Preparation Saves You Money

Attorneys deal with "fact patterns." If you present your facts to an attorney like a stack of cards thrown up in the air and dropped down on his head, if you ramble all over the place in a two-hour meeting and hand over a set of unorganized documents, be prepared to shell out a lot of money to have that attorney pick up and organize that jumbled deck of cards.

Major companies take the best approach. They have their in-house counsel handle such organization and presentation for the company. If you're an individual or a small business, you should do the same before talking with an attorney. Begin by organizing your documents, presenting the facts to your lawyer as clearly and succinctly as possible. If you don't take some time to organize what you're handing off to an attorney, you may look at your first bill and say, "My God! Who is this paralegal, and what was he doing for $2,000?" Then you'll probably hear, "Well, you gave us this set of documents, and you don't want me billing you at my full rate trying to put these in order, do you? I can't do anything on your case until the documents are in some order."

Right from your first contact with an attorney, remember that you have a story to tell. It has important elements and peripheral issues, and you need to start making some decisions about which documents are important, which letters are important, and so on. If there are letters, documents, other written articles, tapes, videos, or other items that your lawyer should see, pull them together in a logical order, think about your presentation to your lawyer, and prepare—before you go to see the lawyer.

Bring a full set of documents to your lawyer. They could include your calendar, notes, letters, memos, anything you think may be relevant to your case. If your suit is about an insurance policy, bring the policy. Have all the pages and attachments of the policy with you, because the lawyer is going to need to see them. Don't just rush out the front door and take everything but the exhibits. Think about what the lawyer might need. Err on the side of being overly inclusive. I like chronologies and time lines I can refer to that are in concrete, written form. The first meeting will be much more effective if you bring everything—as long as everything is organized well!

Also, type out the full names of the players in your story, and give their addresses and phone numbers. If you don't provide that information, your lawyer or his assistant must spend a lot of time calling you: "Do you have that last name? Do you have that address?" And they'll do it one player at a time. If you're paying hourly, that's costing you more money. So think about the obvious—names of defendants, witnesses, where they work and live, where they should be served with a complaint or a subpoena, the basics.

Photocopy all your documents (rather than asking your lawyer to copy them for you at a high rate), then put them into folders with labels.

Put your overview and chronology of the facts and documents on the cover or as the first page of each folder. When you meet with the attorney, go in with an outline for your discussion. Tell generally what your story is, what your goals are in suing, and what your questions are for the attorney. Then give the attorney the documents; show him what you have and how it's organized. He'll realize and appreciate that you've done this preliminary work, and he'll observe that you're an intelligent client. Ask him to look your materials over and get back to you on whether he's interested in the case. If he is, ask him to give you a rough idea of what he thinks it would cost. Then you can have your second meeting with him.

Often people considering a lawsuit have suffered a traumatic incident. Maybe someone they loved was hurt or killed by accident. Maybe they had a bad experience in surgery, so their leg isn't working correctly. Maybe their business got put under, or maybe someone stiffed them for a lot of money. Maybe they're getting divorced. Whatever the case, the litigation almost always involves some strong emotional issues. Those issues should not drive the litigation.

Too often they do, though. When that happens, clients go to an attorney and essentially say the same thing over and over again: "That person is wrong! That person is wrong!" They say it in so many different words and so many different ways, and meanwhile the lawyer's meter is running. Don't confuse your attorney with your therapist. Think about how to use him efficiently right from the first meeting.

Should You Send a Demand Letter?

Before you file a lawsuit, consider having a lawyer send the parties on the other side a letter that outlines your grievances, puts them on notice that you're contemplating legal action, and demands that they take appropriate action to resolve the problem in order to avert a lawsuit. This is called a demand letter.

For example, assume you have a simple contract case. You had a contract to deliver 10,000 widgets for $10 each. You delivered the widgets, and your customer failed to pay the $100,000 that is due. You go to your lawyer and complain that the customer isn't returning your phone calls. You suspect the customer has a cash flow problem but won't file for bankruptcy. You just don't think your customer is taking you seriously. Rather than running to court and filing a complaint—which may cost you thousands—your lawyer can write a demand letter like the sample in Figure 1.

In some instances demand letters are critical to protect certain rights and to ensure that you are entitled to certain relief at trial. For example, if someone defames you, in some states you must make a formal demand for a retraction before you sue. If you don't demand a retraction but just charge on ahead and sue, you may not be able to recover certain damages you could have otherwise obtained. In this

Figure 1. Sample Demand Letter

Dear Widget Company:

> My name is Joe Smith of the law firm of Smith, Jones & Smith. I have been retained by Mr. Widget Maker. On or about [date], Mr. Widget Maker entered into a contract with your company. This contract requires that upon delivery of goods, your firm will make immediate payment in the amount of $100,000. Your company is in material breach of this contract. Delivery was made, and payment was not received.

> If you make immediate payment by cashier's check within five business days, my client will accept such payment and will consider this matter resolved. However, if my client has not received payment within five business days, our firm will file suit in Los Angeles Superior Court on or before the close of business on [date].

> It is not our intention to run up your litigation costs. Rather, it is our intention to enforce our client's rights. Our client upheld his end of the bargain. We look forward to your upholding your end of the bargain. If you have any questions at all, please don't hesitate to contact us. But please be assured that we do not intend to sit on our client's rights.

> Sincerely,

> Joe Smith, Esq.

instance, a demand letter can become a crucial piece of evidence that affects the value of your case.

That said, not every situation is appropriate for a demand letter. In many instances you can pretty much tell ahead of time that the other side is just going to view a demand letter as the warning flare of a coming lawsuit. The person who wronged you will use it as an opportunity to get his own lawyers in the loop, get them up to speed, and see if they can do some timely damage control to make him look less guilty. Meanwhile you'll just receive a "Get lost!" response to your letter, and you've given him time to brace himself for your suit.

Don't Buy a Worthless Demand Letter

It would be unfortunate to go through the sometimes costly process of having a lawyer draft a demand letter when you're pretty sure you're just going to have to pay for a complaint anyway. Parties who are going to stonewall you in response to a demand letter generally are the type who are experienced at putting on a defense intended to drive up your fees. Some large corporate defendants or insurance companies accustomed to being sued can be accustomed to dragging out the legal process, looking for ways to delay, file motions, oblige you to bring motions, and do everything they can think of to compel you to spend money on your case. If you're going to be stuck in this situation, your mind-set must be to spend your money only on matters that are directly associated with getting your case into a courtroom.

Many people think, "Well, according to my litigation budget, I could pay out $7,000 for the first sixty days of my lawsuit, between the researching, drafting, filing, and serving of my complaint. Maybe there's a way around that." Your antennae should go up if your lawyer says, "Why don't we first send out a demand letter and see what happens." While demand letters may make sense and can help avoid a lawsuit in some situations, before paying for one, you should go through a thoughtful inquiry process with your lawyer—and on your own—to try to assess whether a demand letter has any realistic chance of bearing fruit.

A demand letter could cost anywhere from $200 to $2,000 or more, depending on the lawyer's rate, how detailed the letter is, and how much legal research goes into preparing it. If you're pretty sure all you're going to get as a response is the very predictable, "Sorry; drop dead," then you should skip the demand letter. Don't get sucked into having a demand letter go out simply because it's cheaper than paying for a complaint. You probably know your opponent best, and if you believe that it's unlikely the demand letter will succeed, don't spend money just to find yourself still at square one.

What May Work; What Never Will

If you do decide to send a demand letter, the letters with the best chance of success delineate a strong set of facts, stated in an articulate, non-rhetorical fashion. Be sure to make a reasonable settlement demand. The other side will do a cost-benefit analysis. If you send a letter saying, "I want x dollars," then the other side will probably consider a number of factors before answering, such as their exposure, their likely liability, the cost to defend your case, the likelihood you can hang on until your case goes to trial, and your lawyer's reputation.

A letter that outlined your case well and made a modest demand could be successful. Say you were wrongfully terminated and asked for $60,000—$30,000 this year and $30,000 next year. Your former employer might look at your firm but respectful, well-crafted letter and decide to avoid the cost and potential embarrassment of defending your claims; $30,000 this year and $30,000 next would be less than the company would pay to defend the case, let alone to pay a verdict at trial.

If you send over that same letter but demand $150,000, then your former employer's cost-benefit analysis may lead management to say, "We can pay a really good defense firm $70,000, and there's a chance they'll bury this guy and he'll get exhausted or frustrated and go away. If I have to make a choice, I'll pay the $70,000 to the defense firm. I'm not going to pay $150,000 to this guy, because I need to get upper management's approval for a settlement that big, and $150,000 settlements look bad on my corporate report card."

A $150,000 settlement is a lot more than a $60,000 settlement, and a number of large corporate defendants will pay what is called a "nuisance value" settlement to get rid of a potentially troublesome suit. A nuisance value settlement is one in which the defendant in effect says, "Look, we think the lawsuit's absolutely meritless, but at a minimum it will cost us five or ten grand to secure defense counsel, so we'll give you two, three, or seven grand to go away."

Defense Mentality

Sometimes your lawyer will know enough about the institution, the corporate defendant, the insurance carrier, or the individual defendant to give you some odds on what the likely outcome is. In other situations, you and your lawyer may be writing to a defendant you know very little about, and you don't know what's going on behind the facade—especially if it's a corporation. This is why demand letters are usually a crapshoot.

Here's are some examples of how defense thinking might go, all in the same company.

We're StarStruck Studios, and we've just been taken to trial in a high-profile case, and our lawyers publicly state again and again that the lawsuit has no merit and will fail miserably. We fight the plaintiff tooth and nail, investing a million dollars of our company's money into the defense. We take on a plaintiff's contingency fee firm that meets us blow for blow. We go to trial and begin to fully realize that the plaintiff is going to win a multimillion-dollar verdict against us.

Meanwhile, in comes a letter from your lawyer, who has a claim from you that isn't nearly as strong as the claim in the lawsuit that we're going to lose—and suddenly we've got cold feet. Maybe a memo comes down from upstairs, chewing us out and telling us to try to settle those cases earlier. Well, your demand is reasonable, and it's your lucky day. We're running to the table to settle your claim.

Now, a year later we have a new head general counsel or a new head of the parent company. He sees that a lot of lawsuits have been filed and quick settlements handed out, and he doesn't like it. It's bad for his bottom line. Also, he just went through a management course that says effective management should send a message out to the plaintiffs of the world that if we're going to get sued over and over again, we're not going to be settling early. So he sets the new policy: "No more freebies.

You want so sue us and get some money? You're going to have to go the distance."

A sophisticated in-house counsel and companies that have been sued several times know that many plaintiffs can't afford to go the distance, and that some contingency fee lawyers may lose interest in a case if the defendant makes them work too hard. Contingency fee lawyers will often be anxious for a quick payout and early settlement. They want to exert just enough to win the case and not much beyond that. If they are fighting a defendant who churns out discovery motions and protective orders and countless letters, suddenly the contingency firm may realize that one of its attorneys is working full-time on that case with no immediate revenue coming in. That case may not look so appealing to the firm anymore. Big corporate defendants understand they can wear down the contingency fee lawyers and their clients in this way.

Some companies adopt a strategy that, until they get to the point where they're thirty days away from a trial, this is just another lawsuit. They get sued so often, to them it's like getting the morning newspaper delivered. Their view is "Another lawsuit? Fine. Put it in the docket, we'll deal with it, and let's just see if the plaintiff can go through our marathon course of tough meetings, discovery motions, Motions for Summary Judgment, and long-winded letters from our defense lawyers. And, hey—we can always whip out our checkbook later and settle. But why do it now? Maybe we'll get a judge in our corner, who throws out the case; maybe we can grind down the plaintiff or his lawyer, and they'll be forced to fold."

To Demand or . . . ?

A demand letter probably won't be a shot in the dark if you go to a lawyer who says, "I've dealt with that insurance company before. I know that if I send a letter over to this person with this set of facts and evidence, it's likely to get a positive response."

At other times you, the client, may have knowledge about the potential defendant that makes it much easier to predict how a demand letter will be received. For example, a client of mine who had been terminated knew her employer very well. She knew that if the letter were written in a certain way and said certain things, the employer would be likely to settle. She knew what the cost-benefit analysis was going to be on the other side—because she had been making that type of analysis herself before she was terminated. You couldn't ask for better intelligence than that. She knew what keys would unlock her former employer's door and how to present the request so that it had the best chance of getting the right response.

In some situations you're bluffing and aren't going to be able to sue for one reason or another. In this case, the demand letter is simply your last, best hope: If you wave around this lawyer's name, this lawyer's letterhead, these legal terms, and these ominous warnings, maybe the other side will think you're serious. Maybe they'll make you an offer. If you don't really plan to sue, there may be no harm in trying a demand letter. But remember that sending out a demand letter can be like kicking a sleeping dog—the attacked may fight back. In fact, you could end up getting sued yourself. For example, say the other party felt they had grounds to sue *you*, but had decided not to bother. In comes your demand letter, and now they decide that if they're going to be in a lawsuit, they might as well sue you before you sue them.

Another valid purpose for sending a demand letter is to provide a psychological release for a client who needs it. Maybe you can't afford or don't want to put your family or company through a lawsuit, but you do need to have your position heard by the people who wronged you. Judges often talk about the importance of giving parties their day in court—not their judgment, but a day when they can be heard. There's a psychological benefit to having your say, taking your blast. And sometimes if you cannot realistically afford a lawsuit, a demand letter is a relatively cheap way to assert your principles. Then you can have the satisfaction of letting the other parties know that their actions did not go unnoticed, and maybe you'll sue them someday.

Handle with Care

Do not disclose the contents of your demand letter to anyone other than the person for whom it's intended. One of my clients had a zealous attorney who sent out a demand letter to a corporation and copied it to another company that the corporation did business with. Then the corporation sued the client for tortious interference (harming a corporation's relationship with another company). My client and his attorney had been hoping to make a quick strike and see if they could settle; instead, they got an armful of trouble.

If you want to go on record with a demand letter but don't have the funds to prosecute a case, the last thing you want is to find yourself being sued as a result of that letter. But if you throw a little jab in a demand letter to a potential defendant, and you send off a copy of that letter to another company or to a bank that does business with that potential defendant, you may find yourself on the receiving end of a suit. Suddenly you'll have a lot at stake—and few, if any, contingency fee lawyers in any town will take on defense work. Don't do anything rash just to experience a temporary rush.

Also be careful about the contents of your letter, as demand letters can be used as evidence. Sometimes a demand letter can be structured in a way that it constitutes a "settlement discussion," and this is preferable. Settlement discussions are protected from being admitted into evidence, and you may wish to have your demand letter kept out at trial. The reason for preventing settlement discussions from being introduced at trial is to encourage people to talk to each other, to try to work out and settle their differences outside of a courtroom. One side's lawyer in a settlement discussion might say, "OK, my client will pay you x dollars if your client does this. What do you say?" If such settlement discussions could be introduced at trial to try to argue, "The other party must be guilty because, look—they offered to pay me money!" then this would prevent people from ever entering into settlement discussions.

The problem generally starts when there is posturing before a case begins. That posturing can later become an issue. In short, be very careful about what you, or your lawyer, put in writing prior to filing a suit, whether in a demand letter or otherwise.

If you find a trial lawyer you really like and decide to send a demand letter, think of that letter as a litmus test for how that lawyer is going to conduct himself throughout your case. And if you do send over a demand letter, don't go to bed at night thinking there's going to be a present under the Christmas tree in the morning. If someone ever did a study, I'm sure he would find that only a low percentage of demand letters are met with, "OK, I'll pay."

5

Nuts and Bolts: Before Filing

This is a court of law, young man, not a court of justice.
—Oliver Wendell Holmes Jr., Supreme Court justice

Once you've cooled off and are ready to take a level, businesslike approach to evaluating your lawsuit, you'll be beyond thinking, "I want to get even!" and be ready to think, "I want to accomplish *x*, and of the various options open, I believe a lawsuit is the best way to do this." At this stage, you have a number of issues to discuss with any attorney you hire or are considering hiring.

Plaintiff, Defendant, and Parties

A party who brings a lawsuit against another party is called a plaintiff, while the party being sued is called the defendant. A "party" to a lawsuit simply means a person, business, or government agency that is a plaintiff or defendant in that lawsuit.

Someone who is a witness or is in some way related to a plaintiff or defendant is not a party (although these people can be termed "third parties"). Only those people or entities directly involved and named as plaintiffs or defendants in the lawsuit itself are referred to as parties.

Your Claims or Defenses

Once you have retained an attorney and you and your attorney have completed your initial consultation, it will become incumbent upon the two of you to decide on your claims (as plaintiff) or defenses (as defendant).

A claim is a legal "cause of action." To understand what that means, you need to understand how the law came into existence. The U.S. system of justice is patterned after the English common law system. Hundreds of years ago the courts in England realized they needed to formally decide under what circumstances a party who was injured or had suffered a loss should be legally entitled to recover from another party. So the courts began defining different pockets of conduct that would give rise to a right to take a matter to court and recover damages. These pockets of conduct are called causes of action. So causes of action are types of conduct that the law recognizes as actionable. If someone acts in one of these certain defined ways, you can sue him and you may be entitled to recover damages or receive some other form of relief.

Your claims or causes of action are the assertions or allegations that you intend to make at court. They are, in short, the substance of your lawsuit. If you were in a car accident and contend that your car was damaged because of the negligence of another driver, your claim might be for "negligence." If you maintain that another party to a contract did not follow through and perform as promised under the contract, then you may be asserting a claim for "breach of contract." A countless number of claims can be asserted, and the type of claim depends largely upon circumstances.

If you are instead a defendant in a case, you will most certainly want to assert a defense to counter a claim. For example, if you are being sued for moving out of an apartment before the lease terminated, you may want to argue as a defense that the landlord forced you to move out, in which case you may offer a defense called "constructive eviction." Or maybe you'll assert a defense that the landlord did not work hard enough to find a new substitute tenant—the landlord had a "failure to mitigate damages"—so he's not entitled to collect some or all of what he's suing for.

Claims You Can Make

While many people describe a lawsuit in terms of the emotional issues involved, the truth is that a lawsuit is made up of a set of claims, which are countered by a set of defenses to those claims. The claims must be couched in terms of causes of action formally recognized under the law. There is no such thing as a claim of "that person really pissed me off." You won't see a complaint that has a heading saying, "They snookered me." Rather, there are claims for such things as "intentional infliction of emotional distress," "tortious interference with a prospective economic advantage," "conversion," "fraud," or many thousands of other causes of action.

Identifying your precise claims is an area where you obviously need a lawyer's help. A lawyer went to law school for three years to learn these different types of claims and defenses. For certain basic, common types of claims and defenses that do not involve complex fact patterns or a substantial amount in controversy, court forms are available to the parties. These court forms often allow you to assert a claim or defense just by checking the appropriate box. With the exception of these small-claims or municipal court types of proceedings, though, you almost certainly need the advice and counsel of an attorney in determining what your claims and defense might be.

To ensure a uniform system of justice, the courts and legislature have carefully defined "elements" for each cause of action. All these elements must be present to satisfy the definition of that cause of action. To succeed in a trial or any other legal proceeding, you will need to establish that you have satisfied each of the elements of your claim. In other words, you must present proof to the jury or the judge that supports each element of any claim you assert. For example, if you are suing for breach of contract, you will need to establish five elements:

1. There was a contract.
2. The contract imposed a duty.
3. The duty was breached.
4. The breach was "material."
5. The breach caused you damage or injury that could not have otherwise been avoided.

Those are, in general terms, the essential elements of a cause of action for breach of contract.

The same is true of a defense. To be successful with any given defense, you must present evidence to prove each of the required elements for that defense, as defined by law.

The Ingredients That Matter

As your case proceeds, you and your attorney will often discuss the "story" of your case, without referring to the specific legal claims and defenses involved. However, every time the court analyzes or considers your case, it will focus only on the legal claims and defenses. It will not be interested in any part of your "story," unless that story relates specifically to the claims and defenses at issue. When the case is submitted to the finder of fact (such as a judge, jury, or arbitrator), that person or persons will consider whether or not the plaintiff or the defendant has satisfied the "burden of proof" (discussed on pp. 61–62) with respect to the claims and defenses at issue. Simply stated, at the end of your case, you will be required to show that you have in fact satisfied each of the elements of your claim or your defense.

If you were building a house, you would first hire an architect to put together a set of architectural drawings. The builders who later construct the house use these drawings as a point of reference; when the house is finished, it conforms with the architectural drawings. In a lawsuit, your claims or defenses are like the architect's drawing. When the lawsuit is ultimately presented to the finder of fact, the evidence should support all the elements of any claims or defenses asserted. For this reason, it is important that you and your lawyer spend time considering the different claims or defenses that could apply. You must assert the right claims or defenses; if you assert the wrong ones, you might not be able to assert the correct ones at a later date.

It is imperative to understand that litigation is not simply about convincing the jury that you are right and the other guy is wrong. It's not about being more vocal or more aggressive or more assertive. It is about proving your case. To do that, you must provide the judge or the jury with admissible evidence that supports each of the elements of your claims or defenses.

That may sound hypertechnical, but in truth it's like following a recipe in a cookbook. If you are baking a cake, the recipe tells you that you need a certain number of eggs, a certain amount of milk, a certain amount of cake mix, and so on. Lawyers have cookbooks for lawsuits, too. There are legal research materials, jury instructions, and numerous form books that state what each of the necessary elements is for any given claim. You as a client should not abandon your attorney or delegate the process of determining what claims apply in your case. This should be a team effort, and just as you would have to follow correctly the recipe to have a properly baked cake, you need to know what instructions the court has set forth in order to have the proper elements of a cause of action.

If your lawsuit recipe calls for two eggs and a gallon of milk, and you don't have two eggs, it doesn't matter if you have five pounds of butter. You're not making that cake. If you don't have all the required ingredients to allege a cause of action, it won't work. And if you're not talking about cooking, but about injury or loss, that can sometimes sound unfair. You may say, "Well, look, the truth of the matter is I lost a ton of profits. So what if I don't have a contract!" But no matter how bad you feel, you may be flat out of luck if, according to the law, you don't have the requirements for your cause of action.

Often a party to a lawsuit does not wake up to the reality of what his lawsuit is really about from a legal perspective—in terms of the claims or defenses that actually apply—until many months after the case has been filed and reams of depositions and other discovery have taken place. Be certain your attorney reviews with you at the start all of the different claims or defenses that could apply in your situation, and make sure that you understand the elements of each. Ask your attorney what you have to prove and what type of evidence you must present in order to succeed. You must develop an understanding of these basic legal goals in the structuring of your lawsuit.

What Relief Is at Issue?

To succeed as plaintiff, you need to prove your claims at trial. For example, let's say you're suing for defamation, and you go to trial. You successfully show all legal elements needed to establish defamation: that what the defendant said was untrue and that he knew or should have known it was untrue or acted with reckless disregard for the truth or falsity of his statements. The jury agrees with you. So you've shown that you were defamed, and you've established that the defendant is liable for defaming you.

To prove a claim, you simply establish what is known as liability. Liability means that a party is, in fact, responsible for the consequences of his conduct. If the defense is successful and the plaintiff's cause of action is not proved, then there is no liability, and the case is over.

But if the claim is successful and the defendant is therefore found liable, the issue becomes, What is the remedy? How do we redress this situation? How can we remedy it and make the plaintiff whole again? That remedy is termed relief.

There are essentially three kinds of relief that you can obtain in a lawsuit. The first, and what is most often sought, is some form of monetary damages. This means the defendant pays you money for his conduct.

Relief can also come in the form of an order by the court. For example, if you were a celebrity and someone were publishing naked photos of you without your permission, you could ask the court for an order prohibiting the defendant from publishing those photos. Or maybe your neighbor has put a fence on your property; you could ask the court to issue an order that he remove the fence.

The third kind of relief is called declaratory relief because it comes in the form of a declaration of rights by the court. You might ask for this if you wanted the court to determine an issue that doesn't directly concern monetary damages. For example, let's say two songwriters are having a dispute about a song; one of them is claiming he wrote the song by himself. After rendering a verdict, the court might issue a declaration that the song was written by Writer A instead of Writer B. Or your case may entail a boundary dispute, and you may ask the court to formally declare exactly where the boundary lies.

Relief—what you're suing to obtain—is the other crucial area (besides your claim) to understand going into a trial. In Chapter 6, I'll discuss relief in much greater detail, including the various kinds of damages you might seek. In addition, you need to be aware that the different types of relief you can ask for are often interrelated. A doctrine called the election of remedies, for example, essentially states that if you seek and receive one particular remedy, you may not be entitled to another one for the same claim. Asking for a certain kind of order, for example, may preclude you from also asking for money based on the same claim. You will need to go through the issue of damages conscientiously with your attorney.

Burden of Proof

In every lawsuit, both parties will try to convince the decision maker (judge or jury) that they are right, that their version of events should be accepted, and that their facts support a claim or a defense under the law. For a case to go forward, one side has to go first and put certain basic facts before the jury to establish its claims. That responsibility is called the burden of proof.

For example, California law includes the following jury instruction:

> A plaintiff in a civil action will have a burden of proving by a "preponderance of the evidence" all the facts necessary to establish the essential elements of their claim.

The instruction continues:

> "Preponderance of the evidence" means evidence that has more convincing force than that opposed to it. If the evidence is so evenly balanced that you're unable to say that the evidence on either side of an issue preponderates, your finding on that issue must be against the party who had the burden of proving it.

So the party who asserts a claim or a defense carries the burden of proving that assertion through a preponderance of evidence. If the evidence looks like a tie, then the party asserting the claim or defense will not have met the burden of proving the assertion, and the jury cannot find in that party's favor on that claim or defense.

Some people will define *preponderance of evidence* simply to mean that you must prove that something is "more likely than not." Juries may conclude that they're not certain who is telling the truth, but it seems more likely than not that this person is telling the truth. They find in that person's favor on that basis alone.

This differs from the level of proof needed to make a finding in a criminal case, where it's "proof beyond a reasonable doubt"—a much higher standard. Jurors are permitted to have lots of reasonable doubts in civil trials. If it simply looks more likely than not that the defendant violated someone's rights as alleged, they can find the defendant liable.

Statute of Limitations

Whether you are considering filing a lawsuit or have just been served with a suit, one of the first issues your attorney will need to examine is the relevant statute of limitations. The statute of limitations is the time period specified by law within which an action must be filed. If you are wronged but don't file a lawsuit before the legally required time period expires, with a few exceptions, you will be legally barred from suing.

The idea behind the statute of limitations is that it's better to resolve matters sooner than later. People die, witnesses move, evidence gets lost, people's memories get hazier over time. If you're going to sue Bill Smith, it is more fair to do it now so he can inspect the evidence while it still exists and interview the witnesses while they're still available and can recall details. While you typically don't want to rush to court to file, you usually want to file suit sooner rather than later, especially if a lot of witnesses are involved in your matter.

Statutes of limitations are generally set by state or federal legislatures, and they vary depending on what kind of claim you wish to bring and whom you're suing. Not only do these statutes vary from state to state, they may be changed from time to time. In general, they are seldom less than a year. As an example, here are some general statutes of limitations in force in California:

- For property damage, the statute is generally three years from when the damage occurred.
- For oral contracts, you must file within two years of the date the contract was breached.
- For written contracts, you have four years to file from the date of breach. (Written contracts can be anything from a detailed, formal legal agreement signed by the parties to a messy repair estimate a roofer asked you to initial before he started work. If you made an oral agreement with someone and later simply signed a receipt of delivery, this might constitute a written agreement.)
- For personal injury, you must file within one year of the injury or, if you didn't discover it at the time it occurred, the discovery of the injury.
- For fraud and medical malpractice, the statute is three years from the date of discovery.
- If you want to sue a city, county, or state agency in California, a statute of limitations generally requires you to take certain actions within six months of an occurrence.

Be sure to check with a lawyer for your own specific situation. In some instances the statue of limitations can be suspended, or "tolled." For example, the statute may be tolled when a party is imprisoned, insane, living out of state, or a minor.

Discuss right away with an attorney what the statute of limitations is on your matter. Most lawyers will know the statute of limitations, but it's not always cut-and-dried. You should not assume that the lawyer will always consider the applicable statute of limitations. Don't wait until a month or two after you've retained the lawyer to ask what the statute of limitations is for the claims you will be asserting. You need to go over this right away, as it may affect the timing of the filing of a complaint (if you're considering filing one) or the assertion of defenses or the filing of your own complaint against the plaintiff (if you're a defendant).

Sometimes a lawyer will be so focused on the merits of your case that he may not calculate the statute of limitations until some point after your case has been filed and accepted. A problem could arise later, when more discovery has been taken or when your lawyer sits down to prepare for trial; he may realize that he didn't plead the best causes of action to fit your facts. If the statute of limitations has passed, it's hard to amend the complaint to include a new or additional cause.

Have your lawyer give you in writing a specific date when the statute of limitations will run out on your claims. Put that date on your calendar or somewhere where you will see it. If you are within a few months of that date and the lawyer still hasn't filed a complaint, start to get nervous and make sure he's going to get the right complaint on file in time.

If You're a Corporation or a Partnership

If you are a corporation bringing suit, make certain your corporation is in good standing in your state. This means ensuring that you have taken care of all proper corporate duties, such as filing the appropriate certificate with the state and paying your taxes. It's important to know that in most state courts a corporation has the authority to appear as a plaintiff or a defendant only if it is in good standing.

I have seen mom-and-pop corporations get stuck because they failed to keep their records or taxes up-to-date or to pay their franchise or some other tax. When they file an important lawsuit, the other side moves to dismiss on the grounds that the corporation is not in good standing. The court throws out the lawsuit on that basis. It's just too easy to log onto a computer and see if a corporation has complied with all the requirements to be a corporation in good standing.

Even worse, if your corporation gets sued and is not in good standing with the state, you may have no right to defend yourself. The case is over. With few exceptions, you may lose, even if you are completely blameless. I've had clients whose corporation gets sued, and they're in arrears on their taxes because it's a defunct entity. They realize, "Oh my God, I can't defend myself because I'm not in good standing!"

If you are in a partnership and want to bring a suit, you may need to first determine who owns the rights to the suit. That's not always clear. You could be a dentist or doctor in partnership with others, and you want to bring suit on behalf of the partnership. For you to be able to sue, the other partners may have to agree to join in.

Insurance Coverage

Another issue you definitely want to investigate and discuss with an attorney is whether you have any kind of insurance coverage that could pay for your damages or for your prosecution (or defense) in a lawsuit. Do you have any insurance policies? Homeowner's? Renter's? Auto? Business? An umbrella policy? It is always a good idea to have an attorney review your policies as soon as possible to see whether potential coverage exists. Never assume you do not have coverage, as you may be pleasantly surprised.

Find out if you have insurance coverage that would help offset some or all of your damages. You may well be able to collect on your own insurance policy, even if another party was responsible and even if you're pursuing that other party and expect to be reimbursed by him or his insurance company. The common example is a car accident where the other party was at fault. Your own insurance carrier has an obligation to reimburse you based on any coverage you had in place for medical bills and auto repairs. Some policies have a "right of subrogation" clause, which basically means they're entitled to recoup some or all of what they pay out on your behalf, should you later collect a settlement or award from the responsible party.

Another reason to have your attorney review your own insurance policies is to find out whether there is even a remote possibility that you have some kind of insurance coverage that would cover your legal fees. If you're a landlord, for example, and a tenant sues you alleging you were negligent in some way, you probably have an insurance policy on your building that may require your carrier to pay the costs of your defense, as well as any judgment. You paid for this coverage. Now is the time to use it.

If you invoke your insurance policy and there is coverage, the insurance company will have a substantial say in how your case is handled. Sorting out the rights of the insurer versus those of the insured can become very complex. In some situations, it is important to hire not only a litigator but also an insurance specialist to review your policy and inform you of your rights.

If you're a defendant, whether or not you have insurance may affect how hard you're willing to fight and whether you're going to litigate a case through trial or try to settle early. If you do not have insurance coverage but the plaintiff thinks you do, you may want to voluntarily disclose that you do not have insurance. Sometimes the plaintiff will lose interest and drop the lawsuit when he realizes there isn't a deep pocket covering you.

You might read your insurance policy and conclude that you don't have any coverage under that policy pertaining to your situation. But you may well be mistaken, and there may actually be stated or implied coverage of which you're unaware. The area of insurance law is complex, changing, and expanding all the time. There are law firms that specialize in interpreting insurance policies and helping enforce the terms (where necessary), especially when those terms might be interpreted to cover the costs of litigation. An entire book could probably be written on this subject alone, so whether you're a plaintiff or a defendant, you should have your attorney review your policies. If necessary, get an expert in this specialty to analyze your coverage and advise you what to do.

Selling the Rights to Your Lawsuit

Under the law, you are generally permitted to assign the rights to your lawsuit. "Assigning" means that you agree to prosecute your lawsuit, and any damages or recovery will go to a third party, usually in exchange for a payment. In the same way that companies factor and buy accounts receivable from other companies, there are sophisticated people who specialize in purchasing certain kinds of claims.

A famous example of selling an interest in a lawsuit was the case of *Intex Plastic Sales Co. v. Charles Hall.* Charles Hall invented and built the first water bed in 1968, as part of a master's degree program at San Francisco State University. Some twenty-plus years later, Hall was sued by Intex Plastic Sales Company, a subsidiary of a Taiwanese company, in an attempt to declare Hall's patent invalid. Hall then countersued on a patent infringement claim. As Hall's legal fees mounted, he realized he could not continue to press his case unless he could come up with several hundred thousand dollars. A group of investors acquired part of Hall's right to enforce his patent. In March 1991, a six-person federal jury ruled that from 1982 to 1988, Intex had infringed on Hall's 1971 patent. Hall and the investors who had paid to prosecute his lawsuit eventually received $6.8 million in damages and interest from Intex. Additionally, Hall and his investors were then able to force other companies that had infringed on his water bed patent to pay royalties as well.

One thing to keep in mind is that a claim for punitive damages may not usually be assigned.

Jurisdiction

If you're going to sue, you'll need to have a lawyer help you figure out whether you're suing in the right court and in the right state. This depends on which court has jurisdiction, that is, the authority to hear your case. There are two types of jurisdiction: personal jurisdiction and subject matter jurisdiction.

Personal jurisdiction concerns whether you have a right to sue the plaintiff in a given forum —a particular county, state, or country. For example, let's say you flew to England, ate at a restaurant, and were made sick by some improperly prepared food. You flew back to your home state of Alabama and decided to sue the English restaurant in Alabama. You may well, under the law of Alabama, have a cause of action for negligence or for some other form of personal injury. But unless the English restaurant is part of a chain that's also in Alabama or has had some business dealings in Alabama that would relate to this claim, you most likely don't have a right to sue the English restaurant in Alabama. You don't have a right to file a lawsuit in Alabama because the set of facts and circumstances entirely occurred in England, not Alabama.

Here's another, less extreme example. Let's say you, a resident of Virginia, are in a car accident in Washington, D.C. The person who hit your car (the defendant) doesn't live or work in Virginia and didn't have any dealings with you in Virginia concerning the car accident. As much as it might be convenient for you to sue the other driver through a Virginia court, you would not likely be permitted to do so. Only the court in the neighboring District of Columbia would have personal jurisdiction over the other driver, since that is where the accident occurred.

Personal jurisdiction requires at the most basic level that defendants have some minimum contacts with the forum in which they're being sued, which means they have to have either had some dealing in the forum directly connected to the incident in question or be conducting some form of business in the forum in which the suit is being brought. This requirement is important to consider, because if you file in the wrong state, the court will bounce your case out of that state. If you live in Oregon and have an Oregon lawyer you like, you probably would prefer to file in Oregon. But if the incident occurred in Vermont, you may not be able to have the defendant hauled into Oregon. Instead, you may have to sue in Vermont. That can be quite a hurdle.

The other kind of jurisdiction, subject matter jurisdiction, involves just what its name suggests: what the lawsuit is about. The law is set up so that certain courts have jurisdiction over certain subject matter, meaning some claims belong in state court and some belong in federal court. With certain exceptions, state courts do not have the right to decide cases that have to do with federal law. If your case has to do with a violation of federal antitrust laws, it's unlikely a state court will have the right to hear or decide that case. Subject matter jurisdiction determines whether you can file that case in state or federal court.

Venue

In some situations, two or three different states might have both personal and subject matter jurisdiction for your matter. Perhaps you have to decide between filing suit in federal or state court. Within a state you can file your lawsuit in two or three different counties. In each situation, the issue becomes, Which is the most convenient forum? A discussion about the most convenient place to sue involves choosing the venue, is the specific circuit, district, or county within a state or within the federal court system.

The analysis of where you should sue, among acceptable alternatives, turns on issues such as these: Where did the incident in question take place? If it's a contract claim, where was the contract negotiated?

Where was performance to have occurred? Where was the contract breached? Where do the parties reside? Where do the witnesses reside? Does one particular state or county have a strong public policy concern or interest in the dispute?

If you sue a person in the wrong county, state, or country, or if you sue a person over whom you don't have personal jurisdiction, there are a number of motions that the defendant could immediately file to dismiss the suit or have it transferred to another court. Again, it helps to have a lawyer experienced in litigation matters, because if you pick the wrong court or sue a defendant in the wrong state, it can be a very costly process to have your lawsuit dismissed and then transferred or refiled. You could spend a fortune in legal fees before you make any headway at all. Therefore, have your lawyer explain very carefully to you the exact court where the lawsuit should be brought to and ask him to explain if there is any chance of the lawsuit being dismissed because it should be brought in another court.

Judge, Jury, or Administrative Proceeding

Is your case more suitable for a jury trial or for a trial where there is no jury and the judge determines the verdict? Not every case has a *Perry Mason*–type ending with a jury of your peers in the box. In some cases, in fact, you're not even entitled to have a jury; a lawyer would have to advise you whether you have the kind of case where juries aren't allowed. For example, if you were asking simply for declaratory relief—a declaration from the court regarding the rights of the parties—typically that does not involve a jury.

Bench trials (cases in which you're asking the judge to make the decision) often go to trial much sooner than cases where you want a jury. That's because a judge doesn't need to worry about having a group of jurors available. If the judge is available, he can try the case. In addition, bench trials are less expensive, because you don't have to pay jury fees, you don't have to prepare elaborate jury instructions, and the judge can loosen the rules of evidence to make the trial go faster.

A judge will be much more schooled on the law and how it should be correctly applied than a jury will be. The truth is, juries don't always understand and apply the law properly. A jury trial can often be more about swaying a group of people to your position using emotion. Judges, on the other hand, are not persuaded by charisma, charm, or a great closing argument. They are more scientific in their review of evidence and less influenced by oratory. If you have a case that looks strong on the law and the facts, and if you're not looking for a huge punitive damages award—such as those often awarded by juries swayed by passion and argument—you may opt for a bench trial. If, for example, you have a business dispute that you simply want resolved as quickly and cost-effectively as possible, talk to your lawyer about having your case decided by a judge rather than a jury—in a bench trial. Not only will your case probably go to trial sooner, you're likely to have a more legally accurate decision, and the process will be less expensive.

Do not assume that you automatically have a right to a jury trial. You have to specifically request it and pay the jury fees by a certain time; if you fail to meet stated deadlines, you can lose your right to a jury trial altogether. Each jurisdiction has specific rules as to how you preserve this right. In some jurisdictions you need to make a demand for the jury when you file your first set of papers, the complaint. Other jurisdictions specify a time period by which you must file a request and post jury fees. Make certain that your lawyer goes over with you your state's requirements to ensure you don't lose your right to a jury trial, if you want one.

Some matters need to be presented to an administrative agency rather than a court. For example, certain workers' compensation claims must be presented to a labor department. Certain administrative claims that have to do with your electric or water bill often must go first to a government agency. A tenant who wants relief for a housing code violation may have to submit the matter first to a governmental agency or department before filing suit. Most matters relating to government or to rights that usually arise under some federal or state statute, unemployment issues, labor issues, issues having to do with the Department of Motor Vehicles—many of these kinds of agencies require that disputes be submitted to an administrative body before you can litigate in civil court.

If you believe your matter might involve some kind of violation of a government-related rule, ordinance, or regulation, make sure that you're talking to a lawyer who has some background in administrative issues.

In these situations, you may have to first exhaust your administrative remedies before filing a lawsuit. If you ignore a commission or some board set up to handle your kind of dispute, but instead just file suit, your case may be summarily thrown out on that basis.

Cases before administrative agencies are very different from court cases. Often administrative proceedings do not involve formal rules of evidence. Sometimes they can be less expensive and move more quickly. Usually a hearing officer instead of a jury makes the decision. Again, if your case must go before an administrative agency, talk to a lawyer who has some background in administrative matters.

Choice of Law and Venue Provisions

If your lawsuit arises from a contractual issue, look at that contract carefully. It may contain a provision that you're not permitted to file a suit at all, but must arbitrate any disputes. Other contracts allow you to sue but specify which court will have jurisdiction. You may or may not be able to overcome such provisions.

Does the contract have a choice of law provision that says the law of a particular jurisdiction will apply in any legal disputes? Is the contract subject, for example, to the laws of Illinois? Does your contract have a venue provision, stating that you have to litigate the case in a particular jurisdiction? If it does have these types of law and venue provisions, you should be careful when you're talking to lawyers about them.

Why? Well, let's say you're in New York and have a contract dispute, and the contract has a California choice of law and venue provision. Chances are you aren't going to get on a plane and see a lawyer in California to ask whether that provision can be enforced. You're going to see a New York lawyer because he's closer to you. You may ask, "Does this clause mean I really have to litigate this issue in California? Is there something I can do to overturn this clause?" Some lawyers may have a personal bias toward answering, "I may be able to find a way around that choice of venue clause." And they may—or may not.

You may find that those clauses are not so easily overcome. You may spend a lot of money getting up to speed with and developing a relationship with your lawyer in New York, and he may file your suit in New

York, only to have a court say, "Wait a minute, the contract says this has to be tried in California!" Your case gets bounced. Then you have to start over 3,000 miles away, going through all the same steps—talking with people, checking references, interviewing lawyers, and asking them their opinion. The inordinate amount of money you spent back in New York is largely wasted.

If you have a choice of law or choice of venue provision, that's a huge red flag. It's your time and money, but as the client, you should know that if your contract contains clauses like "You must arbitrate," "You must litigate in State X," "The law of State X will apply," and "Service has to be on such-and-such a person," you should not blindly accept the word of an attorney who says he thinks he can dance his way around those clauses. Courts tend to enforce those clauses.

State Versus Federal Court

As previously mentioned, you may have the option of bringing your case in federal or state court. That choice arises if your dispute is a federal question involving federal statutes. It may also arise if you have diversity of citizenship, and the amount in dispute is larger than $75,000. Diversity of citizenship essentially means that the parties in the suit are from different states. To avoid giving any one party an unfair home state advantage, a federal court may hear your case. A federal district court is not part of any state court system but is part of the integrated federal court system with its own codes and rules.

If you have the option of bringing your suit in federal court or of having a state suit against you transferred to federal court, you need to weigh the advantages and disadvantages of filing in federal versus state court. Obviously, no lawyer can advise you properly without knowing all the facts of your case. Many important issues can come into play. You'll need to consult with your lawyer to decide. That said, there are some general differences between the courts that you may want to factor into the thinking you do with your attorney.

The way a complaint is drafted doesn't differ a lot between state and federal court, except that if you're in federal court, you're often operating under federal statutes and what is often called "federal question jurisdiction." As a lawyer, I have to look at the nuances of a statute in order to make sure I'm pleading the cause of action correctly.

In contrast to many state courts, federal court requires the defendant to file a specific, line-by-line, answer to the complaint (whereas in many state courts, a "general denial" set forth in a few sentences is allowed). That means the defendant will have to respond to your complaint line by line, denying or admitting each of the allegations. Federal court also tends to have a shorter time period for responding to a complaint: twenty days instead of the thirty you get in most states. In addition, you generally have to make your demand for a jury trial in your complaint (or else you will waive your right to a jury trial, and a judge will hear and decide your case). In certain state courts, you don't have to make a demand for a jury until several months later in the process.

Probably the biggest difference I've noticed between state and federal courts is in the systems themselves. For one thing, when you walk into federal court, you see a picture of the President and the Vice President of the United States, so you know you're in federal court. Aside from the federal courts themselves tending to look a bit nicer, the judges may have a little more experience than the typical state judge. Federal courts usually have more funding than state courts, and it shows in the level of work the court puts out.

A federal court judge generally has law clerks right out of law school, people who were at the top of their graduating class and who will do a two-year internship clerking for that judge. These clerks thoroughly research everything that the lawyers submit to the judge. Every one of the briefs is carefully read and reviewed. The decisions of the judge also tend to be very carefully written. You can see that legal issues are really being considered in fine detail at the federal level.

Because state funds tend to be more limited, state judges don't have the same kind of clerk resources available. So the judges themselves often work up the cases, read the papers, do the research. They frequently have a heavier docket, and sometimes it's obvious they're rather short on time when they're hurrying you to get to the point. The result is that they may make more mistakes than a federal judge because they didn't have time to read the papers closely or didn't pull the cases down and read what they said. They didn't compare a lawyer's argument with what the case actually claims, to determine whether that lawyer's interpretation of the case is really valid. On more than one occasion, I've seen a state judge who doesn't appear to have closely read the papers, and he's issuing rulings based primarily on instinct. That's much less likely to happen in a federal court case.

In state court, a jury can reach a verdict by a certain majority of the jurors agreeing (in California, for example, eight out of twelve jurors must agree to reach a verdict). In federal court, though, the jury must be unanimous in order to reach a verdict. So in federal court, if you're a defendant, all you need is one juror to side with you and the plaintiff can't win; in state court, the plaintiff only needs the established majority to win.

If I had a case where I had a choice to file in federal or state court, I would probably base my decision in part on what kind of jury I'd be likely to get in each court. If I were representing an underdog or a member of a minority group, I would probably file in state court in downtown Los Angeles. The jury pool will be more inner-city-based, so it potentially will have more minorities. I expect this downtown Los Angeles jury to deliver a "Robin Hood" kind of verdict favorable to my underdog or minority client. Also, the state court system in California has a commitment to trying cases by a certain time, so the case may get to trial sooner than in federal court.

I would also probably choose state court for plaintiffs whose case is relatively weak but has an emotional appeal, and if the client will sell well to a jury. Many large cities have a higher percentage of state court judges who are so overwhelmed with their docket that a weak case will sometimes slip by them. They don't have the resources to screen out a lot of weak cases, and it's easier to err on the side of letting someone have his day in court and letting a jury make the decision. If you're likable and your case has emotional appeal, you could be in a good position to win.

Federal court judges rarely allow an undeserving case to proceed. With almost every federal court judge, his team of clerks is more likely than not going to detect a case that's legally weak and stop it from going to trial. On the flip side, for a defendant with a really strong defense and an opportunity to remove the case from state to federal court, if you're a little concerned about the Russian roulette nature of busy downtown state court systems, you might want to remove your case to federal court, where you know it's more likely to get a careful review. The frailties of a legal theory will show up more reliably in federal court.

"Now about your loss
of consortium claim . . ."

Nuts and Bolts: Damages

I don't know if I want a lawyer to tell me what I cannot do.
I hire him to tell me how to do what I want to do.

—J. P. Morgan, American financier

Essentially, whatever you are suing to recover is called your "relief."
Usually your relief is money, but you could also seek an order from
the court telling someone to do or not to do something in order to
address your injury. For example, rather than—or in addition to—
seeking money, you may want to ask the court to issue an order saying, "Defendant will not publish or distribute this photograph," or,
"Defendant shall remove said fence from the plaintiff's property."

In deciding what damages to recover, you and your lawyer need
to pay attention to a legal concept called election of remedies. Stated
simply, election of remedies means the choice of what relief you
want. Some situations require you to make such a choice. Maybe the
court will issue an order that the defendant do or not do something;
maybe you can obtain a judgment ordering the defendant to pay you

money. In certain instances, you can't have both. You have to elect what kind of relief you want.

What Are Your Damages?

In your complaint you allege the defendant's misconduct, and you must prove at trial by a preponderance of evidence that it is more likely than not that the defendant committed the wrongs you're alleging. But that's not all. Once you convince the jury of that, you must also prove exactly how much you were damaged and ask the jury to award you that amount.

Typically, for example, people in personal injury suits sue to recover the monies they incurred for medical treatment, for damage to their property, for pain and suffering, and perhaps for lost income or loss of consortium. So let's say you were in a car accident for which the other driver was at fault. You might sue to recoup the costs associated with an ambulance ride, charges for hospital and other medical examinations, and the costs of treatment and therapy to recuperate. You'll probably also sue to recover the cost to properly repair or replace your car, and you'll ask for compensation for the pain and suffering you've had to endure as a result of your injuries. If you weren't able to work for a period because of the accident, you may ask to be compensated for lost income. If your injuries were serious and long-lasting enough to affect your marital relationship with your spouse, you might be entitled to an award for the loss of consortium (and your spouse may conceivably have a claim for their loss, too).

If you lost money when the defendant breached a contract, you would be entitled to an award for what you would have received had the defendant honored the contract, as well as any other damages the contract might entitle you to, such as an award for attorney's fees.

If you suffered severe emotional distress as a result of the defendant's conduct, you may sue to recover money for this, too. If the defendant's conduct was outrageous, beyond standards of decency, and/or fraudulent, and if the defendant acted with the intent to trample your rights, you may ask the jury to award you punitive or exemplary damages—forcing the defendant to pay you as punishment. Punitive damages are awarded in addition to compensating you for your regular damages.

The relief you seek for your damages is the sum of money you affix to the damage itself. It may not be difficult to assess how much damage you suffered when a contract said the defendant was to pay you $100,000, but he didn't pay a cent. That damage is $100,000. But if as a result of not having the $100,000 at the time the defendant was supposed to pay you, you suffered other damages as a consequence—maybe a related project fell through—there may be arguments for additional damages, if you can show that the defendant should have foreseen that these additional damages could result from the breach.

It's easier to figure out what a $100,000 breach of contract case is worth than what a broken arm is worth, or how much damage was caused by a contractor's lousy work, or how much money you lost as a result of being sexually harassed, distressed, and driven out of your job. A number of very specific considerations come into play. If you broke your arm, the considerations include the impact on your earnings. Are you a professional tennis player who was earning $500,000 a year before you broke your arm? Or are you just an average Joe who had a broken arm?

In some situations there are schedules that delineate exactly how much damages you may be entitled to. Different areas have statutes and schedules that set caps for how much you can recover for various causes of action. Therefore, it's critical that you talk with a lawyer who is not only familiar with your particular kind of claim but also your particular injury, and who can inform you right away when such statutes apply.

Forms of Monetary Damages

There are various forms of monetary damages. Terms you may encounter include actual, compensatory, consequential, continuing, excessive, exemplary, general, liquidated, nominal, presumed, punitive, special, and treble damages.

Actual or Compensatory Damages

Damages that are "real," meaning the amount is to compensate for the plaintiff's real loss or injury, are called actual damages. The term contrasts these damages with "nominal" or "punitive" damages. Thus, actual damages are not for purposes of punishment or making a nominal award. Rather, they restore what you lost.

Damages that compensate the injured party for the injury sustained, and nothing more, may also be called compensatory damages. *Actual* and *compensatory* are two terms for essentially the same type of damages.

Consequential Damages

Sometimes a person causes damages that, in turn, cause additional damages. Consequential damages are any damage, loss, or injury that does not flow directly from the defendant's act, but instead from consequences or results of the act. If you broke your arm as a result of someone's negligence, you should be compensated for all of the medical care to your arm; that's an actual damage. If you are a major league pitcher whose contract is up for renegotiation and the new contract is impacted by the injury to your arm, then the additional loss would be consequential.

Continuing Damages

In some cases damages accrue from a single injury but are ongoing. The legal term for these ongoing damages is *continuing damages*.

Excessive Damages

If a court finds that damages awarded by a jury are grossly in excess of the amount warranted, the court may determine the damages are "excessive." Thus, *excessive damages* is a term used after the fact.

Exemplary or Punitive Damages

If the defendant aggravated the wrong to the plaintiff by engaging in violence, oppression, malice, fraud, or wanton and wicked conduct, the court may award exemplary or punitive damages. These are damages awarded over and above what will compensate the plaintiff for his loss and are intended to solace the plaintiff for mental anguish, hurt feelings, shame, or degradation, or to otherwise punish the defendant for his behavior. The idea is to "make an example" of the defendant. Punitive damages are often set as a percentage of the defendant's net worth and are usually in some relation to the amount of compensatory or actual damages.

A wide variety of rules relate to punitive damages, and in some jurisdictions the jury may not consider punitive damages until a second stage of the proceedings. That is, you may first have to win your case, prove the defendant acted with malice or was otherwise oppressive, then have the jury consider a separate sum for punitive damages. If you're going to seek punitive damages, you need to discuss with your attorney the special rules that apply in your local jurisdiction.

General Damages

The basic set of damages that you typically would expect to recover from an incident are called general damages. These are the damages that the law itself presumes to have occurred from a wrong that's been complained of. General damages may be established by statute (laws passed by the state or federal legislature) or in case law (the courts' written decisions).

Liquidated Damages

Often a contract provides that if there is a breach of the contract, the person who caused the breach must pay a specific dollar amount. In those instances, that amount is referred to as liquidated damages.

Nominal Damages

In an action where there's no substantial loss or injury to be compensated, but still there's been a technical invasion of rights, the court may award nominal damages. Typical nominal damages are one dollar.

Presumed or Statutory Damages

Sometimes the law can presume damage from certain conduct. If, for example, you slander someone by telling others that the person committed a crime, then damages are presumed. You don't have to prove that you were damaged by this false allegation; damage is presumed by law. In some instances a statute specifies the sum of money you will recover for this damage.

Special Damages

Lawyers often talk about "special damages," especially in personal injury cases. These are actual damages, but they are not the necessary result of the injury complained of. Rather, as the name suggests, they are damages by reason of special circumstances or conditions. An example of a special damage might be a form of emotional distress damages in a personal injury case: someone defamed you, and you suffered extreme emotional distress as a result. Special damages must be specifically pleaded and proved.

Treble Damages

Some statutes, especially federal statutes such as antitrust laws, allow you to triple your damages. In a way, damages are like punitive damages; they award more than the actual loss.

Be Reasonable in Your Request

When determining your damages, don't claim too high an amount in damages. Juries don't like it when they believe a plaintiff is overreaching. You may have a great case, the defendant may look terrible and very guilty, but you may look unreasonable if you stick in everything but the kitchen sink and say the defendant is responsible for all of your ills. In addition to being likable, you want to appear reasonable to a judge and jury. Avoid putting in nickel-and-dime damages; forget about the $14 parking charge from something you had to do because of the defendant's misconduct.

Your attorney can ask you on the stand about monies you had to spend and about your belief that the defendant's conduct forced you to spend them. You'll look very reasonable to a jury if you're not trying to claim every last cent the defendant cost you. Impressing a jury can help ensure that you will get 100 percent of what you are requesting.

You also need to be sure that your damages are not too speculative. The law doesn't permit a jury to award damages that are purely speculative. For this reason, defendants often assert that the plaintiff's damages are too speculative. Perhaps you don't have a specific track record of your profits in order to argue lost profits, or your damages theory may be too difficult to establish. If your start-up company was put out of business by a big corporation, how are you going to prove what your lost profits were if you haven't yet had a profitable year on your books? Or if you're a movie producer suing because you were denied a credit, it may be very hard to establish your loss of future earnings as a result of having been denied the credit.

Finally, your lawyer will have to look into whether there are limits on damages for your particular claim. Certain states have placed caps on medical malpractice damages. A lot of people assume that if something goes wrong and involves some negligence, they're automatically entitled to receive punitive damages. That's not necessarily the case. You should probably have a sobering discussion with your attorney about punitive damages, because they're not awarded as often as they once were. In some states, voters have passed initiatives (backed by insurance companies) that reduce the amount plaintiffs can be awarded for a variety of claims.

Attorney's Fees

Your attorney's fees can be seen as a "damage." They're a necessary expense related to the defendant's misconduct. In the United States, however, the prevailing party does not automatically recover attorney's fees from the other side. He can recover court costs, but that's limited to charges such as court reporters, transcripts, cost of exhibits, and other costs associated with the acts necessary to bring the case to trial and a resolution. However, if you're suing someone over a contract with a clause that says the prevailing party should recover its attorney's fees, then you will in all likelihood be able to recover some of them. Additionally, certain statutes provide that if the other party violates the statute, then you can be awarded your attorney's fees. Just always keep in mind that cases in which the prevailing party is awarded their attorney's fees are the exception—not the rule!

In a handful of instances, you may be able to recover attorney's fees by statute. That's something you want to discuss with your attorney, and you'd certainly want to know it at the outset of your case, as it would affect every aspect of your analysis. If you feel your case is strong and know you are going to recover your attorney's fees, you might be willing to pay more for your representation.

Additionally, if you have a contingency fee agreement, you need to address how an award of attorney's fees will affect your attorney's percentage. Will the percentage of recovery include any attorney's fees recovered? Will the attorney's percentage be more overall if you recoup attorney's fees? Also, how will the court determine a reasonable amount of attorney's fees in a contingency fee case, where you're not actually paying your attorney up front? This is why it is very important for your contingent fee lawyer to send you monthly bills showing the time they have put in on your case, even if they are not charging you hourly. If there is a basis for recovering attorney's fees, your request for relief will include a request for those attorney's fees. You will always ask for court costs.

Damages from the Defendant's Perspective

Even if you have a solid defense and believe the plaintiff will never prove that you're liable, you have to take into account that the judge or jury may see things differently. There is almost always the possibility— even if remote—you will get hit with a liability verdict and significant damages. You must factor this into your equation and take a hard look at the worst-case scenario.

Some defendants decide to admit liability because they realize they have weakness on the liability portion of their case; that is, they realize they're going to have a problem defending against the cause of action the plaintiff has asserted. Nevertheless, the defendant might choose to litigate the case simply because the plaintiff's demand (his request for relief) is too substantial. The defendant honestly believes that he can prove the damages are less than what the plaintiff asserts they are. Thus, some cases are litigated not because the parties disagree on whether there's liability, but because they disagree on the issue of damages.

Damages and Discovery: Opening Pandora's Box?

An entire book could be written just on the subject of damages. Determining the value of a breached contract, the net worth of an ex-spouse, the reasonable cost to repair something that was faulty, the actual amount of royalties the studio should have paid if it had given an honest accounting—these sorts of issues are important and can be argued ad nauseam. People make very good livings doing nothing but assessing the value of various kinds of damages. You may well need to have such experts brought in for your matter. (For more on experts, see Chapter 14.)

When determining which damages you want to claim, you must understand up front that you are going to have to prove your damages: first, that the damage exists, and second, that the defendant caused it. The defendant, in turn, will try to show that any damages you may have suffered are either exaggerated or faked, and/or that they were actually caused in whole or in part by something or someone other than the defendant. Even if you can prove that the defendant is liable for his misconduct, you must also prove the connection between the defendant and any damages. Thus, when you sue, you not only put the facts surrounding the defendant's liability at issue, you also put the facts surrounding the damage you claim at issue.

If you claim the defendant's actions led to your broken leg and want to be compensated for it, the defense now has the right to have its expert examine your leg, and will want to obtain copies of everything that might be relevant to the injuries you're alleging. You might be forced to turn over the name of each doctor you've seen in the past five or more years, and then the defense lawyer will subpoena all your medical records, including records you may believe are totally irrelevant. They'll pore over your OB-GYN records, your urology records, your chiropractor's records, your plastic surgeon's records—in short, every medical record of yours they can get their hands on. They're on a fishing expedition, hoping to find evidence that they can point to as an alternative source of your problem. The defendant's medical expert will see you for an appointment. His job, everyone will understand, will be to help the defendant counter your claims and, probably, to try to help the defense prove that you're actually a liar and a fake, and/or that your injury was preexisting, so the defendant shouldn't have to pay for your medical treatment.

Likewise, other kinds of claims will give the defense team access to information about your personal or business life. If you are seeking compensation for emotional distress, the defendant has the right to review your therapist's or psychiatrist's files. You may be examined by the defendant's psychologist or psychiatrist, who may then testify that you are a liar and are faking injuries. If you are seeking compensation for lost work, the defendant will be entitled to fully examine your employment history, potentially including confidential files. If you're a freelancer, the

defense may even talk to your clients. The defense team may find someone to testify that you lost work because you're sloppy or careless or not
committed to your work. If you're filing a lawsuit as a company, you
have to be especially careful. The defense may want to look at all kinds
of business records to establish a more favorable (to its side) explanation
of why you lost profits. The defendant might even tip off the IRS if the
search turns up something fishy.

There is an exception as to what discovery can be taken when a
damage is put at issue. That exception is punitive damages. In some
states, if a jury finds the defendant acted with malice or indifference to
your rights, you may be entitled to receive a portion of the defendant's
worth in the form of punitive damages. In California, for example, a
jury can award you as much as one-third of a defendant's net worth. If
you're entitled to one-third, then you need the right to find out how
much the defendant is really worth. You may conduct your own discovery into the defendant's financial worth in order to come up with this,
but only with the permission of the court. To take net worth discovery
of the defendant, you have to first file a motion and convince the judge
from the evidence that there is a "substantial likelihood" that you're
going to prevail at trial. This is a fairly ambiguous standard, subject to
the judge's interpretation. The judge will give the benefit of the doubt
to the defendant in this situation.

Plaintiffs generally wait until a short time before trial—near the
end of discovery, when they've assembled the trial evidence they'll
need—to file a net worth motion against the defendant. If the plaintiff
wins the motion, he will have the right to subpoena any and all of the
defendant's financial and banking records and to depose any accountant
or employee who might have knowledge about the defendant's financial
situation. If the plaintiff loses the net worth motion, he will still have an
opportunity to take some net worth discovery—once he wins the case.

Generally, when the plaintiff has lost the net worth motion, his
lawyer will subpoena the records he wishes to see in order to take net
worth discovery (bank records, tax returns, balance sheets, etc.), but
the subpoena will order the defendant simply to bring these materials
to trial. If the jury finds in the plaintiff's favor and determines that
punitive damages should be awarded, the defendant is supposed to
hand over copies of previously subpoenaed items relating to his net

worth, and the judge may give the plaintiff a short period to conduct discovery. Then evidence of the defendant's net worth will be presented to the jury, which will determine how much to award the plaintiff. It may be important to file a net worth motion before the close of discovery, even if you lose the motion, in order to preserve your right to take net worth discovery.

"Ex parte, res judicata, equitable estoppel, res ipsa loquitur . . . Why don't these guys speak English?"

Nuts and Bolts: The Complaint

The purpose of law is to prevent the strong from always having their way.

—Ovid, first-century Roman poet

In its simplest form, a complaint is your opportunity to put the defendant and the court on notice, in writing, of the basic information in your lawsuit. It tells who you are suing, what the defendant did or failed to do that occasioned the lawsuit, what legal claims you are making and what broad legal theories support those claims, where you are suing (in what court), what type of relief you are requesting, who's representing you, and in some jurisdictions, whether or not you're demanding a jury trial (as opposed to a bench trial, where a judge hears the evidence and renders a verdict). Your complaint will be filed with the court and formally served on the party you're suing.

Its chief purpose is to notify the other party and the court in sufficient detail about the hows and whys of your lawsuit.

Filing your complaint is like stepping up to the tee and taking your first swing at a golf ball to get the game started. Before taking that first swing, you need to consider a few things: Where's the green? Which way is the wind blowing? Are there any trees, sand traps, or lakes to look out for? Which club should you use? Just as you take time to consider before swinging your golf club, you and your attorney need to study the course you're about to begin playing, aim carefully, and consider the hazards that may lie ahead.

What's in the Complaint?

In most jurisdictions the courts used to be concerned about the technical wording of the complaint; they required carefully drafted legal pleadings setting forth in abundant detail a number of necessary facts and issues. Most jurisdictions today, however, allow a much simpler form of pleading called a notice pleading. The basic concept of a notice pleading is to put the defendant on reasonable notice of what he's being sued for. Generally you don't put all or even most of your facts in the complaint, but keep it relatively succinct and to the point, with enough details to state your claim. If you tried to put all fact, details, and evidence into your complaint, it could be a hundred pages long.

A demand letter will say, generally speaking, something like, "You said this. You defamed me. I want a retraction. I want $20,000." A complaint is a more dressed up version of this. It contains separate, enumerated causes of action (your allegations and the specific legal theories you're suing under), a statement of damages (enumerated in specific or general terms of what the defendant's acts or omissions cost you), and a "prayer for relief" (a request to the court of what specifically or generally you'd like to be awarded).

In the example of being defamed, you would probably have a cause of action for defamation and perhaps one or two other related causes of action or alternative theories. For example, you might have a cause of action for intentional infliction of emotional distress, alleging that the defendant intended to harass you along with his defamation. Your complaint would also state what damages you suffered as a result of each individual cause of action. At the end of the complaint the prayer for relief might say, in essence, "I want special damages . . . I want a retraction, and I want the amount of damages I prove at trial."

At other times you want to use the complaint to send a specific message to a defendant. If you think your claim is extremely strong and you have the advantage over the other side, then perhaps you'll put a little bit more information in the complaint as a "sneak preview" of what might be disclosed to certain third parties—if your suit isn't settled quickly.

Some individuals go into a lawsuit with the idea that they're going to file suit and just see what happens. Their funds may be limited, or maybe they can't find a contingency fee lawyer for their matter, but they at least want to launch a lawsuit and see whether taking the step of filing the complaint alone will bring some kind of settlement. This approach works sometimes, but is shortsighted and carries some risk. (See the discussion of counterclaims and cross-complaints in Chapter 8.)

Getting It Right the First Time

A complaint is like a foundation for a house, and a complaint that's poorly written is like a foundation that's not properly laid. A poorly drafted complaint could occasion all sorts of problems for you later. Initially, it may invite a motion to dismiss part or all of it on any of a number of grounds, including that there isn't sufficient detail to support the legal claims you're asserting. For instance, if you want to file a complaint in California for breach of a written contract, you must attach every part of that contract as an exhibit incorporated by reference, or else your cause of action can be dismissed "without prejudice" (meaning you may fix and refile it). In other words, if you simply fail to attach a complete copy of the contract in question to your complaint, the other side can file a motion to dismiss your suit on that basis alone, and the judge will dismiss the suit without prejudice. If you lost your copy of the agreement and couldn't attach it to the complaint, then you would have to allege the facts and circumstances in precisely the right way, stating why you can't attach the agreement, or else your case could still be thrown out.

There are many rules and procedures, which vary from jurisdiction to jurisdiction. A good attorney should know them or be able to find out what they are, and draft your complaint properly. The last thing you want is a complaint that's slapped together in a rush and thrown out on a technicality equally fast. You would have to spend more time and money refiling and re-serving the complaint, just to get back to square one.

Typically, the easiest complaints to draft are for what I would term a mundane commercial dispute: You had a contract with Company X; the company was supposed to deliver fifty widgets but didn't; therefore, Company X breached the contract, and you were damaged by y dollars. The body of these kinds of complaints often includes a brief summary of the contract the plaintiff is attaching, a cursory review of what the essential terms are, allegations of the breach, and a statement of what the damages are. Those can be direct, to-the-point complaints that simply put the other side on notice. I call this "debt collection litigation."

Your case may be a little more complex or may contain causes of action that require more detail and explanation in the complaint in order to be sustained. For example, if you decided to plead fraud against a defendant, you have a high burden to meet in drafting your complaint. Under the law, fraud must be pled with specificity; that means you must provide abundant detail about who, what, when, where, and precisely how fraud entered into the defendant's actions. The court isn't going to let you sue someone for fraud unless you can allege exact facts to back up your claim. Expect just about any defendant who's sued for fraud to attempt to dismiss the complaint on the ground, among others, that you haven't alleged sufficient facts to support a claim of fraud. Or perhaps you're alleging a civil conspiracy, that two or more people plotted to violate your rights, and one had a role in the misdeeds of the other. Well, your lawyer had better feel confident that the facts of your case are strong enough to support a conspiracy, and then he'd better express those facts in enough detail to prevent that cause of action from being thrown out at the outset.

The Complaint as Public Document

Perhaps you or your company is prominent, and your lawsuit is going to have publicity value. Maybe you're a prominent singer who claims that your record company has violated an important state statute and is preventing you from getting money you deserve. Your lawsuit may be as much for the publicity you'll receive as anything else. That means you're going to want a detailed introduction in the complaint, describing who you are, what your career history and accomplishments are, and who the defendant is. You probably want to put your dispute in perspective so that the press will be able to report your lawsuit with just the right emphasis and importance (i.e., the right spin). Some plaintiffs file a complaint with the intent of making a public statement about the defendants and their misconduct.

If your lawsuit is going to draw public interest, you might consider whether there are aspects of your relationship with the defendant that you don't want in the public eye. For example, I was involved in a case where a performer had confidential information that he wanted to preclude a former agent from disclosing to the press. We had to deliberate seriously about whether filing the complaint would expose the confidential information we were suing to prevent the agent from disclosing. The lawsuit would have essentially said, "I am suing because I want an injunction against this person, because he has breached a fiduciary duty and a duty of confidentiality by disclosing sensitive and very private personal information about me that I entrusted to him as an agent." Then, of course, we would have to put the sensitive, very private personal information into the complaint—where the public, including the curious press, could find it and put it into all the tabloids.

Before filing, we decided that we would seek an order sealing the file, a difficult order to obtain. Most judges are hesitant to seal the file. An order sealing your file makes the court papers off-limits to anybody other than the most basic court personnel who have to handle it. No third parties, like the general public or the press, are permitted to read or copy the complaint. There are a number of situations where a client might want his complaint filed under seal. Maybe your case is very personal; maybe you have trade secrets that are an issue in your litigation, and you don't want your competition to have access to your secrets.

We got the order sealing the file, but the client had to decide whether this was enough assurance of privacy to move forward with his suit. Today most court systems scan their complaints into a computer database and store this data on-line in a court computer system. The good news is, that's a lot more efficient than only having it on paper. The bad news is, if you file a complaint and get an order sealing it, there's no longer a guarantee that it will stay private. I was recently in court when the judge made an order sealing a file and then said, "You know, there's no way for me to know who has access to our computer database, and we can't track down everybody who may have accessed it at any given time or who could have downloaded or hacked into it . . . Just so you understand."

Step by Step Through the Complaint

So that you can understand what each term in a complaint refers to, let's go through Figure 2, which is the cover page of a sample complaint. (This complaint conforms to today's California Superior Court rules; complaints in other jurisdictions will vary.) At the top of the complaint is the name and address of the attorney representing the plaintiff. Below that is the name and location of the court where the case will be heard. (This information appears on the summons as well.) Sometimes defendants become very confused when looking at these two lines; some think the name and address of the attorney suing them is some-how affiliated with the court. They call the attorney for the other side and start talking freely with him. If you're sued, don't talk to anyone but your own lawyer.

The complaint then sets forth the name, or "caption," of the case. This is the name(s) of the parties (people or other entity) suing and being sued. The caption is the shorthand name of the case; in our example, it's the last names of the initial plaintiff and initial defendant: *Smith v. Jones*. This, along with your case number (described on p. 95), is how your case will be identified throughout its lifetime. Despite the short caption, a lawsuit may have more than one plaintiff and multiple defendants. Some partnership disputes, for example, have ten different defendants.

Figure 2. First Page of a Sample Complaint

```
1 | FOX, SIEGLER & SPILLANE
    GERARD P. FOX, ESQ., SB# 99999
2 | 1880 Century Park East
    Suite 1114
3 | Los Angeles, CA 90067
    (310) 229-9300
4 |
    Attorneys for Plaintiffs
5 | JOHN SMITH and PEGGY SMITH
6 |
7 |      SUPERIOR COURT FOR THE STATE OF CALIFORNIA
          FOR THE COUNTY OF LOS ANGELES, WEST DISTRICT
8 |
9 | JOHN SMITH AND PEGGY SMITH   ) CASE NO. SC 159 322
                                 )
10|              Plaintiffs,     ) COMPLAINT FOR
                                 ) (1) SLANDER PER SE;
11|      vs.                     ) (2) VIOLATION OF THE
                                 )     IMPLIED COVENANT
12| JOE JONES and MARY WHITE,    )     OF QUIET ENJOYMENT;
    and DOES 1 through 25,       ) (3) WRONGFUL EVICTION;
13| inclusive,                   ) (4) INTENTIONAL
                                 )     INFLICTION OF
14|              Defendants.     )     EMOTIONAL DISTRESS
   _____) (5) CONSPIRACY
15|
16|      Plaintiffs John Smith and Peggy Smith ("Smith" and
17| "Peggy Smith", respectively; collectively, "plaintiffs")
18| allege as follows:
19|
20|                      THE PARTIES
21|      1. Plaintiffs are a married couple who resided
22| together at 12345 Main Street, Los Angeles, California,
23| from January 1, 1997, to August 5, 1999.
24|      2. Upon information and belief, defendant Joe Jones
25| ("Jones") resides at 12345 Pine Street, Los Angeles,
26| California. Jones owns and, for all times relevant hereto,
```

Doe Defendants

The caption in Figure 2 includes "DOES 1 through 25." Complaints often list such "Doe" defendants. It means that the plaintiff wants the opportunity to add more defendants to the case if he decides other people are also liable for the allegations in the complaint.

For example, let's say you go to a doctor for a series of tests because your wife is concerned about your heart, and she doesn't want you overexerting yourself. You see a cardiologist, who checks you into the hospital and gives you a battery of exams. He releases you with a clean bill of health. The next day you decide to play a game of basketball, and you collapse on the court with a fatal heart attack. Now your surviving spouse decides she wants to sue, but she doesn't know who conducted the cardiogram; she doesn't know exactly who, out of those who examined her husband, is possibly at fault. Was it the doctor? A nurse? Someone at the lab? She may know some of the defendants, but she doesn't want to limit the possibility that she'll discover information as the case progresses and realize there are other people who should be held liable and named as defendants as well.

So Doe defendants are unnamed defendants for whom you are, essentially, reserving a place in your complaint. You are putting the court and other side on notice that there may be some other defendants who are going to be added and brought into the case. (In fact, without going too far into what is a complicated area, failing to name Does could potentially cause problems related to the statute of limitations. If you didn't name any Does and the statute passed, and then you wanted to add someone new to the case, you might have some difficulty doing so.)

A lot of lawyers misunderstand the use of Does. If, for example, when you file a suit you have no reason to believe there are any other defendants, and then you later find out there is another party who should be added, you can make a motion for leave to amend to add him. The fact that you didn't have any Does listed doesn't prevent you from doing so. The Doe concept is chiefly for a situation where you know or feel strongly that another party is also liable, but you don't know his name or identity yet. In fact, the most proper use of Doe would be to say, "I'm suing Jane Doe, a woman in her late thirties who has brown hair, who was present at such and such a place on such and such a date . . ." You're essentially saying you know what the person looks like, who the entity is, but haven't figured out everything you need to properly identify her.

It's important for your lawyer to remember to dismiss out Doe defendants before you go to trial. You're never going to sue "Jane Doe." If you left a Doe in your pleading, the other side might successfully argue that they aren't liable or aren't fully liable, because you believe there is another defendant whom you've been unsuccessful in identifying, and that person is partly to blame.

Case Number and Title

To the right of the caption block, you'll find your case number. When a complaint and summons are filed, the court will stamp them both with a unique case number, usually a letter or two, followed by a long number. This is an important number to keep around for future use. If you ever decide to go down to court to look at the court file on your case and find any specific documents, you'll need that case number. Everything at the court during the life of your case will be identified by your unique case number.

Beneath the case number is the title of the case. Each of the causes of action is listed here so that you can see, at a glance, what the complaint is complaining about.

The Complaint Itself

Below this caption area, the complaint begins. The body of the complaint will begin with the plaintiff alleging information about the parties in the lawsuit. It will first identify the plaintiff, whether he's a person or corporation, where he resides, and briefly provide relevant information about him. Then it will give information as to the identity of the defendant(s), and it may describe them in terms of the time period relevant to the issues in the complaint.

Each paragraph in the complaint is numbered, and each line of each page is numbered. This is to help the parties and court when they later debate issues in the complaint. One lawyer or the other can say, "On page 7, lines 22 to 27, Plaintiff alleges that . . ."

After naming the parties, the complaint may explain why this particular court was chosen. This concerns "jurisdiction" and "venue"—in other words, the reasons why this defendant can be sued in this court.

Depending on how complex the case is, once the complaint has presented the background information about the parties involved (including the Doe defendants), it may give some background information on allegations common to all causes of action, or it may simply list each cause of action. Each cause of action is a separate group of paragraphs under a separate section in which the plaintiff outlines facts and allegations, then describes the legal theory for suing the defendant on the basis of the allegations (see Figure 3).

After all of the causes of action have been listed, there will be a summary of the damages the plaintiff is seeking. In Figure 4, this summary begins with the word *WHEREFORE*.

Figure 3.   Complaint Excerpt Showing Causes of Action

```
 1| shame, mortification, hurt feelings, and severe emotional
 2| distress in an amount to be proved at trial.
 3|     33. As a result of the above-described words, Peggy
 4| Smith has suffered a loss of consortium as well as severe
 5| emotional distress in an amount according to proof within
 6| the jurisdiction of this court.
 7|     34. Jones made the defamatory statement, as alleged in
 8| Paragraphs 11 and 26, knowing that the statement was false
 9| and without a good-faith belief in the truth of the matter,
10| with hatred and ill will toward plaintiffs, and with the
11| intent of inflicting emotional distress and injury to
12| plaintiffs. Accordingly, Jones's conduct in making the false,
13| defamatory statement alleged was despicable and willful and in
14| conscious disregard of plaintiffs' rights, with malice within
15| the meaning of Civil Code section 3294, thereby entitling
16| plaintiffs to the award of punitive and exemplary damages.
17|
18|                    SECOND CAUSE OF ACTION
19|     VIOLATION OF THE IMPLIED COVENANT OF QUIET ENJOYMENT
20|                        (Against Jones)
21|     35. Plaintiffs reallege each allegation contained in
22| Paragraphs 1 through 34, inclusive, as if fully set forth.
23|     36. As alleged in Paragraph 4, plaintiffs and Jones en-
24| tered into the Rental Agreement for rental of the premises.
25|     37. Beginning on or about February 1999 and continu-
26| ing until August 5, 1999, as alleged in Paragraphs 7
```
                                  -11-

Figure 4.   Complaint Excerpt Showing Summary of Damages

```
 1      66. As a direct and proximate and foreseeable result of
 2  Jones's and White's scheme and conspiracy as alleged herein,
 3  plaintiffs have sustained and will continue to sustain
 4  substantial injury in an amount according to proof at trial.
 5      67. Jones's and Black's conduct in harassing plaintiffs
 6  by conspiring to make, and making, threatening and intim-
 7  idating telephone calls to plaintiffs for the purpose of
 8  causing plaintiffs to vacate the premises, as alleged
 9  herein, was intentional and willful, and in conscious dis-
10  regard of plaintiffs' rights, was intended to and did cause
11  plaintiffs severe emotional distress and anguish, and was
12  malicious and oppressive within the meaning of Civil Code
13  section 3294, thereby entitling plaintiffs to the award of
14  punitive and exemplary damages according to proof.
15
16      WHEREFORE, plaintiffs pray for judgment against defen-
17  dants as follows:
18      FOR THE FIRST CAUSE OF ACTION plaintiffs pray for
19  judgment against Jones as follows:
20      a. Actual damages according to proof;
21      b. Punitive damages according to proof;
22      c. Costs of suit, including attorney's fees;
23      d. For such other relief as is fair, just, and
24  equitable.
25      FOR THE SECOND CAUSE OF ACTION plaintiffs pray for
26  judgment against Jones as follows:
```

–19–

Verified or Unverified?

Some jurisdictions offer a choice between filing a verified complaint and an unverified complaint. If the complaint is signed by a lawyer but not by the plaintiff, it's called an unverified complaint, because technically it has not been formally "verified" by the client. Since the point of the complaint is primarily to notify the other side about the causes of action and who's being sued, you as the client are generally not required to sign it under penalty of perjury. You're typically not obligated to swear that everything in the complaint is absolutely correct. The attorney signing the complaint essentially means, "I'm signing this as an attorney, and I'm aware of my general obligation not to assert claims that are frivolous, to do some due diligence, and to present the causes of action to ensure the court and the other side are placed on proper notice."

If the complaint is signed under penalty of perjury by the plaintiff himself, it's called a verified complaint. Signing the complaint under penalty of perjury means, "These are the facts; they're correct as they appear here, and I'll swear to that." Filing a verified complaint forces the defendant to respond in like manner when he answers; he must also verify his answer (see Chapter 8).

If your lawyer signs your complaint, the defendant can respond through his lawyer. In California, for example, you can respond to a complaint with what's known as a general denial; you deny that the allegations in the plaintiff's case are true. But if you're a defendant and receive a verified complaint, you must go through the complaint line by line and say specifically what you admit and deny. If a paragraph says you live in Los Angeles, and you do, you would say that you "admit" that allegation. If a paragraph says you lied about important facts, and you didn't, you would say that you "deny" that paragraph. If there is an allegation that you aren't certain is true or false, you would say that you don't have enough information to answer it at this time. In federal court typically all defendants must respond to a complaint in this way—admitting, denying, or stating they don't have enough information to answer.

Answering a verified complaint can be an arduous process. Some plaintiffs decide they really want to stick it to the defendants and make them go line by line to deny everything in the complaint, so they sign the complaint themselves. If you're thinking of filing a signed (or verified) complaint, you should understand that a potential drawback is that pleadings are generally considered a judicial admission. Sometimes when your attorney is drafting your complaint, he doesn't know your case perfectly yet, so he makes a mistake about a name or a date, and it goes into the pleading you've signed. It's easier to excuse mistakes on a complaint when it's just an unverified complaint signed by your lawyer. But if it's verified and sworn by you, the judge may think, "Well, you had a chance to correct any errors before you signed it, but you verified it and swore it out . . ." If there are mistakes in your complaint and you sign it, it could potentially be more harmful than if you had not chosen to do so.

In a case I handled, the judge dismissed based on a disagreement over the meaning of a single word. The judge interpreted a certain word one way; we said we meant it another. But the judge used the fact that the complaint was verified to dismiss the complaint, based on how he interpreted the word.

You have to be cautious about whether to file a verified complaint or not. Some courts will give some wiggle room at the early stages of a case, but when you verify a complaint, the idea is that you're setting the allegations in stone. Since you're doing that, the judge may not allow you any wiggle room.

Exhibits to the Complaint

At the end of the complaint, your lawyer will generally attach those exhibits referred to in the body of the complaint. If you're involved in a contract dispute, you must attach the contract you're suing on. If something in writing is at issue, or if you're in a copyright dispute about, say, a picture, a magazine article, or a book, you will likely attach this to your complaint. Now, obviously, if you're suing about a crane that was defective, you're not going to attach a crane to your complaint.

Some parties go overboard and attach every piece of correspondence, every piece of paper that will be entered into evidence. Remember, a complaint isn't supposed to be a written submission of the case you're going to present at trial. It's not supposed to contain every exhibit. The basic rule of thumb is that if you're suing over a contract, a guarantee, a note, or some significant legal instrument, then you'll attach that. If you're suing over proprietary rights and there is documentation that can be attached, generally you want to attach that as well.

Amending Your Complaint

If you forgot to include something in your complaint at the time you filed it, many jurisdictions permit you to amend your complaint and reserve it, so long as the defendant has not yet filed his answer (see Chapter 8). Amending your complaint in this instance is fairly simple: your lawyer fixes the complaint, re-serves it, and files a copy at court. Now everyone will disregard the original complaint and focus on what will be referred to as the "first amended complaint." It's not unheard of for attorneys to spot a problem or deficiency a short time after they file. If so, they take this free opportunity to correct your complaint.

What happens if you want to include additional causes of action or other information in your complaint after the other side has already answered? There are two ways you can still amend your complaint. Either the defendant can agree to allow you to amend the complaint, or you can file a motion with the court for permission to amend the complaint. In general, when you want to amend your complaint, it's because you want to allege extra facts or causes of action. Very few defendants are going to say, "Oh, you want to add a cause of action against me for fraud? No problem. Go right ahead!" Instead, they'll force you to file the motion.

In it, you ask the court for permission to amend the complaint and state the reasons why you should be permitted to do so. Generally, the defendant will oppose your motion and argue reasons you should not be permitted to amend the complaint. This can get expensive, and if you get a fair distance into your case and have taken some discovery, some judges might decide that you waited too long. They will deny your motion, and you're out of luck.

Most jurisdictions have rules against splitting causes of action that arise from the same facts. For example, if you're in a car accident and have claims that relate to emotional distress and physical injury, you can't decide that you want to litigate the physical injury claims now and the emotional distress claims later. If a set of claims arises out of the same general set of facts and circumstances, and you knew about the potential claim but didn't assert it at the same time, you could face a problem when you try to assert the related claim at a later date.

How Quickly Should You File?

Plaintiffs tend to want to get their complaint on file as soon as possible. It's satisfying to know the other party has been served with a lawsuit and realizes you're serious about enforcing your rights. Therefore, plaintiffs often feel a sense of urgency to get the complaint on file.

The first and foremost consideration governing when to file a suit is the applicable statute of limitations—the deadline for filing your complaint. If the statute is going to run out in less than a month on your matter, you had better be sure your attorney is working in high gear to get your complaint on file, or you're going to lose your right to sue. This is why I stress the importance of having your attorney inform you in writing the applicable statute of limitations for your situation.

Naturally you need to consider how much time a lawyer needs to get your particular complaint on file. In my experience, if you set an unreasonable time frame because you want to "sue those jerks as soon as possible," a lawyer who wants to keep your business will rush to get the complaint out for you. But rather than the more senior lawyer, you may get a junior lawyer on your case. You may also get a rush job, and the complaint is the last thing you want rushed. Why? Because just before your case goes to a jury, your lawyer will begin filling out your pretrial paperwork, including the jury instructions. The instructions that will be submitted to the jury are married to the causes of action in your complaint. The jury is going to try the causes of action you sue for, nothing more or less. If your lawyer rushes through your complaint to get something on file fast but leaves out something important, you may be out of luck. Maybe you got hit by a car, and your damages are the cost to repair your car, your pain and suffering, and your lost income for the time you couldn't work. Maybe you want the jury to also give you money for the emotional distress of the experience, but if you didn't plead emotional distress in your complaint, it won't be submitted to the jury.

Is Your Lawyer Stalling?

A reasonable amount of time for your lawyer to get your complaint on file can depend on a number of circumstances, such as what you and your lawyer have agreed to do, whether your lawyer feels he needs to complete some special legal research before filing, and what his work schedule is like. You may find a lawyer you like, hire him, and then discover he's about to start a four-week trial and won't be able to start work on your matter until after that. For the right attorney, waiting probably isn't a problem.

Also, your lawyer may need some room to learn your case and about you. It takes a while to get a feel for a set of circumstances. Maybe the client hasn't told the lawyer everything about some element of the claim or about a weakness in his case, and the lawyer wants to think about it. Sometimes the lawyer might see—in a document, an agreement, or an arbitration clause—something the client doesn't notice.

Watch out for situations where your case is not a high priority to the lawyer and languishes for months. Perhaps there is technically no statute of limitations problem, but maybe waiting five months to file your suit will look a little weird when you get to trial; if you were so upset about something, why did you wait so long to file? Or maybe you're concerned that there could be developments that could hurt your case during the five months your attorney does nothing.

How do you know when your lawyer is taking a reasonable amount of time and when he is stalling for no good reason? Of course, good lawyers are busy, and few good ones are going to be able to drop everything immediately and devote themselves just to your matter. Think of it as reassuring to know your lawyer has other clients, other people who also think he's worth depending on. Ask your lawyer what he projects to be a reasonable period of time to get your case on file; if that seems logical to you, go with it. Obviously, his estimate has to be well within the statute of limitations, and it can't leave you in any disadvantaged position.

As the work is supposed to be moving forward on your complaint, ask your lawyer what's happening. If you get sensible answers—"I'm looking into the issue of whether to sue in this state or that state," or "I'm looking into whether there's an administrative remedy," or "There's an arbitration clause here, and I'm considering that," or "I think we really need to do some investigative search of the defendant"—then you know that there's a reason for the time being taken. But if you get what seems like a bunch of double-talk or lame excuses, then maybe he's too busy for you and your claim. Rather than wait until you're running up against a statute of limitations problem, you might begin looking for someone else to handle your case.

In cases that are not cut-and-dried (such as a routine breach of contract), it is often useful to do some legwork and investigate your claims before filing suit. You may try to do some of this yourself, or perhaps your attorney will put on his detective hat and snoop around for you. He could get information from the Internet, speak to witnesses, or look at public records.

However, sometimes it is more cost-effective to retain a private investigating firm that, for a fee (ranging from a few hundred to a few thousand dollars), will dig up previously unknown facts or "dirt" to strengthen your case. The type of information these investigators provide might include whether a person has ever been a plaintiff or defendant in any case, whether he's ever had any judgments, bankruptcy, tax liens. They'll provide information about any corporate officers or directors of any entities they're involved with, any fictitious names, licensing, education, banking relationships, educational background, employment verification, third-party creditors, unreported liabilities, personal and business addresses, current business interests. They'll also do searches on local and national publications for articles, do discreet investigations if needed to determine current lifestyle, look at divorce records, search for warrants and arrests and DUI convictions on various local levels, investigate the potential defendant's character and reputation within respective industries, and determine his current personal and business addresses. They may also investigate other sources of income a potential defendant may have, other business interests or hobbies, whether he operates other entities under an assumed name or alter ego. They'll even attempt to interview the subject directly if you wish, as well as contact any references the person has supplied on various documents. In short, you can use these services to get a full financial picture of a prospective defendant and find out exactly with whom you might be dealing.

If you have an attorney, make sure to coordinate with him any investigation you are conducting. Also, be careful not to violate another's rights while trying to enforce your own.

The most important information retrieved by investigators typically relates to the identity and character of possible defendants and witnesses, and a defendant's potential for paying on a judgment. This information can also help you decide when it's best to file suit. You could also find out whether the defendant has insurance coverage before going through more formal channels later on to discover this. Clearly you do not want to find out a particular defendant has no assets after spending thousands of dollars on a worthless judgment. So work with your lawyer and study a case before filing suit.

Why You Must Understand the Legal Jargon

It is critical that you do your best to understand every sentence in your complaint *before it is filed.*

Let's take a look at a couple of reasons why. If you're like a lot of plaintiffs, your lawyer drafts a complaint and files it, and now you're thinking, "Hey, great! I sued! Fantastic! Send me a copy of the complaint." When you get the complaint, you read it, and there's a factual story in the beginning, what I call the sexy part: "On Monday John ran a red light and ran into Jill's car." You think, "OK, great! That's what happened." Then you get to the boring part. You may not understand much of it because it is a lot of legalese that gives you a headache: ". . . which therefore on the aforesaid date, approximately and directly caused the injury . . . and which aforesaid damage will be proved at the time of trial . . . and is being pled in the alternative . . . and on an alter-ego theory . . . and Defendant Johnson's employer, as respondeat superior . . ." You may start wondering what all that legalese means.

If you have any question about what something in your complaint means, have it answered immediately, before your complaint is filed. Most people read the complaint and see all the parts that relate to them or their business, and that all looks good. Or perhaps they spend time with their lawyer correcting some of these factual things: "It's Jack, not Jill, and it's Tuesday, not Monday." But equally important—and sometimes *more* important—is the legal jargon. You should absolutely know what all of it means and have your lawyer explain to you every aspect of what's happening. When the case goes to trial, it doesn't go to trial on the theory of "Hey, you wronged me! I'm mad! Give me money!" The trial is framed by the pleadings, and only those pleadings that appear in your complaint will be tried, just as only the defenses the other side puts in its answer will be tried.

The procedural rules in a lawsuit operate to try to promote fairness at trial. (I say "try" because that's not what the rules always do.) Judges take a dim view of sandbagging; they are not supposed to let either side in a lawsuit introduce something at trial that was not presented correctly and in a timely way. Each side has to be put on notice of any allegations or defenses of the other, so that each has the opportunity to investigate and prepare a response to everything that might be presented. When you allege something in your complaint, the other side will then have the opportunity to conduct discovery all about that. Your opponent can depose people, subpoena documents, hire investigators, talk with experts, and do almost whatever he wants to check out and try to poke holes in your case. If your complaint omits a crucial allegation or claim, the judge won't allow you to spring it on the other side at trial. This is why the complaint is very important.

Let's say that, like most clients, you don't understand all the legal jargon. Your lawyer explained that the defendant will get your complaint and then have thirty days in which to file his answer denying your allegations (see Chapter 8), or maybe he'll just settle right away.

But wait! The defendant files a Motion to Dismiss your case. Instead of filing an answer or sending you a settlement check, he sends a stack of documents that are half the size of a phone book, citing legal cases to argue points of law that you don't know anything about—something about your having admitted a fact that is at odds with your theory for recovery. What should you do? Well, your first reaction may be to turn to your lawyer. However, this is your lawsuit and it has your name on it. Don't only depend on your lawyer. Read the material yourself and take the time to understand it.

For example, if you are suing a maze of corporations, know clearly who you are suing and why. The law now provides that if you sue a person or corporation without a proper basis and simply disregard your responsibility to investigate whether there was a basis, the defendant can sue you for malicious prosecution and recover their defense costs. I've seen far too many situations where intelligent people actually had no idea exactly who their lawyers had sued and why. Always remember that it is your name listed as "plaintiff"—not your lawyer's.

Also, if you sue the wrong person or corporation the first time and your case gets dismissed, you may not have the opportunity to get it right a second time. Chances are you either ran out of funds or took too much time and blew the statute of limitations.

Inviting Trouble

Here's a scenario you want to avoid: A couple discovered some rather dangerous construction defects in their new home. The couple decided to bring suit. They found a lawyer, who looked at their case and put together a big lawsuit with all sorts of causes of action and various allegations including fraud, and seeking punitive damages against the contractor. The couple didn't totally understand the causes of action, and they didn't ask the lawyer why each claim was being asserted and whether it was necessary, and how each claim helped the overall case. The couple figured, "He's a lawyer; he seems to know what he's doing. We'll leave all that to him."

What was actually going on was that the lawyer—partly out of habit and partly out of his interest in developing an area of law in order to make a name for himself—had thrown into the complaint a novel claim that he felt his clients had a pretty good chance of being able to assert. Unfortunately, throughout the life of the case, this claim was controversial, so it drew fire from the other side, caused motions to be filed, and essentially dwarfed the other claims. Perhaps the judge in the case thought the claim was specious and then began to wonder whether the couple's solid claims also were specious. In any event, the clients later realized that what they really wanted was the money it would take to fix their house plus the reimbursement for their living expenses during the time they couldn't live in the house, some related expenses, and their legal fees. Although it initially felt good to sock it to the builder with the litany of causes of action, the couple later wished that they had asked more questions at the start to understand the nature of the fight they were picking with their complaint.

Ask your lawyer, "Is there a chance any of these causes of action will be thrown out?" If the lawyer says, "Well, this one may be a bit iffy . . .," then think about what your exposure might be for keeping that claim in and whether you want to face the possibility of having to pay to oppose a motion to dismiss that cause of action. You want to try to ensure that your attorney isn't overlawyering your case and exposing you to potential costs and motions you prefer to avoid. You also want to be sure you're not rushing into filing a big complaint just for feel-good reasons.

The Summons

If you were being sued, you would receive a summons along with a copy of the complaint. A summons is a court form putting you on notice of the fact that you are being sued, and telling you some basic facts that you must know as a defendant. Everything in the court system is notice-based. When you have a hearing, you have to show the court that the other side was given notice of your motion. The court system is premised on the idea that a person has a right to defend himself; he has a right to know what's going on.

At the top of a summons you will usually find the following words in black, bold letters: **You are being sued.** For a first-time defendant, a summons can be very intimidating. It's an official government form informing you, among other things, of the name of the person suing you and how many days you have from receipt of the complaint to respond to it in court.

Respond in Time

If you receive a summons and feel completely and utterly overtaken by everything else, and if you don't understand the summons and complaint because they seem frighteningly complicated, what you must focus on is the response time. Usually you have a short period in which to respond to a complaint—generally, twenty or thirty calendar days (that is, generally counting any weekends or holidays as part of the time period). Twenty or thirty days might seem like a lot of time if you were taking a cross-country road trip with five young children, but if you've been sued, that twenty or thirty days can pass very quickly.

I've seen cases where a receptionist at a dental office gets served with a complaint against the dentist. It's a small practice, the dentist's been out of school for only a few years, and it's the first time he's being sued. He's too busy to focus on it immediately, and by the time he sits down to review what's in his In box, three days have clicked by, and maybe a weekend has passed as well. He gets angry when he looks at it, and he tosses it in the corner of his desk and leaves it for a few days.

A week has now passed, and maybe his assistant reminds him that he needs to call a lawyer, so he gets the name of someone and puts in a call. They play telephone tag for a week, then finally set up an appointment to meet. By the time the dentist decides on a lawyer and is beginning to discuss the matter, it could be just a few days before the response is due. Now his lawyer is really up against the wall to draft and file a good response. The lawyer may have to ask the plaintiff's lawyer for an extension—which the plaintiff's lawyer may not agree to. Don't put yourself in this position. When served with a lawsuit, read it carefully and start the process of finding the right lawyer for your case now!

The summons explains that within the given time period you must file with the court a typewritten response, if you want the court to hear your case. Here is the advice right off the standard summons issued in California Superior Court:

> Sending a letter or making a phone call to the court will not protect you or your assets in a lawsuit. Your typewritten response must be in proper legal form if you want the court to hear your case. If you do not file your response on time, you may lose the case, and your wages, money, and property may be taken without further warning from the court. There are other legal requirements. You may want to call an attorney right away. If you do not know an attorney, you may call an attorney referral service or legal aid office listed in the phone book.

So if you fail to file a response within the mandated time period, you will be in default. And if you're in default, that means a judgment can be entered against you—even if the case has no merits. Why? Because the judge has no reason to know that the case is meritless. He hasn't heard from you. You didn't respond in the time frame the court gave you, so you lose by default.

You can move to set aside a default, if you give good cause. It takes time, though, and the plaintiff can move to enter a default judgment against you, and then there's a hearing at which he presents his proof and at each step the plaintiff has to give you notice. The further you let it go, the more you'll have to do just to get yourself back to zero—which in this case means being a defendant in a lawsuit. The process of setting aside a default is very expensive and time-consuming and not easily done.

Get Help with the Details

The summons advises you that you have to file a typewritten response but doesn't tell you that there are all sorts of other specific rules and regulations about the size of the paper, how it must be lined and the lines numbered, how the margins at the top of the page must be set up, and how the papers need to be attached in just such a way, using just the right binding. In short, what the summons is really telling you is that you'd better find yourself a lawyer. If you can't find a lawyer you can afford, then you'd better find a pro bono lawyer (a lawyer who works at no charge for low-income people), because very few people can effectively represent and defend themselves outside of small-claims court.

One reason you need a lawyer is that there are so many require-ments. It probably took me, a lawyer, a full day to read the small single-spaced booklet of rules for filing a complaint or any kind of legal pleading in California. You must use a particular font and a certain num-ber of lines per page; you must place two holes at the top of each page in exactly the right place; place a forked clasp through the two holes and join them together in the center. In other words, it would be difficult and time-consuming for the average person to know how to file an accept-able response in court without a lawyer.

In many states, along with a summons, you will typically receive paperwork that can be confusing even for a lawyer. California Superior Court gives you a grid of different judges' names in tiny print, instruct-ing you how to look at the last two numbers in your case number in order to know which judge has been assigned your case. Obviously, it's important who your judge is going to be. As lawyers will tell you, some judges are pro-defendant, some pro plaintiff; some are Republicans, some Democrats; some are known to be hostile, others to be nice; some worked as defense lawyers for insurance companies, others as plaintiff's attorneys. Each judge has his own personality and his own take on your kind of case. An experienced lawyer may have some additional insight into your case, based on his knowledge of your judge.

Serving Your Complaint

In nearly every jurisdiction, when you first sue another person or a cor-poration, you have to serve your summons and complaint personally on the defendant. (There are some exceptions I'll describe in a moment.) Once the defendant has been served and his lawyer files a response to your suit, you no longer need to have personal service on the defendant. Your lawyer can serve papers on his attorney by fax, mail, or messenger.

Service is an issue of crucial importance. If you sue someone but don't serve him the complaint to let him know, he has no way of knowing he's been sued, no way of defending himself. For that reason, the court makes specific requirements about how another party is to be served any court documents.

Typically, attorneys hire a professional attorney service experienced in serving people, but service can take place in many ways.

States may vary in their definition of what constitutes valid service. To avoid disputes about whether the party actually received the complaint, personal service is the preferred if not the mandated method. The server must be over the age of eighteen and be able to attest that he served the complaint—physically handed it to someone.

People play all sorts of games to try to avoid service, if they suspect a lawsuit is imminent. They may open the door, see it's a process server, and try to shut the door, then the process server will throw the complaint at their feet. In some jurisdictions that may be a valid service; in others it wouldn't be. Generally, if you have made certain attempts but can't serve the complaint personally, you may try to serve it by mail and hope to get back an acknowledgment of receipt. If that doesn't happen, the court may allow "service by publication," where the court lets you put notice in some kind of a periodical or newspaper the defendant would be likely to see it, and that will constitute valid service. Because these rules of service are fairly intricate, you should consult an attorney.

My clients are often surprised when they see I've budgeted $200 or so in service and filing fees. They'll say, "But wait! The filing fee is only $14." Then I have to explain that there's the messenger service to take the complaint down and file it, and then the process service is probably going to make numerous attempts to serve the defendant. Someone may have to sit in a car in a parking lot where the defendant parks, or outside of his office building or house, and you'll be charged by the hour for that time. Once the process server has served the person, then the service firm will fill out a report—and charge you to do that—called a Proof of Service. The form is necessary because you have to prove to the court that the person was served. The form has to be filed within a certain period of time, showing that notice has been given.

If you are suing a corporation, you have to serve the corporation's designated agent for service of process. Usually you can find out who this person is by checking with the office of the secretary of state. Every corporation has to register with the state who their designated agent for service is. In general it is not difficult to serve the corporation's designated agent for service. Part of his job is intended to be accepting service for that entity, and it's rare that you run into any games. This type of information can be secured over the Internet by going to the website for your secretary of state.

Service Games

The games that the parties can play are not limited to the defendant trying to avoid service. I've seen situations where the plaintiff is familiar with the defendant's daily routine, and has intentionally misled the process server so that he keeps missing the defendant. After many unsuccessful tries, the plaintiff's lawyer goes into the court and says that they have been unsuccessful in serving the defendant and want an opportunity to serve by publication. When the judge agrees, the plaintiff is secretly hoping that the defendant won't read the paper where the notice appears, and the plaintiff will win by default. The plaintiff is playing games with service and using it to try to win not on the merits of his case, but through trickery.

I defended a case where someone knew that my client, being in the entertainment business, would not be in his house more than one or two months out of the year. So the server knocked on the gate to the house, supposedly on three different occasions. When my client wasn't home to accept the complaint, the plaintiff apparently went to court and told the judge—who was older and unsympathetic to the rock and rollers of the entertainment business—that he was being frustrated in serving my client. The judge said, "Fine, I'll let you serve by publication." The plaintiff's attorneys asked, "Well, your honor, can we put the notice in *Daily Variety*?" And the judge said "yes."

The only problem was that since my client was in the music business, if there were any place where he would see the notice, it would be in a music trade paper like *Billboard*, not *Daily Variety*, which is more for TV and film. My client never saw it, the plaintiff got a default judgment, and we had to file to get the judgment overturned. We showed that the plaintiff did, in fact, know that my client was out of town and should have known that my client was more likely to read a different trade magazine.

The classic situations, though, are the defendants who evade service and become quite professional at doing it. They frustrate plaintiffs by causing them to wonder whether it's all worth it because they're spending a fortune just trying to track the defendant down. Halfway through a case, one of my clients named an additional defendant, a friend of the central defendant who had been in the case for some time. When we went to serve the new defendant, he did everything possible to avoid service. He locked himself in his house and refused to answer his door. We had a process server at his house around the clock, waiting to catch him. The server could see that the man was home, but he couldn't get him to come to the door or a window. The man had his lawyer call me and say that our process server was trespassing and would be reported to the police.

This was fast getting expensive. Fortunately, my client came up with an idea. He was on friendly terms with his UPS driver, so he asked him for a favor. The driver agreed, and one day after he finished his shift, he drove his truck over to the man's house, walked up the steps with a package under his arm, and rang the bell. Well, even a man who's trying to evade service is going to open the door for UPS, and bingo—the UPS driver handed him the package and told him he'd been served. (Inside the box were the complaint and summons.) Not everyone trying to serve an evading defendant has a friend who works for UPS, but you can see how expensive things can become.

If You Are the Defendant

If you know that someone is trying to serve you with a complaint, you don't have to go out of your way to make it easy to serve you. But if you intentionally avoid service, and it can be proved you did so, certain jurisdictions have rules that will sanction you; you could have to pay the additional costs incurred because you turned this into a game.

"You've been served."

Nuts and Bolts:
The Defendant's Turn

When you have no basis for an argument, abuse the plaintiff.

**—Cicero, first-century Roman statesman,
orator, and writer**

When you are served with a complaint, do not ignore it. It is not junk mail. If you fail to respond to it in a timely, correct manner, you will have major problems. In the last chapter, I explained how failing to respond to a case within the allotted time period can allow the plaintiff to win his case against you by default. The plaintiff then is able to have a judgment awarded against you, potentially in the full amount he asked for. You cannot get a default judgment reversed by saying, "Gee, I was busy . . .!" You must file papers called a Motion to Set Aside Default, and when you see your bill and find out what your attorney has charged you, you'll regret that you did not respond promptly in the first place.

After being sued, you have to make several critical decisions quickly. First, you need to find a good lawyer. When you're the plaintiff, you have the luxury of taking your time when choosing a lawyer, but when you're a defendant, you only have twenty days (in federal court) or thirty days (in most state courts) to respond to a lawsuit. And finding the right lawyer, as we discussed, can take time.

If you've just been sued and are facing a tight deadline, a lawyer you want to represent you may have you in an uncomfortable position. He can easily say, "I need a $10,000 retainer." If you have a week or two to respond, and your back is against the wall, then you may have no choice but to shut your eyes and write the check. However, if you start looking for a lawyer immediately, you are more likely to find one you like for a $2,000 retainer. You don't want to get leveraged into a relationship with a lawyer you wouldn't otherwise retain but for time constraints.

Strategy: What's in Your Best Interest?

After you are sued, you must determine how you want to handle the lawsuit. Do you want to settle? Do you want your attorney to contact the other side and try to resolve it in some form acceptable to you? Do you want to say, "Mea culpa! Mea culpa!" and write a check to the plaintiff? Do you want to fight? Do you want to go into a courtroom to prove that you're not liable and show that the plaintiff is mistaken or a liar? Do you want to go into the trenches and look for every legal device and motion possible to try to wear that plaintiff down, and hope that by sticking it to him enough, you can shake him?

You don't have the luxury of too much time to think, but you should try to take a dispassionate inventory of where you are and where you'd like to be. People who have been sued are generally mad as hell and not thinking too clearly, and most lawsuits are not cut-and-dried. But maybe you recognize that you did do something that makes you liable for most or all of the allegations. Maybe if you consider the case from a juror's point of view, you see there's a pretty good chance you're going to lose. You might think, "How much money do I want to spend defending this lawsuit if it's pretty likely I'm just going to lose in the end?"

Most lawyers aren't going to suggest this to a defendant who walks into their office, but you might want to consider whether it is in your best interest to try to settle the case fast and at a low number. Sometimes saying, "I'm sorry," and paying some money to nip a lawsuit in the bud will serve you better than paying a bunch of legal fees and then facing a big judgment. I have seen countless cases where a defendant decides to mount a tough defense, pays his attorney a fortune to throw up every imaginable legal roadblock, and then loses. Or just before trial, the defendant realizes he's going to lose, but now when he tries to settle, the plaintiff has incurred such huge legal fees that it would take a huge amount to settle it. I wonder whether those defendants later say to themselves, "You know, I could have gotten rid of this matter two years ago for twenty grand, but instead I spent fifty grand defending myself, lost the case, and got an order to pay out sixty grand, and I'm looking at paying another eight grand to appeal the verdict. What the hell was I thinking?"

Sometimes defendants opt to litigate just to buy themselves time. When one of my clients got sued, she called me and said, "Oh my God, I didn't provide this person an accounting. I do owe him money, but it's going to take me a while to put some cash aside so I can pay him what I owe. I don't want to risk losing my home, and there are some side issues and some technical defenses I could raise to put up a decent fight. I doubt I'll win, but it will take three or four years for a case like this to get to court where I live, and I could litigate with the guy for two years, and then I'll have the money to pay him. If we do that, I can sleep at night." In a case where she was liable but some issues weren't clear-cut, this client knowingly used some technical defense, allowed by the litigation process to stall for time to get money together to pay the plaintiff. However, keep in mind there is a fine—but important—line between a "technical defense" and a frivolous defense.

Formulate your defense strategy quickly. You want to go through many of the same processes as a plaintiff, but speedily. In addition to doing a cost-benefit analysis, study your insurance policies and show them to your lawyer. Perhaps you have coverage under your homeowner's or other policy to pay for your defense. If you think you do, contact your carrier, or have a lawyer do it for you, and get the company involved immediately.

Filing the Answer

The defendant must file an answer to the complaint within the time specified on the summons. Therefore, you and your lawyer need to pick through the allegations in the complaint and draft a document that denies, generally, all of the allegations in the complaint. As noted in the previous chapter, in some jurisdictions the plaintiff may file a verified or signed complaint. If you have received a verified complaint, then you have to actually read every sentence and in your answer state, "I admit that," "I deny that," or, "I lack sufficient knowledge at this time to give an answer one way or another." (Those are really the only three answers you can give to an allegation when filing your answer.)

Your answer will also include what are known as your affirmative defenses. The term *affirmative defense* refers to a legal theory that the defendant plans to offer at trial to shield himself from liability such as an argument that the time period allowed for filing such a claim has passed. While some affirmative defenses are fairly obvious, you have to be a lawyer to know what many of these are. Some typical defenses include the following examples:

- Truth—For example, in a slander case, you maintain that what you said was not slander but something true.
- Failure to state a claim—The facts alleged don't contain the necessary elements to establish the cause of action.
- Waiver—The plaintiff waived his right to sue you for this.
- Equitable estoppel—This fancy legal term is just a way to say, "It isn't fair for you to be able to say or do that now."

Remember, everything that is going to happen in your lawsuit is subject to the rules of notice. If it's fair for the defendant to be on notice of the claims against him, it should also be fair for the plaintiff to be put on notice of the defendant's basic defenses. This is why the defendant must put the legal theories in his answer, alerting the other side to the legal arguments he's going to assert.

After you are seven months into the lawsuit, go back and take a look at your complaint or answer. See if your legal theories have changed, now that you know more about the facts. A plaintiff might realize he had a fact wrong, so he wants to amend the complaint. As the defendant, you may want to amend your answer to include a new affirmative defense.

Procedural Technicalities

A number of issues have the potential to get the plaintiff's complaint dismissed, or at least partially struck. First, there's the issue of service. Was it made properly? Maybe the complaint was served on your neighbor, not you. Maybe the complaint didn't list the correct number of days in which to respond. Maybe someone made a mistake in filling out the summons, and there's an error somewhere. The circumstances of service might provide your attorney with the ability to argue that service was not proper, so the complaint has not yet been served, technically.

Because several crucial decisions must be made at the answer stage, you should hire an attorney early on. A young lawyer might spend a day or two researching your possible responses, and a night or two drafting them. Put that on top of the time he may need to organize your file, and you can understand how your lawyer needs a big window of time to prepare properly. Don't do your lawyer the disservice of waiting until the last possible moment and then saying, "Here's the complaint. Now the first thing you have to do is go get me an extension." That's going to cost you additional legal hours on your bill.

Preliminary Motions

In some situations you're not going to file an answer but instead will file one of several different preliminary motions. There are maybe two, three, or four dozen ways to respond to a lawsuit that don't just involve a simple answer. You might decide to challenge jurisdiction or venue. You would challenge jurisdiction if you think you don't have sufficient contacts with the state for the plaintiff to be able to sue you there. Maybe you live in Montana and the plaintiff sued you in New York. If you've not had minimum contact with New York (as defined by statute), a New York court doesn't have the right to hear the case.

Then you might want to file a Motion to Dismiss for Lack of Personal Jurisdiction. Your lawyer can also research the choice of venue—whether you've been sued in the right county, in the right courthouse within the county, in the right branch. Are you (correctly) in federal court, but in the wrong federal court? Maybe you'll file a Motion to Dismiss based on venue: if the plaintiff's lawyer made a mistake and shouldn't have filed in that venue, the judge will throw out his case or transfer it.

Before filing a motion to move your case to a different court, you may want to consider with your lawyer whether you're better off in staying in the court. Court branches in the same system can differ in the way the courts are run, how cases will be heard, how soon you'll go to trial, and the judges at one courthouse versus another. There can even be a huge difference in the jurors. If you sue in Westchester County versus Manhattan, you're going to see a huge difference in the jury pool. To an outsider it may seem all the same because it's all the New York metropolitan area, but Westchester County jurors are very different from New York City jurors, just as Orange County jurors differ greatly from jurors in the downtown Los Angeles court, even though it's all Southern California.

You may have to decide whether a suit filed in state court should be moved to federal court. This would entail filing a formal Motion to Remove. If you're already involved in a related arbitration, you might file a Motion for a Stay (to delay the case filed against you from going forward until the arbitration is resolved). If another party hasn't been joined to the lawsuit against you, you could file a Motion to Dismiss for Failure to Join an Indispensable Party. Or you might have an arbitration clause or other clause in an agreement with the plaintiff, so you need to file a motion in order to enforce the provisions of that agreement as they might relate to the litigation.

Maybe you find out your case is being heard by a judge who, based on your attorney's experience, will be unfriendly toward your positions. Most jurisdictions provide for your right to disqualify (remove) a judge from hearing your case. In California it's called a Section 170.6 Motion, and you get essentially one free pass if you swear out an affidavit saying, "I think this judge might be biased."

If you're being sued by a corporation, remember (as discussed in Chapter 5) to check with the secretary of state. Look up that corporation and find out whether or not it's in good standing with the state. In lawsuits between small companies, one or the other of them is sometimes not in good standing. You can file a motion to dismiss on that basis, and the case might get thrown out.

You may want to file a motion challenging some valid, technical problem in the complaint. In federal court, the rules for pleading are more relaxed, and if the plaintiff generally pleads out a cause of action competently, there is a limited basis by which the defendant can have the claim dismissed or force the plaintiff to rewrite the complaint.

Demurrers

In states like California, where the rules of pleading are a little more antiquated, a defendant is allowed to file a motion called a demurrer. In a demurrer the defendant can make arguments about the language in the complaint and ask the judge to dismiss part or all of it. If the plaintiff's lawyer was slightly asleep when he drafted the complaint and didn't put in all the correct magic words under one of the causes of action, the complaint actually gets dismissed "without prejudice." This means that the plaintiff has twenty days in which to amend and refile the complaint. For the plaintiff, it feels terrible to have to start over, fix the complaint, refile it, and wait for the defendant to take another swing at it.

If you are a plaintiff and your lawyer was a little sloppy in drafting your complaint, and it was dismissed on demurrer, make sure he isn't sloppy on his second try. The judge just may decide to dismiss your case permanently and not give you the right to try again.

Of course, few lawyers, if ordered to redraft a complaint, are going to say, "Hey, that was my fault. I won't bill you for that." You may not even know what the heck's going on when some or all of your case has been dismissed with leave to amend. The lawyer may tell you, "Oh, the judge just said to clean it up a little bit. I need some more facts from you. So we're going to refile it." Right, and then there will be that $5,000 in extra billing. This is another reason it pays to find a solid set of lawyers and to stay on top of their work. If you've paid a lot for work that turns out to be shoddy, you may decide that the lawyer himself should bear the cost to get it right.

In fairness, even a good lawyer who's doing a good job can have a complaint or part of a complaint thrown out. You may decide to assert

what constitutes a really cutting edge claim or a claim where the facts
are not entirely clear. Maybe your lawyer has told you that under the
law you need more specific facts in your complaint, but you don't have
all the information right now, so the other side files a motion and your
case is dismissed.

Regardless of what jurisdiction they're in, large defendants are
going to look for ways to throw up hurdles to test how much money you
have or how much of a commitment your contingency lawyer has. A few
defendants may say, "Hey, if the plaintiff hasn't drafted his complaint
correctly, let's not file a motion pointing out the problems and educating him about why the elements of his cause of action won't work once
he gets to trial." These kinds of defendants take the position of skipping
a demurrer because it would teach the plaintiff how to draft the complaint more correctly. Why would I file a motion and educate the plaintiff about the elements of his cause of action? But I would say that most
defendants with resources think this way:

- They didn't attach *all* of the contract: Demurrer!
- They didn't plead with sufficient specificity because when they
  said on page 7, line 12, "Defendant repeated the misrepresentation on April 4 . . ." they didn't say specifically what the misrepresentation was: Demurrer!
- They didn't say on page 9, line 23, "On Friday, June 7" what the
  misrepresentation was: Demurrer!
- They've put forth inconsistent causes of action, as between this
  claim and this other claim, and under the law you can't necessarily do both: Demurrer!
- They've got the dollar amount of punitive damages; you can't do
  that in California: Motion to Strike!
- They've got the wrong middle name of the defendant in the caption: Motion to Strike!

This could go on for three months until your lawyers finally get it right,
and the other side keeps picking, picking, picking. This could cost you a
lot of money, which is exactly the point.

Countersuits

In most jurisdictions if you want to file a countersuit—that is, you as the defendant want to sue the plaintiff back—the time to do so is when you file your response. In addition to or in place of suing the plaintiff back, you might make a counterclaim or a cross-complaint against another defendant, for indemnification or for contribution.

The difference between a counterclaim and a cross-complaint has to do with what jurisdiction you're in. A lawsuit by the defendant against the plaintiff is called a counterclaim in federal court but a cross-complaint in many states. In federal court, a cross-complaint is a complaint filed by one defendant against another defendant. Sometimes people use those terms interchangeably, especially in California.

As a defendant, you might file a cause of action for indemnification against another defendant on the theory that the damage done to the plaintiff wasn't your fault, but the other defendant's fault. This happens often in construction defect cases. The general contractor gets sued, and he cross-complains (or countersues) against every one of the subcontractors—the people who delivered the supplies or the wood or the nails. Of course, the most basic countersuit is the always-popular defendant sues plaintiff: "Hey, you sued me, so I'll sue you!"

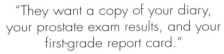

"They want a copy of your diary, your prostate exam results, and your first-grade report card."

Nuts and Bolts: Written Discovery

A man without money needs no more fear a crowd of lawyers than a crowd of pickpockets.

—William Wycherley, 17th-century English dramatist

At one time, cases were tried without each side knowing much at all about their opponent's evidence until the time of the trial. The plaintiff and defendant would show up at court, bringing their witnesses and supporting documents. There was a tremendous element of drama and surprise because each had no way of knowing before the trial began how the other side was going to prosecute or defend its case. As a result, there were usually surprise witnesses, surprise documents, surprise smoking guns. These days it is rare that you see any surprise smoking guns (old *Perry Mason* reruns aside). With the modern rules of discovery, by asking the right questions you should be able to figure out what witnesses and evidence are likely to be submitted at trial by the other side long before your trial begins.

What Is Discovery?

Discovery is just what the word suggests—a chance to discover something about the other side's position. As a party in a lawsuit, you're entitled to find out all of the factual basis for the other party's claims or defenses. You have the right to ask about the existence of documents, witnesses, and any other evidence the other side has to support their claims and defenses. The other party can do the same with you. Everything you might know about or want to submit to the jury, the other side has a right to ask you about, and to locate and examine it.

Discovery changes the whole dynamic of a lawsuit and a trial. If there is fair discovery, there should be no shockers for either side about the evidence the jury will see. By the discovery cutoff date (a date the court sets after which no more discovery will be allowed), everybody will have the same packet of facts, at least in theory. It's a little like exams that law school students are given. At the start of the exam, the professor hands out a packet of facts to everyone, and each student has to use the same given set of facts to answer questions. The idea in a lawsuit is that everyone is supposed to end up with a complete set of all the facts and documents that relate to the legal issues in question, including damages.

To get the facts and documents, each side is allowed to ask questions of the other side, both in written form and during a deposition (see Chapter 11). The witnesses must be identified; the factual support for certain positions will be determined; you'll see what the defense is predicted upon, what it is, and whether the other side is aware of the existence of certain documents; and the plaintiff must explain his calculation of damages. You can even ask another party if he actually wants to admit a particular fact, and thus save the time from having to prove that fact at trial.

If both sides of a lawsuit end up knowing everything the other side knows, a trial becomes a question of shaping your evidence and assessing the best spin to give it: How do you get something into evidence? Where is your case strong, and where is it weak?

That's the ideal. But frequently parties will try to play games with discovery.

What Is Discoverable?

What is someone permitted to ask you about, in writing or in a deposition? What files or things of yours can the other side see? In other words, what are the limits on what a party in a lawsuit can discover? Can you examine everything, or does it have to be relevant to the lawsuit?

The standard in discovery is not whether something is "relevant" to the lawsuit, which is an ambiguous term to start with. After all, what's relevant to me may be entirely irrelevant to you. The discovery standard generally is that the information sought must be reasonably likely to lead to the discovery of admissible evidence. Evidence does not have to be admissible to be obtained in discovery; the idea is that you should be able to discover any information that may lead to something that *is* admissible.

For example, you may be able to find out in discovery whether a party took a polygraph exam. You might even get lucky and see the results of the test. But a polygraph exam is not admissible in a trial. So while the lie detector test itself may not be admissible at trial, you might unearth relevant information or statements by asking about the test.

If someone objects to providing certain information, the side requesting the information merely has to show a judge that it's reasonably likely to lead to the discovery of admissible evidence. Some judges have a heavy docket and don't have time to figure out enough about the facts in your case to determine whether something is "reasonably likely" to lead to admissible evidence. Therefore, if a request doesn't sound too far-fetched, most judges will allow the request and require the other side to respond.

Forms of Discovery

There are three primary forms of written discovery:

1. Document requests—a request to the other side to produce documents relevant to the litigation
2. Interrogatories—written questions for the other side to answer in writing
3. Requests for admission—asking another party to admit certain facts

Document Requests

One side may send the other a formal request that all documents relating to the lawsuit be identified and provided for copying. These document requests try to set forth with some specificity the categories or groups of documents believed to be relevant to the case, and to ask the parties on the other side whether they possess any of these type of documents. Typically, the other side may just send over copies of the requested documents, or the documents will be made available at the client's place of business, or their attorney's office for inspection and copying. Generally the attorneys work out how the documents will be copied. If the documents requested are voluminous or used in the course of business, they may end up being inspected "on-site."

In discovery, the word *documents* refers to anything that's written, capable of being seen on a screen, or printed out and to anything physical that might be relevant to the lawsuit. People typically ask for documents like memos, letters, files, calendars, bills, receipts, notes, medical records, x-rays, business cards, photographs, posters, videotapes, audiotapes, the contents of a computer hard drive, etc.

However, "documents" can include a wide array of items, not simply what most people commonly think of as a document. You can request anything that's tangible—that's capable of being touched, seen, heard, smelled, or tasted. If something large or cumbersome such as a work of art is at issue, you can require that you be given the opportunity for an on-site inspection. You can demand a walk-through and permission to take pictures or a video.

If you believe the other party has documents relevant to your case, your lawyer will serve him with what is known as a Request for Identification and Production of Documents (see Figure 5). This will request that the party produce documents for copying on a given date, and it will identify which documents or category of documents are being requested.

When you're served a Request for Identification and Production of Documents, you'll have a certain number of days in which to respond in writing, either agreeing to or objecting to the request, and number of days before which you must produce the documents. These deadlines are generally set by statute in the state where you're litigating. In California, for example, a party will have thirty days in which to respond in

Figure 5.   Sample Request for Identification and Production of Documents

---

```
 1  BLACK, BLUE AND GREENE
    HARVEY GREENE, ESQ., SB# 99998
 2  2311 Legal Park North
    Suite 889
 3  Los Angeles, CA 90099
    (818) 555-6400
 4
    Attorneys for Defendant
 5  JOE JONES
 6
         SUPERIOR COURT FOR THE STATE OF CALIFORNIA
 7
         FOR THE COUNTY OF LOS ANGELES, WEST DISTRICT
 8
 9  JOHN SMITH and PEGGY SMITH,)  CASE NO. SC 159 322
                               )
10             Plaintiffs, )  REQUEST FOR
                               )  IDENTIFICATION AND
11     vs.                     )  PRODUCTION OF DOCUMENTS
                               )
12  JOE JONES and MARY WHITE, )  DATE: June 29, 1999
    and DOES 1 through 25,     )  TIME: 10:00 A.M.
13  inclusive,                 )  PLACE: 1880 Century Pk. E.,
                               )  Suite 1114
14             Defendants. )Los Angeles, CA 90067
15  _____
16     PROPOUNDING PARTY:  Defendant, JOE JONES
17     RESPONDING PARTY:   Plaintiffs, JOHN SMITH and
18                         PEGGY SMITH
19     SET NO:             ONE
20     TO PLAINTIFFS, JOHN SMITH and PEGGY SMITH, AND TO
21  THEIR ATTORNEYS OF RECORD:
22     Defendant, JOE JONES, requests that plaintiffs produce
23  the following described items for inspection and copying,
24  pursuant to California Code of Civil Procedure, Section
25  2031.
26
27     The following described items are believed to be in
28  the possession, custody, or control of plaintiffs or
29  plaintiffs' attorneys, are not privileged and are relevant
30  to the subject matter of the action, and are reasonably
31  calculated to lead to the discovery of admissible evidence
32  in this action.
```

-1-

Figure 5.   Continued

```
 1 ||    The items requested for production are as follows:
 2 ||    1. Any and all reports by practitioners of the heal-
 3 || ing arts (including but not limited to physicians, sur-
 4 || geons, chiropractors, physical therapists, optometrists,
 5 || and psychotherapists) who examined, treated, and/or con-
 6 || sulted with you for injuries sustained as a result of the
 7 || accident forming the basis of this lawsuit.
 8 ||    2. Any and all statements or bills by practitioners of
 9 || the healing arts and/or medical facilities prepared in
10 || connection with the injuries you allegedly suffered as a
11 || result of the accident.
12 ||    3. Any and all statements, in any form, of persons who
13 || witnessed or claim to have witnessed the accident, and/or the
14 || events immediately prior to or subsequent to the accident.
15 ||    4. Any and all statements, in any form, secured or
16 || obtained in any way from this answering defendant, its
17 || agents, officers, servants, or employees.
18 ||    5. Any and all reports by law enforcement agencies re-
19 || garding the occurrence of this incident, including but not
20 ||limited to investigative reports and supplements thereto.
```
-2-

writing to a document demand in which to produce the documents. (If the demand was served by mail, the statute gives an additional five days for the party to respond.)

If you serve a document request on another party, and he fails to object in writing within the allotted time period, with few exceptions he automatically waives his right to object and must produce the docu-ments—even if they are normally privileged, such as tax returns or commercially sensitive information. If you refuse or fail to produce the documents requested, the other side may file a Motion to Compel (described later), and you could face monetary sanctions if the judge determines you did not have a proper basis for withholding the documents.

You never can prevent the other side from destroying documents that you want to see. It's against the law, as it constitutes suppression of evidence, but shredding documents still does happen. Thus, your document request can only accomplish so much.

Document requests, along with depositions, are two of the most important tools of discovery, and documents play a significant role in most court cases. A party served with a document request must produce everything responsive within his "custody, possession, or control." Thus, if you're requesting financial records and the party doesn't have them in his offices, but his accountant has them, he has a duty to go to the accountant and get the records and turn them over to you for copying. Those records are considered "in his control" in the sense that he can call the accountant and ask for the records.

It's not unusual for there to be arguments about what constitutes custody, possession, or control. A major business with multiple branches in different states might want to argue in court about what's in its possession, custody, and control and what can be brought within the scope of a request made in Wisconsin when the documents may actually be in Florida.

If you're trying to conduct your case cost-effectively, you probably don't want to send out more than two sets of document requests. The first set should be a starter set. You ask for and get the most basic groups of documents. Then you can really start investigating and begin to see what the other side has. Once you've secured the basic information, you can send over another set of requests in order to get any other documents you've learned about, but still do not have.

In the beginning of the case, you don't know enough about who the players are on the other side, how their files are set up, what names they may use for documents, and what categories of documents exist. When you send over your document request, the other side only has to produce those documents you've referred to. You may not know about the existence of certain other documents. So you begin with a starter set, which should be enough for taking the first round of depositions. Your lawyer will have those documents to question witnesses about.

For example, say your case has to do with a construction defect. In the beginning you may request the basic paperwork concerning the construction job at issue. You may later find out that a subcontractor was involved and that the real issue turns on electrical wiring. So now you'll be asking for a very specific set of documents, maybe having to do with the electrician or other subcontractors, and having to do with all their files.

Often you may not know how to refer to a given set of documents in order to properly identify them to the other side and get copies. For example, in a medical malpractice case, you asked for documents from the defendant. Later, when deposing a cardiologist who was brought in during surgery, you hear about something they call the "Riff report" and realize you didn't receive this document in your first request. Or maybe you don't know about documents stored in computers and don't know how to identify them in order to have the other side produce them. Most organizations have internal names for their documents and special ways they store files in their computer system. In depositions you find out about these files—what they're called, where they're kept—and then you can send over another request to get them.

When the lawsuit involves a corporate defendant, I send over document requests to get the basic documents, nothing fancy. Then I'll take a deposition of the person most knowledgeable about my client's claims at the corporation, and while I'm deposing him, I'll ask, "How do you set up your files? Who's in charge of your files? What terminology do you use in the company for certain documents? When and how often do you use the computer? How do you use E-mail? What's on your hard drive? How does this stuff get printed out?" This type of deposition is similar to doing exploratory surgery on the other side. You learn how the corporation is set up and where its information can be found. Then you can make more precise follow-up document requests that use exact terminology.

It's important to use the right terminology when making document requests. If you don't, the other side may not produce the things you're looking for. Someone may omit things you're really interested in because you didn't ask for them properly: "Oh, if you'd asked for *that*, we would have given it to you, but you didn't specify clearly that was what you wanted." The other side is generally not under obligation to provide documents that you don't ask for. (In many Federal Courts there are rules in place that require a party to come forward with all documents that support their claims or defenses at an "Early Meeting of Counsel.")

A lot of lawyers in the beginning of a lawsuit speculate as to what the other side might call their documents and what documents might exist. Then they send out far-reaching requests. The problem with this is that if the other side objects, he forces an expensive discovery battle. I'll talk about discovery skirmishes later in this chapter.

Interrogatories

Interrogatory is a fancy word for "question," and is derived from the word *interrogate*. Interrogatories are written questions served on the other party, which the other party has a certain number of days to answer in writing—or to object to and supply a reason for not answering.

While some interrogatories seeking basic information can be helpful, for the most part I'm not a big proponent of extensive use of interrogatories. The kind of interrogatories you typically see, and that I consider a good usage, are those seeking information like this: "Please list the names and addresses of all witnesses of whom you are aware . . ."; "Please specify your damages . . ."; "Please state the basic facts supporting this claim or defense . . ."; "Please list all insurance policies in effect during . . ." Those types of interrogatories are fine because they seek basic information.

The thing to remember is who answers interrogatories. In theory it's the other party, the other corporation, the corporation's representatives. In reality, though, their lawyer writes answers to any interrogatories you send over. A lawyer will write a lawyerly answer to an interrogatory question; it usually has little substance and a lot of posturing and legal jargon.

Have you ever put something fat and juicy in the microwave and had it come out shrunk down to a little lump? Well, that's what happens when a client answers a question through his lawyer. The client reads the question and spills out a lot of information, then the lawyer writes, "I object on the grounds that this question has component parts in violation of Local Rule Number 23.41, and additionally I believe it impinges upon the attorney work product privilege because the process of determining who is a witness requires me to opine as to who is a relevant witness. We do at this time, however, know that John Schmidt and Jane Day are witnesses, but we are continuing our investigation. There are other people who may be potential witnesses, and we will supplement at an appropriate time if allowed by the law blah blah blah."

The lawyer hedges the client's bets to prevent the client from being pinned down. In a deposition, though, if I ask the client, "Who were the witnesses?" the client has to answer without the help of his or her lawyer and answer fully right then for the record. If he's trying to be vague or to hedge, I can follow up with questions. That makes for a much more useful answer for me, and one much harder for him to later try to change.

You generally want to ask any important specific questions to the client in person and in a deposition. You can, but do not have to, ask specific questions in interrogatories. That's why I generally recommend that cost-conscious plaintiffs ask a handful of basic, simple questions in interrogatories—and only questions that no one could reasonably avoid answering—and then just wait for depositions.

An exception is when the other party is a large corporation; then using interrogatories actually saves you money. If you serve interrogatories on a corporation, you can avoid having to depose twenty different people to find far-flung information. A corporation has a duty to go to its employees and pull together the information you're requesting.

There are two kinds of interrogatories: form interrogatories and special interrogatories. Most jurisdictions use form interrogatories, which are mostly designed for personal injury or medical malpractice cases, though they can be used in other instances as well.

Form interrogatories are just what the name implies: a preprinted list of questions frequently asked in lawsuits (see Figure 6). They are drafted by an advisory panel put together by a court in a given jurisdiction. The court asks the panel to draft a list of the most common questions asked. The questions generally ask for the respondent's name, address, driver's license number, social security number, ability to speak English, involvement in other lawsuits, names of the witnesses, location of documents relevant to the case, names of the doctors he has seen, and so on. To get answers to these questions, your lawyer just checks off the boxes by the questions he wants answered and sends the form to the other side.

Special interrogatories, on the other hand, are questions that you and your lawyer think up, specific to your case. Most jurisdictions limit the number of special interrogatories you can serve—perhaps twenty or thirty or thirty-five—and most jurisdictions try to keep the number of interrogatories down. For many years parties in civil litigation would serve some 200 interrogatories on the other side. Even if the questions were redundant or irrelevant, the party receiving the interrogatories

Figure 6. Excerpt from a Sample Form Interrogatory

ATTORNEY OR PARTY WITHOUT ATTORNEY (Name, state bar number, and address):	TELEPHONE AND FAX NOS.
ATTORNEY FOR (Name):	

NAME OF COURT AND JUDICIAL DISTRICT AND BRANCH COURT, IF ANY:

SHORT TITLE OF CASE:

FORM INTERROGATORIES Asking Party: Answering Party: Set No.:	CASE NUMBER:

Sec. 1. Instructions to All Parties

(a) These are general instructions. *For time limitations, requirements for service on other parties, and other details, see Code of Civil Procedure section 20.30 and the cases construing it.*

(b) These interrogatories do not change existing law relating to interrogatories nor do they affect an answering party's right to assert any privilege or objection.

Sec. 2. Instructions to the Asking Party

(a) These interrogatories are designed for optional use in the superior courts only. A separate set of interrogatories, *Form Interrogatories—Economic Litigaton* (form FI-129), which have no subparts, are designed for optional use in municipal courts. However, they also may be used in superior courts. See Code of Civil Procedure section 94.

(b) Check the box next to each interrogatory that you want the answering party to answer. Use care in choosing those interrogatories that are applicable to the case.

(c) You may insert your own definition of **INCIDENT** in Section 4, but only where the action arises from a course of conduct or a series of events occurring over a period of time.

(d) The interrogatories in Section 16.0, Defendant's Contentions—Personal Injury, should not be used until the defendant has had a reasonable opportunity to conduct an investigation or discovery of plaintiff's injuries and damages.

(e) Additional interrogatories may be attached.

Figure 6.   Continued

Sec. 3. Instructions to the Answering Party

(a) In superior court actions, an answer or other appropriate response must be given to each interrogatory checked by the asking party.

(b) As a general rule, within 30 days after you are served with these interrogatories, you must serve your responses on the asking party and serve copies of your responses on all other parties to the action who have appeared. See Code of Civil Procedure section 2030 for details.

(c) Each answer must be as complete and straightforward as the information reasonably available to you permits. If an interrogatory cannot be answered completely, answer it to the extent possible.

(d) If you do not have enough personal knowledge to fully answer an interrogatory, say so, but make a reasonable and good-faith effort to get the information by asking other persons or organizations, unless the information is equally available to the asking party.

(e) Whenever an interrogatory may be answered by referring to a document, the document may be attached as an exhibit to the response and referred to in the response. If the document has more than one page, refer to the page and section where the answer to the interrogatory can be found.

(f) Whenever an address and telephone number for the same person are requested in more than one interrogatory, you are required to furnish them in answering only the first interrogatory asking for that information.

(g) Your answers to these interrogatories must be verified, dated, and signed. You may wish to use the following form *at the end of your answers.*

I declare under penalty of perjury under the laws of the State of California that the foregoing answers are true and correct.

_____   _____
          (DATE)   (SIGNATURE)

Sec. 4. Definitions

Words in **BOLDFACE CAPITALS** in these interrogatories are defined as follows:

(a)   (*Check one of the following*):

    ❑ (1) **INCIDENT** includes the circumstances and events surrounding the alleged accident, injury, or other occurrence or breach of contract giving rise to this action or proceeding.

    ❑ (2) **INCIDENT** means (*insert your definition here or on a separate, attached sheet labelled "Sec. 4(a)(2)"*).

(b) **YOU OR ANYONE ACTING ON YOUR BEHALF** includes you, your agents, your employees, your insurance companies, their agents, their employees, your attorneys, your accountants, your investigators, and anyone else acting on your behalf.

(c) **PERSON** includes natural person, firm, association, organization, partnership, business, trust, corporation, or public entity.

Figure 6.   Continued

(d) **DOCUMENT** means a writing, as defined in Evidence Code section 250, and includes the original or a copy of handwriting, typewriting, printing, photostating, photographing, and every other means of recording upon any tangible thing and form of communicating or representation, including letters, words, pictures, sounds, or symbols, or combinations of them.

(e) **HEALTH CARE PROVIDER** includes any **PERSON** referred to in Code of Civil Procedure section 667.7(e)(3).

(f) **ADDRESS** means the street address, including the city, state, and zip code.

Sec. 5. Interrogatories
The following interrogatories have been approved by the Judicial Council under Code of Civil Procedure section 2033.5:

CONTENTS

1.0 Identity of Persons Answering These Interrogatories
2.0 General Background Information—Individual
3.0 General Background Information—Business Entity
4.0 Insurance
5.0 [Reserved]
6.0 Physical, Mental, or Emotional Injuries
7.0 Property Damage
8.0 Loss of Income or Earning Capacity
9.0 Other Damages
10.0 Medical History
11.0 Other Claims and Previous Claims
12.0 Investigation—General
13.0 Investigation—Surveillance
14.0 Statutory or Regulatory Violations
15.0 Special or Affirmative Defenses
16.0 Defendant's Contentions—Personal Injury
17.0 Responses to Request for Admissions
18.0 [Reserved]
19.0 [Reserved]
20.0 How The Incident Occurred—Motor Vehicle
25.0 [Reserved]
30.0 [Reserved]
40.0 [Reserved]
50.0 Contract
60.0 [Reserved]
70.0 Unlawful Detainer [See separate form FI-128]
101.0 Economic Litigation [See separate form FI-129]

Figure 6.   Continued

1.0 Identity of Persons Answering These Interrogatories
❑ 1.1   State the name, **ADDRESS,** telephone number, and relationship to you of each **PERSON** who prepared or assisted in the preparation of the responses to these interrogatories. (Do not identify anyone who simply typed or reproduced copies of the interrogatories or your answers.)

2.0 General Background Information—Individual
❑ 2.1 State
(a) your name;
(b) every name you have used in the past;
(c) the dates you used each name.
❑ 2.2 State the date and place of your birth.
❑ 2.3 At the time of the **INCIDENT,** did you have a driver's license? If so, state:
(a) the state or other issuing entity;
(b) the license number and type;
(c) the date of issuance;
(d) all restrictions.
❑ 2.4 At the time of the **INCIDENT,** did you have any other permit or license for the operation of a motor vehicle? If so, state:
(a) the state or other issuing entity;
(b) the license number and type;
(c) the date of issuance;
(d) all restrictions.
❑ 2.5 State:
(a) your present residence **ADDRESS;**
(b) your residence **ADDRESSES** for the last five years;
(c) the dates you lived at each **ADDRESS.**
❑ 2.6 State:
(a) the name, **ADDRESS,** and telephone number of your present employer or place of self-employment;
(b) the name, **ADDRESS,** dates of employment, job title, and nature of work for each employer or self-employment you have had from five years before the **INCIDENT** until today.
❑ 2.7 State:
(a) the name and **ADDRESS** of each school or other academic or vocational institution you have attended beginning with high school;
(b) the dates you attended;
(c) the highest grade level you have completed;
(d) the degrees received.
❑ 2.8 Have you ever been convicted of a felony? If so, for each conviction state:
(a) the city and state where you were convicted;
(b) the date of conviction;
(c) the offense;

Figure 6. Continued

(d) the court and case number.

❑ 2.9 Can you speak English with ease? If not, what language and dialect do you normally use?

❑ 2.10 Can you read and write English with ease? If not, what language and dialect do you normally use?

❑ 2.11 At the time of the **INCIDENT** were you acting as an agent or employee for any **PERSON**? If so, state:
(a) the name, **ADDRESS,** and telephone number of that **PERSON;**
(b) a description of your duties.

❑ 2.12 At the time of the **INCIDENT** did you or any other person have any physical, emotional, or mental disability or condition that may have contributed to the occurrence of the **INCIDENT?** If so, for each person state:
(a) **ADDRESS,** and telephone number;
(b) the nature of the disability or condition;
(c) the manner in which the disability or condition contributed to the occurrence of the **INCIDENT.**

❑ 2.13 Within 24 hours before the **INCIDENT** did you or any person involved in the **INCIDENT** use or take any of the following substances: alcoholic beverage, marijuana, or other drug or medication of any kind (prescription or not)? If so, for each person state:
(a) the name, **ADDRESS,** and telephone number;
(b) the nature or description of each substance;
(c) the quantity of each substance used or taken;
(d) the date and time of day when each substance was used or taken;
(e) the **ADDRESS** where each substance was used or taken;
(f) the name, **ADDRESS,** and telephone number of each person who was present when each substance was used or taken;
(g) the name, **ADDRESS,** and telephone number of any **HEALTH CARE PROVIDER** that prescribed or furnished the substance and the condition for which it was prescribed or furnished.

3.0 General Background Information—Business Entity

❑ 3.1 Are you a corporation? If so, state:
(a) the name stated in the current articles of incorporation;
(b) all other names used by the corporation during the past ten years and the dates each was used;
(c) the date and place of incorporation;
(d) the **ADDRESS** of the principal place of business;
(e) whether you are qualified to do business in California.

❑ 3.2 Are you a partnership? If so, state:
(a) the current partnership name;
(b) all other names used by the partnership during the past ten years and the dates each was used;

Figure 6.   Continued

(c) whether you are a limited partnership and, if so, under the laws of what jurisdiction;

(d) the name and **ADDRESS** of each general partner;

(e) the **ADDRESS** of the principal place of business.

❏ 3.3 Are you a joint venture? If so, state:

(a) the current joint venture name;

(b) all other names used by the joint venture during the past ten years and the dates each was used;

(c) the name and **ADDRESS** of each joint venturer;

(d) the **ADDRESS** of the principal place of business.

❏ 3.4 Are you an unincorporated association? If so, state:

(a) the current unincorporated association name;

(b) all other names used by the unincorporated association during the past ten years and the dates each was used;

(c) the **ADDRESS** of the principal place of business.

❏ 3.5 Have you done business under a fictitious name during the past ten years? If so, for each fictitious name state:

(a) the name;

(b) the dates each was used;

(c) the state and county of each fictitious name filing;

(d) the **ADDRESS** of the principal place of business.

❏ 3.6 Within the past five years has any public entity registered or licensed your businesses? If so, for each license of registration:

(a) identify the license or registration;

(b) state the name of the public entity;

(c) state the dates of issuance and expiration.

4.0 Insurance

❏ 4.1 At the time of the **INCIDENT** was there in effect any policy of insurance through which you were or might be insured in any manner (for example, primary, pro-rata, or excess liability coverage or medical expense coverage) for the damages, claims, or actions that have arisen out of the **INCIDENT?** If so, for each policy state:

(a) the kind of coverage;

(b) the name and **ADDRESS** of the insurance company;

(c) the name, **ADDRESS,** and telephone number of each named insured;

(d) the policy number;

(e) the limits of coverage for each type of coverage contained in the policy;

(f) whether any reservation of rights or controversy or coverage dispute exists between you and the insurance company;

(g) the name, **ADDRESS,** and telephone number of the custodian of the policy.

Figure 6. Continued

❏ 4.2 Are you self-insured under any statute for the damages, claims, or actions that have arisen out of the **INCIDENT?** If so, specify the statute.

5.0 [*Reserved*]

6.0 Physical, Mental, or Emotional Injuries

❏ 6.1 Do you attribute any physical, mental, or emotional injuries to the **INCIDENT?** If your answer is "no," do not answer interrogatories 6.2 through 6.7.

❏ 6.2 Identify each injury you attribute to the **INCIDENT** and the area of your body affected.

❏ 6.3 Do you still have any complaints that you attribute to the **INCIDENT?** If so, for each complaint state:
(a) a description;
(b) whether the complaint is subsiding, remaining the same, or becoming worse;
(c) the frequency and duration.

❏ 6.4 Did you receive any consultation or examination (except from expert witnesses covered by Code of Civil Procedure section 2034) or treatment from a **HEALTH CARE PROVIDER** for any injury you attribute to the **INCIDENT?** If so, for each **HEALTH CARE PROVIDER** state:
(a) the name, **ADDRESS,** and telephone number;
(b) the type of consultation, examination, or treatment provided;

FI-120 (Rev. January 1, 1988)   **FORM INTERROGATORIES**   Page three of eight

had to answer or object to each question. It would become a word-processing nightmare (not to mention very expensive for the client).

Some situations are appropriate for special interrogatories. Sometimes you aren't ready to take someone's deposition but want an answer to a specific question. Sometimes you've already taken someone's deposition and realize you have important unanswered questions or new questions based on evidence you've discovered.

If the other side sends you interrogatory questions, you have a certain period of time in which to answer and/or object to them. If you fail to respond to the questions by the deadline, you may be subject to a motion to compel you to answer the questions and may face a court-imposed fine called a sanction.

Requests for Admission

As their name implies, requests for admission ask another party to admit a certain fact. For example, maybe you're in a breach of contract dispute, and you want the defendant, John Hancock, to admit that the signature on the contract is his. He may send back written admission that it is, in fact, his signature. Now you know that you won't have to spend any time proving this issue in court; he admits it, you agree, end of subject. But if he refuses to admit that it's his signature, and if you later prove in court that it *is* his signature, you may actually recover the costs of proving that fact. In short, requests for admission can be used to force a party on the other side to admit a fact that's harmful to his case.

A number of lawyers, after they win a case, forget to go back and look at their requests for admission and see if the other side is open to a request for the cost of proving a certain fact. If you win and your attorney served some requests for admission, after you wake up hung over from all the champagne at the victory party, ask your lawyer for the requests for admission, because you may get to recover even more money. By the way, it can work both ways. If you send your own denial to a request for admission and lose the case, the other side can pull out that request for admission and get you to pay for something where the jury decided against you.

Requests for admission can also be used against you if you admit something damaging and the other side uses your admission in a motion to get your case thrown out. (For more on this possibility, see the discussion of summary judgment motions in Chapter 13.)

Just as with document requests and interrogatories, if your lawyer fails to answer or objects to the question within the allotted time period, you could be in hot water. In effect, you've now admitted that fact, simply by not answering. To "unadmit" that fact, you would have to file a costly motion with the court, giving a reason why you should be permitted to do so.

Some lawyers shoot out requests for admission early on, but I generally like to wait until much later in the case, after I've had a chance to think about which facts the other side has to admit that help me and my claims (or my defense) most.

Service

To serve another party a demand for production of documents, interrogatories, or requests for admission, your lawyer mails the request or has it delivered to the opposing party's lawyer. That's all there is to it. You don't have to hire a process server or issue any fancy paperwork. You just send it out under the local rules in your jurisdiction, and the other side must respond within the prescribed time period for responding. However, although you can serve another party in the lawsuit this way, if you send a request for document production or a deposition notice to someone who is not a party to the lawsuit, then you must send a court-issued subpoena, and it must be served personally on that third party.

You don't have to serve your interrogatories, requests for admission, and document requests all at the same time. A lot of lawyers do it this way because they're trying to be aggressive, and push the other side, or they feel that they're making a statement. You can save yourself a lot of grief by just sending a general set of document requests and a general exploratory set of interrogatories. Once you get those back, you can identify the first wave of people who should be deposed. Then stop.

Now consider: What more specific questions can I ask? What specific documents do I need? Who are the specific people I need to depose? And now what facts do I think I can get them to admit? Some lawyers, though, would say, "Send out the requests for admission right away! Force the other side to focus on its case and make decisions early on." There are different schools of thought on this. My advice is to go with what your attorney recommends, if you understand his logic and it seems reasonable in your situation.

Discovery Referees

Where parties to a lawsuit fight over whether certain information or documents should be produced, many courts try to resolve the "fight" by using an assistant to the judge, typically known as a discovery referee (or "commissioner"). Using a referee serves two purposes. First, in a court in a major metropolitan area with limited resources, it's a way to delegate the work to somebody else, get it done, and move things along. Second, often you have to personally pay for the cost of the referee, so no taxpayer dollars are spent on resolving these discovery disputes. The court hopes that forcing the parties to pay causes them ultimately to spend enough money on their lawyers and the referee that they'll stop fighting over marginal issues.

The potential benefit of a referee is that he'll have more time than a judge, and should be able to weigh carefully the discovery issue. He'll familiarize himself with your case and the issues, and you may return to that referee several times. A referee can be particularly helpful when you're dealing with a party who's stonewalling.

Of course, a downside is that you have to pay for the referee's time. Also, the referee may not always be as competent as the judge; he may make mistakes about the case or take too long issuing rulings. Some may make an issue much bigger than it needs to be. I recently presented a discovery issue to a referee, and he wrote an opinion as though he were sitting on the Supreme Court. The case involved a fairly simple issue, but referees frequently are retired judges or lawyers looking for ways to supplement their income, and since they're paid by the hour, they may not be in a hurry.

In summary, if you are unsure about whether to fight about certain documents being requested, and your lawyer tells you the judge is likely to refer the matter to a referee, ask yourself whether you want to burn a couple thousand dollars paying for both your lawyer and the referee to resolve the "fight" you are about to pick.

Confidentiality Agreements

As mentioned earlier, a party is not permitted to examine everything he may want to. To look at certain information or conduct certain kinds of exams, you have to show the court special circumstances, and the court must agree to permit the discovery.

The courts are protective in all cases of personal, confidential information, like tax returns, financial documents of a sensitive nature, trade secrets, and other commercially sensitive articles. For example, if you're a writer and have a screenplay that no one has seen, you may make efforts to not have it produced, and the court will probably be sympathetic to you. The court can also issue a confidentiality agreement (called a protective order) that limits the manner in which a document can be used. Sometimes the parties will come to an agreement and submit it to the court to be ordered (called a stipulation for the protection of confidential information). Sometimes the court will, upon motion from one of the parties, issue a protective order itself.

Generally, a protective order states that certain categories of documents must be handled in a certain way by all parties. Typically there is a category called "attorneys only," and the party supplying the documents actually stamps "Confidential—Attorneys Only" on each document. "Attorneys Only" means that only the attorneys involved may see the document, interrogatory answer, or a specific portion of a deposition transcript. There may be a category simply called "confidential," which means the attorneys, the parties in the lawsuit, and any experts can see the document, but not the general public. As part of a court proceeding and part of the order itself, rules will be defined for how to handle each category of sensitive documents.

Some confidentiality agreements have a problem that goes like this: You go to great pains to work out a confidentiality agreement with the other side. You produce a document that only the other attorneys are supposed to see. But later, when they have the document, they decide to attach it to a motion or to an opposition that gets filed, and now anyone who asked for the file at the court filing window could go in and see it. It's no longer confidential. If nothing in the confidentiality agreement addressed the issue of how the confidential documents should be presented to the court, the other side didn't break the agreement by doing this.

A well-written confidentiality agreement goes beyond only the use of sensitive documents between the parties; it has provisions on how to handle the submission of this document to the court. It may stipulate that this class of documents will be filed under "seal," or that only the portion of the document that is not confidential may be shown, and the rest must be redacted (blocked out). Another option is to agree that an unredacted courtesy copy of the document can be handed to the judge at a certain time under certain conditions, in the event a document is to be used in a motion.

Handling the exchange of sensitive information is a world in and of itself. Know that your jurisdiction has specific rules that relate to this; if you have sensitive information you're concerned about keeping that way, talk to your attorney about it early on. A mistake many of my clients make is that they'll hear their lawyer say, "Well, we're going to get a confidentiality order or a protective order, so don't worry." Then they get a copy of the proposed order that looks dry and lawyerly so they throw it in a file box somewhere and forget about it. If it's *your* confidential information; you should really read and understand that protective order, even though it's got a lot of legalese. You may see a hole, and before it's too late, you can tell your lawyer, "Holy mackerel! What about this issue?"

Big corporations generally have in-house counsels who help safeguard the company's confidential information, and often they routinely attach a confidentiality form. If you're an individual or run a mom-and-pop business that's not so sophisticated, though, you need to be careful when it comes to confidentiality agreements. The truth is that litigators who are good trial lawyers may not always be as strong at the discovery end of a case. They may be great in court and at taking depositions but not very good on things like protective orders. You need to spend some time talking with your lawyer about getting a protective order and about the desired scope of the protective order. Then read it before it's finalized, and see exactly how the order is to be used.

A client of mine went down to court himself to ask a clerk about how the documents are processed. The client then came back and told me we needed an additional proviso in his confidentiality agreement based on something he had learned about how certain documents are scanned and placed in the court's computers. This was something I certainly didn't know about. I don't hang out in the file room at the courthouse and know all the procedures. This issue was important to the client, so he found out about it himself. If you're considering obtaining a protective order, you may want to do some legwork in your own local courthouse. If what you see there raises some questions or you discover something important, bring it to your lawyer's attention.

It's your confidentiality that needs to be protected, and you had better take charge to ensure that happens. I've seen protective orders that are complete jokes. I've seen some that simply say that during discovery the lawyers cannot show these trade secret documents to anyone. But the minute the other side wants to have an expert deposed, the expert can read it, review it, and talk all about it in his deposition.

Subpoenas and Motions to Quash

Someone who is not a party to your lawsuit may have relevant information. Maybe it's an employer, a medical office, the police department, the phone company, or any other person or entity you can imagine—anyone other than plaintiff or defendant. For the purposes of discovery, you are entitled to depose such people and the people working there, and you can request documents from them. To set a deposition or request a document, your lawyer may not simply mail or messenger to the other party's lawyer a written demand or a notice of deposition. Someone who is not a party must be subpoenaed. Your lawyer must get a formal subpoena issued by the court, and it must be served personally on the third party.

If a third party objects to being deposed or to producing documents, the court will generally be a little less hard on him than on the parties directly involved in the matter, because he's an outsider to the lawsuit. If he wants additional time, or to limit the subject matter, or to be protected in some other way, the court is generally willing to offer that protection.

If you're a third party and have been served with a subpoena, you have rights you may not be aware of. You can get a lawyer and file a motion to quash the subpoena (to nullify it) or file a motion for a protective order. These motions may have different names in different jurisdictions, but they operate the same way. For example, if you're a bank and someone asks for your records, you might have to adhere to a consumer records protection statute requiring you to notify the consumer that the records are being sought. Once the consumer receives notice, he can file a protective motion or a Motion to Quash. Generally, for a Motion to Quash to succeed, the third party must have good and compelling reasons for not adhering to the subpoena or limiting his response.

Attorney-Client Privilege

By law, communications between attorney and client are privileged. You have a legal right to confide in your attorney, and with very few exceptions, no one can ever find out what is said between you. Most people are aware of this right.

One thing many litigants don't realize, though, is that if a communication between you and your attorney is made in the presence of a third party who is not a part of the attorney-client relationship, then it may lose its privilege. So if you have a friend sitting in while you talk with your attorney, that conversation is not privileged, and it could be discoverable.

If you're a husband and have been sued but your wife's not a part of the suit, if she joins in on the discussion with your attorney, many people assume that the discussion is still privileged. But in some instances you may have waived the privilege because you've disclosed the contents of the communication to a third party—even though that third party is your wife. In most jurisdictions a judge will say that your wife is part of a "litigation team," and thus covered by a spousal privilege.

The term *spousal privilege* refers to the fact that you are also permitted by law to have privileged communications with your spouse.

If you later divulge the contents of a privileged communication, it's no longer privileged. One of the biggest mistakes people make is showing their communication with their attorney to friends and family. Poof—there goes the privilege. If somebody (like the other side) discovers that you've shared these communications with third parties, than they can successfully argue that you've waived attorney-client privilege, and they can depose you and your friend about it and force you to produce a copy of that letter. Thus, you should keep your attorney-client communications very much under wraps. If there's a letter or conversation and it's never been exposed to anyone outside of the attorney-client relationship, it stays protected always, no matter what's in it, no matter how damning it may be.

There are a few very basic exceptions to this. For example, if you sue your attorney later, he gets to defend himself by divulging conversations and other communications with you. If you tell your attorney you're going to commit a crime, than the attorney might be able to disclose that fact as well. If law enforcement has cause to believe that you went to an attorney with the intent to commit a crime, they may be able to pierce the attorney-client privilege.

If your attorney is taking notes when discussing your case with you, writing memos to associates about strategy, or formulating in writing his opinions on what he believes is admissible—all of this falls under what is referred to as the attorney work product privilege. Your attorney's "work product" on your case is also protected and generally privileged.

The main message I have about privilege is, Be careful. If you get a letter from your lawyer and show it to your Uncle Joe at Thanksgiving dinner, you could be asking for trouble. Keep your attorney-client letters private in your house. Don't leave them out where others can see them. Be careful about your use of fax machines. If you're expecting a fax from your attorney, go and get it as soon as it comes in. Don't just let it sit there in the tray, where someone else can read it. And don't share your E-mail between you and your attorney with anyone else. You waive the privilege when you disclose these communications to third parties.

"My client refuses to disclose what
he ate for dinner on Friday the 27th!"

Nuts and Bolts:
Written Discovery
and Discovery Motions

A lawsuit is a fruit tree planted in a lawyer's garden.

—Italian proverb

As I explained in the previous chapter, the idea of discovery is to discover witnesses, documents, and facts about the claims at issue in a lawsuit or about the defenses asserted. Sometimes parties disagree over the relevance or necessity of a given question to be answered, witness to appear, or document to be produced. In such instances, one side or the other may decide to bring the matter to the court's attention to get a ruling on the issue. This is done by submitting the issue in writing to the court. When you bring something to the court's attention, it's called a motion.

Because discovery can be used for strategic purposes—to harass, overwhelm, or overburden another party—a defendant looking to drag things out may try to force you to file a bunch of discovery motions. This is yet another way to inflict a lot of expense on the other side.

For example, some lawyers will serve as many as 250 document requests to the opposing party, not because they really want the documents but simply to harass the opposing party. An experienced practitioner could probably summarize the 250 requests into fifteen or twenty requests and, in so doing, snag every document that's relevant to the case. But that's not the objective when someone serves 250 requests. It takes time to go through, think about, and answer each of those requests. It's possible that you may want to object to the request on the basis that it's burdensome, overreaching, duplicative, and that the other side should be required to go back and narrow the request. If you object and the other side refuses to reformulate its questions, you've got your first discovery skirmish.

When the Other Side Doesn't Comply

Today most jurisdictions have what is called a "meet and confer" requirement, which means that the lawyers on each side are required to make a good-faith effort to compromise the dispute before anyone files a motion. If the meet and confer conference doesn't result in an acceptable compromise, then one side or the other will file a motion. The side who received the request can serve a Motion for a Protective Order, saying basically, "I don't want to respond, and I don't want to be held in default or sanctioned, and here's why I believe I should not be required to produce this material." If that doesn't happen, the side that sent the request can file a Motion to Compel to try to force the parties on the other side to release the documents they refused to produce or answer questions they wouldn't answer. These are two ways of getting to the same point.

In many jurisdictions, the losing side in such a motion could be sanctioned by having to pay the other side's attorney's fees arising from the motion. All courts are looking for ways to force the parties to resolve disputes reasonably. That's why they impose the meet and confer requirement and award sanctions: to compel the parties to get the facts out on the table and not to mess around.

Ultimately, unless you're a large defendant whose motive is simply to exhaust the other side's resources or to delay, nine times out of ten it's in everyone's best interest to get the facts out on the table. Why? Because it allows for a fair evaluation of the worth of the case and a determination as to whether it should settle. In contrast, if you play games with the other side, the other side will play games with you. If you refuse to show up at your deposition until it's convenient for you, the other side will probably start having scheduling difficulties as well.

For Joe Average who runs a small business, or for an individual with a limited budget, the key question is this: How do you use the discovery process to get the information you need in order to be prepared for trial? The real danger would come if you or your attorney just want to go to war. Say the first discovery dispute comes up, and you realize as a first-time litigator that there's a sporting element to litigation. You can identify the winner and loser when the judge says, "Motion granted!" or, "Motion denied!"

If the other side has refused to give you a document, you need to stop and think: Do you really need the document? Is there another way to get it? You can too easily get lost on a side journey in what I call discovery warfare. A lot of plaintiffs and defendants want to kick some butt and just don't get the concept of saving it for the trial. "That's too far away!" they think. "Man, they're not giving us our documents! Let's go in there and *win* that motion!" If you take this approach, you could wind up spending tens of thousands of dollars on fights that may not even determine the outcome of your case.

Discovery can be the biggest pitfall for the righteous defendant or the righteous plaintiff. Discovery is not intended to be a warm-up for the trial. Don't spend $40,000—or even $20,000 or $15,000—to get one document that may not even decide the outcome of your case.

If you're the plaintiff and have a limited budget, keep your document requests simple and few: first a basic set of document requests, then a second set later. If you have limited funds and get caught up in discovery skirmishes because you've tried to do too much too soon, you may exhaust yourself and have trouble serving that second document request later.

A party that wants to stonewall you in the production of documents will look for every reason to object. Don't be unreasonable and over-reaching with your requests; you'll only give the other side more grounds on which to object. If the opposing party's lawyer objects and your lawyer can't work it out with him, then you're looking at filing a Motion to Compel if you really want to get those particular documents. If you want to move forward with your case, do not get embroiled in an expensive side dispute; keep it basic. Ask simple questions that won't likely draw the common objections that a court might agree with, such as that your request is unintelligible, vague, ambiguous, compound, or overly burdensome.

If the other side refuses to produce documents or answer questions, or if you get inadequate production or answers, your lawyer must bring a Motion to Compel within a specified time period. If you don't bring a motion within that time period, then you waive your right to ever enforce your demand.

If you're the defendant and your strategy is to find ways to delay—whether to buy time to evaluate the case and decide whether to settle, or just to stall—you're going to be looking for ways to object. You'll force the plaintiff to clarify his requests, to fight.

Discovery as Harassment

If you're a plaintiff up against a defendant who has more resources than you, discovery is where the other side will wear you down. The defendant will try to make your life miserable. Insurance company defense firms are notorious for this kind of gamesmanship. You file a notice of a deposition because you want a defendant to appear for a deposition, and no date works for him. That executive is in Atlanta, so you can't depose him until September. You schedule him for September 12, and on September 11 you get a phone call: "I'm sorry, he can't make it tomorrow." The defense does this to you until you've gotten $4,000 in legal bills just for trying to schedule the guy's deposition!

You go through the roof and tell your attorney, "I'll fire you if you don't depose this person." So the attorney throws a fit and files a motion to compel the executive to appear for his deposition. Now the executive shows up, but he left some of the documents he was supposed to bring back in Atlanta. Or maybe he didn't realize you were going to need to depose him for two days, so he can't come back tomorrow, and he'll have to get back to you about when he can complete his deposition.

Then the other side deposes you, and even though your case is fairly straightforward, the deposition goes from two, to three, to four days . . . They're taking a month between each deposition session to do more discovery, then bringing you in to ask you more questions. You're upset, and your lawyer files a motion for a protective order asking the judge to force the defendant's law firm to end your deposition. You think the judge is going to help you out because it's gone on so long. But the judge thinks, "You're asking for a lot of money, so you have to answer a lot of questions."

Big corporate defendants use discovery to bury the plaintiff or the plaintiff's contingency fee law firm. They do this with discovery motions and by making discovery difficult and tedious.

Most jurisdictions have been trying to refine their local discovery rules so that discovery can't be used so much for strategic purposes like harassment or for lawyers to gin up more fees. They're trying to find ways to make it work better for good-faith discovery. Most federal courts, for example, now have a process called an early meeting of counsel. Both sides must come to this meeting with every document that's relevant to the lawsuit, a complete list of witnesses, a list of likely depositions, and a proposed schedule for taking those depositions. No formal request is served by either side, but the court requires that both sides bring and exchange this information. In some jurisdictions you're even required to meet and confer on what facts will be stipulated at trial (what facts both sides will agree to as true).

This is the wave of the future for discovery. The federal courts have essentially admitted that there is a possibility for abuse in discovery. They see the added cost to the litigant of having a paper war where somebody heaves 200 requests on the other side, and the other side objects and serves back 55 interrogatories. Before you know it, you've got four discovery motions before the court, and in only two months of litigation not a single fact has been exchanged—just massive briefs.

The best course if you are a plaintiff with a limited budget is to wait until you get all your discovery responses. If you feel that the defense is being evasive or trying to outspend you in discovery, wait until you've made a good record. By a "good record," I don't mean a file of long-winded letters where your lawyer is amusing himself and the world with his immaculate articulation of his position, but a few short letters documenting that the other side is not abiding by its discovery obligations. Get a few of those on a point that is not questionable—not in a gray area, but an area where you have a winner. Maybe the person is not showing up for the deposition, or you've asked five times for this category of documents and have received a different excuse each time. Once you've documented a couple of instances of clear discovery abuse, then pick your moment to file your Motion to Compel, where you can get the judge so aroused that he's going to order the other side to pay you sanctions. Therefore, you will be making the discovery process work for you in a cost-effective way.

Again, be careful about which battles you pick to fight, how much information you ask for, and when you go before the court. It helps when your attorney knows your jurisdiction and your judge, and understands how a referee would work in your jurisdiction.

When They Hit Below the Belt

The large institutions papering you to death are hoping you won't answer right away, and they'll look to file a Motion to Compel. The best way to counter that is to have a lawyer who's not asleep at the switch, who will give them the answers in a timely way. To facilitate that, give all the requested documents to your lawyer right away, and tell your lawyer to send them to the other side. Don't get lazy, and don't let your lawyer get too distracted to get the documents delivered. Sometimes lawyers get busy on other cases and will ask the other side on your case for an extension; then they don't get the papers in, and suddenly you're looking at an expensive motion.

Know the deadlines on your case. Make sure you're keeping your attorney on his feet. Let him know that you don't want delays; you want to respond quickly and take the fight to the other side. You want to preclude the defense's ability to start creating discovery motions.

Early on in your case, you'll get a sense as to whether there will be a professional atmosphere or not. In some instances the lawyers get out of control with their power. They may serve a party at an embarrassing moment, schedule a deposition on what they know to be a particularly inconvenient day, or ask questions that are irrelevant to the case but may cause a witness to break down and cry.

Ask yourself whether your attorney is behaving this way. If your attorney is throwing punches below the belt, then you're going to get hit below the belt. Tell your attorney you don't want to hit below the belt. If people on the other side are hitting below the belt routinely, then you have to pick the most dramatic moment where it's clear they are doing so, and have your lawyer keep a good record of it. Then go to a court and say, "They're not fighting fairly," and see if the judge will put a stop to it.

Don't be surprised if the judge doesn't get it or is too preoccupied with other cases and just doesn't see the injustice that you see. If that happens, you've just got to toughen up, take a few more hits, and keep going.

In some situations someone on the other side may call a witness and misrepresent himself, saying he's you or your lawyer, and pull stunts to try to make you look bad. If those types of dirty tricks take place, ask your attorney what the appropriate response is. It almost never is to go down to the other side's level. In a lawsuit what goes around often comes around.

Conversely, don't be upset with your attorney if he allows a few extensions or offers some professional courtesies to your opponent's lawyer. That might benefit you later. Then again, make it clear to your attorney that you don't want him to grant professional courtesies or extensions without first consulting you.

A Preemptive Strike to Avoid Discovery Fights

Don't dive too fast into the discovery pool; it could be a shallow end, and you could harm yourself. If you're the plaintiff, get in and out as quickly as you can, and survive to have your day in court. People forget that discovery is not the only way to secure information. You can use a private investigator or conduct searches on the Internet. There are investigative services that, for a fraction of the cost of filing motions or paying attorneys, can pull together the information you want. They may not get *all* you want, but they may be more effective at getting certain kinds of information.

One method I have used successfully to help minimize discovery harassment is to invest in preparation. If a plaintiff wants to keep his budget low, I'll tell him before we file the complaint to bring me every document that may be relevant to his case. I ask him to give me a list of every witness and to tell me who's knowledgeable. I ask him to let me write a complaint that tells pretty much the full story. Then I file the complaint, call opposing counsel, and say, "I'm sending you a box of every document relevant to the case, and I'm going to give you a cover letter of every witness we think we'll call at trial. We already know who we think our experts are going to be, and we're ready to provide answers to interrogatories whenever you send them over."

Although it costs my client more money up front to have me do so much preparation on his case, every time I've done it, the other side is blown away. It sends a message that says, "We're not just filing out of the heat of passion. We're not just filing a lousy complaint in the hopes of getting a quick settlement. We're ready to go the distance, and we don't have anything to fear. Here is our case." It tells the other side you're not afraid, aren't hiding anything, and are confident in your position.

This tactic also makes it difficult for the other side to harass you, because you've already given every shred of paper that relates to the case without even being asked. Later, if they decide to serve you omnibus 250-document requests, your lawyer will just type in, "Every document that is potentially relevant to this case has been produced." When they then go to the judge to make noise about it—just to pick a fight and run up your costs—there's nothing to fight over. You've produced everything.

So ask yourself whether you can do this. If not, what are you reluctant to produce? A diary that may be a little embarrassing? Well, you'll probably end up producing it anyway, and you've got something far more important at issue—say, that a contract was breached and you lost two hundred thousand dollars, or your dog got hit by a car and he's dead. You don't care if your opponents see everything. Give them the diary. If you're really concerned about producing something at the start, send over some *standard* confidentiality agreement that will give you some moderate level of protection. You will take the teeth out of their ability to box you in. If they send you one of those 250-document requests, you can go in right away with a Motion for a Protective Order and say, "Your honor, I gave them everything voluntarily. I sent it over and they still served me a 250-document request!" The judge will cut them off at the knees.

This is my special recipe for minimizing discovery harassment.

"Did you suffer any injuries?"

Nuts and Bolts: Depositions

All sides in a trial want to hide
at least some of the truth.

—Alan Dershowitz

A deposition is a meeting where the lawyers on both sides of a case have the opportunity to question witnesses or parties to the case about any facts that might be relevant. Each side is given wide latitude to ask any question that might be even remotely relevant to the case.

While everyone in a deposition may be dressed casually and sitting comfortably around a table, the proceeding is every bit as serious as if you were in court before judge and jury. In fact, some portion of what is said in a deposition often *will* be read in court. Depositions carry the same weight as court testimony, and often if a witness can't be present at trial, relevant portions of his deposition will be read to the jury instead.

Deposition Basics

The testimony you give in your deposition should be the same as what you give at trial. If at trial you give a different answer to a question you were asked in your deposition, the opposing lawyer will take out your deposition transcript and read your earlier answer to the jury. If you make a serious change in your testimony, your credibility could be damaged if you don't have a convincing reason for that change.

In your deposition you will be placed under oath, under penalty of perjury, and asked questions about your best recollection of facts known to you. The questions and answers are recorded by a Certified Court Reporter, who later types up a deposition transcript. Each side purchases a copy of that transcript to use in the case.

Either party to a lawsuit can take the deposition of a witness or of the opposing party. If you wish to take a deposition, your attorney prepares and serves a deposition notice and/or subpoena, setting forth the time, date, and location for the deposition. Your attorney also hires a court reporter to be present to record it.

Being the party who "sets" a given deposition has potential pluses and minuses. The downside is that if you set the deposition, you have to pay the cost of the court reporter. Depending on the length of the deposition, this can be a few hundred dollars or can climb into the thousands. The party who didn't set the deposition only has to pay for a copy of the transcript—on average, only about a third of the amount paid by the party who set the deposition. Because depositions are usually expensive, most plaintiffs prefer to let the defendant set as many depositions as possible.

The benefit to being the party who sets the deposition is that your attorney gets to go first in questioning the witness, and the opposing party has to wait until you're finished before getting a chance to ask follow-up questions. Depending on the witness, this may or may not be an advantage.

Depositions are taken in a lawsuit to gather evidence, to nail you down to a particular version of events, and to assess what kind of witness you would make before a jury. You probably don't need to take the depositions of "friendly" witnesses (those whom you know personally, if you know exactly what their testimony would be). You will want to take the depositions of "hostile" witnesses (people who dispute your version of the facts).

Loose Lips Sink Ships

Soldiers are trained to give only their name, rank, and serial number if captured by the enemy. And there's good reason. The answer to even a seemingly innocent question could cost lives, perhaps the war. In a deposition, a similar mentality applies: the less said, the better.

In a case I once handled, a screenwriter sued a studio for stealing his copyrighted material. My client had written a script and sold a studio the option to purchase the script, but the option had lapsed without the studio buying it. Years later, the studio came out with a movie that was suspiciously similar to the screenwriter's script. One of the people we deposed was the studio head who had been involved in optioning the writer's script. As soon as the deposition began, he came out swinging with a bunch of derisive comments about the lawsuit. He made it quite clear that he had a lot of disdain for my client and his claims. Realizing that this gentleman was arrogant and hotheaded, I started asking him pointed questions with a hint of personal accusation. Rather than just answering with a simple "yes" or "no," he went off on rants. He enumerated reasons why the movie they'd produced was nothing like my client's script and mentioned other people who agreed with him, including another writer who had done a rewrite on the very movie that my client believed had been made from his script. This writer's name hadn't come up in previous discovery, and when we deposed him later, we found out he had been given a copy of my client's script.

Had the studio head been more cool and simply limited the answers he gave me to just the precise questions I'd asked, I might never have found the useful pieces of information he volunteered. But since the guy was hell-bent on proving my client a flake, he spilled out details that ultimately helped us.

Check Your Ego at the Door

Too often people go into their depositions leading with their egos. They're just bursting to tell the other guy's lawyer why they're so right and the other guy's so wrong. They see their deposition as a contest, and use it to present their case. They're dying to show their opponent that he's going to have big problems winning. They're looking for opportunities to take shots at the other guy and score points.

A deposition isn't a battle, even if at times it feels like one. It isn't an event to "win," and you don't have to prove anything. You simply want to get through it without harming your own case. The way to do that is by providing simple, direct, truthful answers to the other side's questions—and nothing more or less.

Your deposition isn't for your benefit; it's for your opponent's. It's your opponent's chance to pin you down on relevant facts and to discover information relating to your claims. If you go in to prove a point, you will only help the people on the other side figure out how you view your case—and how they might defeat it.

Nothing but the Truth

Litigation is adversarial, so each litigant is always looking for ways to wound the other. The "fatal blow" you can deliver to anyone in a lawsuit is to show he is a liar. More than anything else, juries dislike liars, and if someone is proved to be a liar on an important matter, juries assume he's lying across the board. Frequently, they want to send such a person a loud message—a verdict against him.

Inconsistencies are the gold your opponents will be panning for in your deposition. Afterward, when you've been pinned down on the facts and circumstances, the other side will look for evidence and witnesses who will disagree or disprove what you said.

If you're evasive or lie in your deposition, you risk hurting yourself. If your testimony is later contradicted at trial or if you appear to be deceptive, you'll do irreparable damage to your case. One of the instructions the jurors receive before they begin deliberations is that if they decide that someone lied in one instance, they may reasonably conclude that the person is lying on other matters as well. If the jury believes you're lying, it will be very difficult and probably impossible for the jury to find in your favor.

Here are some points you need to consider to give a good deposition.

Speak Audibly

You will most likely be deposed in the office or conference room of the attorney who set the deposition. When you're being deposed, you and your lawyer will probably sit on one side of the desk or table, and the lawyer or lawyers for the opposition will sit on the other. Any of the parties named in the suit have a right to be present in your (or any) depositions, so the person you're suing (or being sued by) may also be seated next to his attorney.

A court reporter will be present. Frequently he will sit at one end of the table so that he can hear everyone equally well. A court reporter is a stenographer who has been approved by the court to transcribe any conversation that takes place during the deposition.

Once you've been sworn in, the court reporter uses his steno machine to take down the questions you're asked, anything you say in response, and any other discussion that takes place during the deposition. If anyone in the room speaks, the court reporter is supposed to record what is said. When the deposition is over, the court reporter types up the transcript and sends you a copy. You then have a certain period of time (usually thirty days) to read your transcript, make any changes you wish, and then sign it under penalty of perjury.

You want to be sure your answers are being recorded properly. The last thing you want to do is make a lot of changes on your transcript that the other side can point to in order to question your credibility. Always speak audibly. You should not answer yes/no questions with anything other than a clear "yes" or "no." Avoid answering by nodding or shaking your head or by saying "uh-huh."

Look Your Questioner in the Eye

Presentation is very important during your deposition. The lawyer for the other side will try to assess how well you would do in front of a jury, so he will evaluate your demeanor. You want to make a good impression, convey your confidence in your claims, and come across as forthright, attentive, and friendly. (Don't worry too much, though; you can expect to be tense and nervous in your deposition.) Even if you despise the attorney who's questioning you and dislike the other party who's sitting right beside him, convey respect and give your full attention to the questioner.

Attorneys who work for insurance companies generally must prepare a report about you based on your deposition performance, for the adjuster on the case. That report will include an appraisal of your credibility, likability, whether you're easily flustered, articulate, warm, etc. In essence, he'll give a professional estimation of how you would appear to a jury. You want to put your best foot forward, and this means acting professional, friendly, and respectful to the other side.

If You Aren't Sure You Understand, Say So

It is imperative that you answer questions truthfully and thoroughly. If you're not sure what is being asked of you, don't answer. Say, "I don't understand the question," or, "Could you be more specific?" or, "I'm not sure what you're asking."

The last thing you want to do if you don't really understand a question is to give an answer anyway. You might inadvertently give information the other side wasn't even thinking about and didn't know to ask about. Perhaps you didn't want to be asked about something, and now you find you've opened the door.

If you answer a question without being certain what was meant, you could help the other side create the appearance of a contradiction: "Look! In his deposition he said x. Now he's saying y!" You will be stuck trying to convince the jury that you misunderstood the question in your deposition and didn't think that's what the questioner was asking for. The damage may be done, and you come out looking like a liar.

Don't Try to Fill the Silence

Many people become uncomfortable if they're having a discussion with another person and the conversation stops dead. They can't stand the silence, so if no one is talking, they try to fill the void with something, anything. If this is you and there's a lot of silence in your deposition, resist that urge to vocalize!

You want to give a concise answer that answers the question as presented. That's all. If the attorney who is questioning you doesn't ask another question, or if he simply sits and looks at you or raises his eyebrows or smiles sarcastically, don't feel that you need to say anything more. Just wait for the next question.

Don't Speculate; Don't Guess

A deposition isn't a discussion. You are there only to say what you heard, saw, said, smelled, felt, or tasted. You are not there to guess, make conclusions, or speculate about what might have been in someone else's mind at one time or another. There's no way you can know that, unless you're a mind reader. Even if you're psychic, the judge isn't going to let you testify about what the spirits told you. (It's hearsay!)

Let's say you're suing because John sexually harassed you at work, and after you made a report about it, he fired you from your job. As part of your deposition John's attorney asks you to explain what John did and said to you. After you answer, he asks if you know why John did those things. Now, you could say, "I think John harassed me because he's a dirty old man who's lonely and can't get anybody to date him, and he fired me from the job to retaliate for reporting him! It was payback for exercising my rights!" But even though that may be true, you have no way of really knowing why John did what he did.

Don't speculate. It's going to be your attorney's job to present the scenario to the jury or argue John's state of mind and his motives, not yours. Your job is only to tell what you know, saw, heard, felt, and said. Don't try to go into someone else's mind.

The dangers of speculating are many. Someone could contradict your speculation. Suppose you said John's a lonely loser, and now here come ten women who date him all the time and think he's Mel Gibson. "Wait, Ms. Victim, I thought you said he was lonely and couldn't get any, and that's why he came on to you. That's not true, is it? What else have you made up?" Don't speculate; let your attorney tell the story and put it all in perspective. If you try to do it, you only open yourself up to trouble. If John's lawyer asks why John did what he did, the correct answer is "I don't know." Don't guess.

Also, never hazard an "educated guess" in response to a question. If another witness has a recollection that differs from your guess, this can also be used against you to show a discrepancy between your testimony and someone else's.

Listen Carefully

LAWYER: Was John with you when you drove to the—

YOU: To the park? No, I went with my friend Phil.

LAWYER: No, I was going to say, "when you drove to the beach," but let's talk about Phil a moment. Who is Phil?

See what happened? You just added an extra twenty minutes to your deposition by bringing up Phil and your trip to the park, and now maybe Phil's going to get a subpoena, too.

Never, ever anticipate the question that's going to be asked. Let the questioner finish the entire question. There's no rush. Why make your opponent's job any easier?

Don't answer more than is being asked. Your deposition is not the day to tell your story. It's the day for you to answer questions simply and honestly. Don't let yourself go off on tangents; don't add any more information than is being requested.

QUESTION: What time did you get home?

WRONG ANSWER: 10:00 P.M. I know it was 10:00 P.M. because I remember that *Channel Five News at Ten* was just starting.

RIGHT ANSWER: 10:00 P.M.

Take Your Time and Be Focused

Focus on answering the question at hand. Don't rush to answer it. Think. It makes no difference if you wait a few minutes before answering a question. The transcript of your deposition will not indicate whether you answered the question right away or thought about it for thirty seconds before speaking. Take your time before answering if it helps, and don't think out loud.

"I Don't Recall"

If you don't recall the answer to a given question, no problem. Just say, "I don't recall." That's a perfectly legitimate answer.

Of course, if that's the answer you give, that's going to be your answer at trial as well. A bad witness is one who answers many questions by saying, "I can't recall," and then when he gets to trial a year later, suddenly he has a vivid memory of events. If someone can't recall a specific event or some important facts, but suddenly at trial he *can* recall, a jury will likely think that person is dishonest and not credible. But if you're in your deposition and your mind is drawing a blank, it's OK to say so.

If you're not sure about an answer to a question and think you might recollect if you looked at something to jog your memory, say exactly that: "Gee, I'm not sure. I'd have to go back and review my calendar [or talk to my coworker or look at my notes or whatever] to remember."

Sometimes you think you *should* know the answer to a question, but it's not coming to you right then. So tell the questioner that. Say something like, "You know, if I thought about it a little more, it might come to me. Right now I'm not recalling." Or, "I could probably recall that better if I talked about it with my [wife/husband/friend/coworker/whomever]."

A word on this kind of answer: The difference between saying "I can't recall" and "I might be able to remember if I [did whatever]," is that you're leaving yourself an opening to give an answer for this question later. You're also opening up the other side to depose whomever you mentioned. (If they can help your recollection, they obviously have some knowledge relating to the question.) Also, if you say, "I'd have to go back and look at my [calendar/notes]," you can pretty much assume that the legal team for the other side will send over a demand to see your notes, calendars, or whatever you've referred to. They will have a right to see this material. If you don't want the other side looking at the calendar entry you were planning to refer to refresh your memory, you'd best not mention the existence of that calendar in this context.

Remember, too, that a deposition is not a game. If you're hiding something from the other side, you're probably only going to hurt yourself in the long run. You owe it to the other party to prepare yourself as well as possible before your deposition. If you have notes or a calendar, review them beforehand. If talking with a particular person will help refresh your memory, then you should do that ahead of time, too.

The other side is entitled to your best recollection, and you should make a good-faith effort to give it. If you aren't prepared and answer a lot of questions with "I'm not sure" and "I'd have to think about it to answer," one of two things might happen. You might be asked to review the materials and/or produce them at another deposition session. Or, if your memory of important issues is substantially better at trial than at your deposition, you're going to look as though you were being dishonest and didn't play fair.

Control the Pace

Do not allow the pace of your deposition to pick up. A tactic many lawyers use when they question witnesses is to get their guard down, then go for blood. They'll ask several simple, friendly, inconsequential questions and lure the witness into answering these questions quickly. Then suddenly they'll ask a question the deponent is not as prepared to answer right away, in the hopes that he'll blurt out an answer without giving it as much thought as he should.

If the questioner is speeding up the tempo of the deposition and asking you questions quickly, slow the process down. Take more time before you answer the questions, or answer more thoughtfully and deliberately. Break the questioner's pace, and don't let him speed it up again. Take the time you need; choose your words carefully; be as exact as possible.

If you want to stop for any reason at any time, just say so. It's your right. The attorneys have a duty to question you and get answers, but they can't prevent you from taking a break whenever you'd like. If you want to talk with your lawyer, go to the bathroom, or get something to drink, just say, "Can we please take a break?" You'll get the break right away.

Do not say, "I need to go to the bathroom; can we take a break?" Remember that a record is being made, parts of which could be read back at trial, and "I have to take a leak" is probably something best not read back in front of a jury. Don't give any reason for wanting a break while you're on the record. Just ask to take a break, and wait for the court reporter to say, "We're off the record," before stating why.

You may wish to take a break to confer with your lawyer, but you don't generally want to say, "May I take a break to talk to my lawyer?" If you're in the middle of a particularly important line of questioning and ask to speak with your lawyer, it may look suspect when it's read back to jurors later. They may think, "Hey, he's being asked important questions that go to the heart of his case. Why can't he just answer the questions? Why does he have to stop the deposition and confer with his attorney?

If what he's saying is true, why doesn't he just say what happened without needing to talk with a lawyer? Hmmm . . ." A few states even have rules that make it improper for you to ask for a break to talk to your lawyer about your deposition.

In a case where I took a deposition of the defendant, before answering just about every important question, she said, "May I talk with my attorney?" The issues of this case came down to this woman's word against my client's; one of the two was lying. My client answered questions in his deposition in a straightforward and matter-of-fact way, but the defendant kept stopping the deposition to confer with her attorney. I knew that I could have a field day with this deposition at trial, because the fact that she couldn't answer a question on her own would look funny. After all, her attorney hadn't witnessed anything, so what could he tell her? She created the appearance that her attorney was telling her what to say and how to answer the questions. What's a jury going to think about this person? "Liar. Nail her."

That's not to say you should never interrupt your deposition to speak with your lawyer. You may have legitimate reasons to confer with your attorney before answering certain questions. For example, an answer that you're thinking of giving might relate to something your attorney told you, which would be privileged, and not something the other side is entitled to hear. You *would* want to lean over and whisper a question to your attorney about whether or not you should give that answer. You certainly don't want to waive privilege, and if you really feel you should talk with your attorney before answering a given question, go ahead and whisper your question to him. But if you're being asked a series of questions about what witnesses were present, who said what, what time it was, etc., you already should have prepared yourself with this kind of factual material. You shouldn't repeatedly stop to confer with your attorney about it.

You want to give accurate answers, so don't be afraid to ask the questioner to repeat a question so you can make sure you understand it. Even if you've begun answering the question, you may lose your train of thought or become unsure about whether you're going off track. You can stop, even in the middle of answering a question, and ask the court reporter to read the question back to you. You can also ask the court reporter to read back your answer, whether you've finished answering or not. You want to give your best answer. If you want to hear the answer you just gave so you can add to it or modify it, go right ahead.

Don't Take Notes

Do not take any notes while you're being deposed. Answer the question as best you can by relying on your memory. Should you take any notes or bring any notes or other materials to the deposition and refer to them in answering questions, the other side will be entitled to see those notes right then and there, and to question you about them.

Eat Lightly and Stretch

If you start the deposition in the morning and take a lunch break, eat a light lunch. You want to keep your mind sharp. Too often the deponent goes out, has a big lunch, heads back to the deposition, and soon feels sluggish and drowsy. You're not going to give your best performance if you're fighting to think clearly.

If your deposition lasts for some hours, you should do whatever might help to keep yourself feeling focused. Is the chair they've given you uncomfortable? Does it hurt your back? Mention your back problem, and ask if they have a more comfortable chair you could use. If you want, get up and walk around during your deposition. There's no rule that says you have to remain seated while answering questions. The record won't reflect that you stood up and stretched or that you remained seated. Just say something like, "Do you mind if I walk around and stretch a little while we proceed?" I can guarantee you the other side is not going to answer, "No, please remain seated; we want you uncomfortable and your recollections as hazy as possible."

Don't Argue

Do not get into any arguments with the questioner on the record. Just answer questions as simply, directly, and succinctly as you can, and nothing more. Be polite, and if the questioner is being rude, do not react. Let your attorney react. That's his job. If the other attorney is trying to get a rise out of you, your attorney should jump in and object, and admonish the questioner to be professional. If the questioner continues to be rude, your attorney may decide that his conduct violates codes of professional conduct, and threaten to end the deposition for that reason.

I have threatened to stop and have actually curtailed depositions of clients when opposing counsel has become abusive. I've told a rude adversary that we will continue the deposition only when he decides to act professionally.

While the other side has the right to depose you, no one has the right to be rude and abusive. In any hard-fought case where emotions run high, there's going to be a certain amount of posturing and confrontation to endure. Sometimes it's a strategic decision on the part of the attorney, and sometimes he just wants to impress his client by showing he can be nasty and a tough guy on the client's behalf. But your own attorney should not permit you to be abused and mistreated. He should stop the deposition and explain his reasons for doing so. Sometimes this is enough to get the other side to act correctly. If not, your attorney will have on the record both the unreasonable, rude conduct of the other attorney and his own (reasonable) explanation of why he wouldn't permit it to continue.

In all events, resist the urge to get into an argument with the questioner or to return his rudeness with rudeness. You want any juror who heard that transcript read to believe that you are as polite, honest, and pure as The Beav in *Leave It to Beaver.*

Don't Swear

Never, ever, ever swear in your deposition. Nothing sounds worse in court than the reading of testimony that contains profanity. A legal proceeding is a serious event. People who use four-letter words in such a proceeding risk losing the respect of the jury. If you swear during your deposition, even in response to a relatively unimportant question, rest assured that the other side will do everything possible to find a way to read your cursing to the jury.

Give Your Lawyer Time to Object

For anything but the simplest questions, you are best served if you wait a few seconds before answering, in case your lawyer needs to object to the question. Your lawyer will most likely have to object to questions you've been asked, and when he does, be quiet and say nothing. Do *not* answer a question when your lawyer has objected until he finishes stating his objection, has any necessary discussion with the other side, and then tells you that you can answer.

Answer Every Question

Unless your attorney specifically tells you not to answer, you have to answer every question you've been asked, even if the question is vague. (Naturally, if you think the question is vague, you can ask for clarification before answering.) Your lawyer may object to a given question, but that is chiefly so that later he can prevent your answer from being used at trial, if it was an improper or irrelevant question.

Take Your Lawyer's Advice

Never answer a question your lawyer tells you not to answer. Your lawyer may "instruct" you not to answer. He instructs you when there is a hard-and-fast legal basis for your not having to answer a question. If you did answer such a question, you might harm yourself or waive a privilege.

Let's say that the other side asks you about a conversation with another lawyer. This conversation is likely privileged.

The most important thing to remember is this: If your lawyer ever instructs you not to answer a question, do not answer that question. You can take a break to discuss privately with your lawyer his reasons for telling you not to answer. After your lawyer tells you not to answer, the questioner may ask you whether or not you are going to answer the question. The right answer is, "On advice of my attorney, I'm not going to answer that."

Even if the other side later decides to file a motion to force you to answer that question, the lawyers must first satisfy meet and confer requirements (see Chapter 10), at which time you could always change your mind about answering the question, if you wished, and avoid any potential sanctions.

Your lawyer objects to questions for different reasons, but essentially he objects to preserve his right to have your answers to certain questions excluded from being read at trial. Before going to trial, the attorneys for both sides mark the portions of a deposition transcript they may introduce at trial. If someone has asked an improper or legally deficient question, your lawyer must make his objection during the deposition, even though no judge is present, so that later he can raise that objection to the court before trial, when argument is being heard about what part of the deposition can be used in the trial. A question might be vague or confusing, or assume things that the deponent has not admitted. Your lawyer should object to any questions like this, so that they can't be used in court. Table 3 lists the objections lawyers generally make and gives some explanation for each.

Attorneys frequently use an objection for lack of foundation to send you, the deponent, a signal. They may be trying to tell you to slow down the deposition, if it's picking up too much speed, so they object to break the pace. When objecting, your lawyer may also be trying to remind you of something you might consider in your answer.

Objections for a question being vague and ambiguous can also be what's known as a "speaking objection." Your lawyer may be objecting not just for the record but to send you a signal, to remind or suggest something for you to consider in answering.

Don't Characterize, Mimic, or Joke

Don't characterize people in your deposition; simply say what you saw, what a person did, what you heard, and so on. Don't say the defendant is "a nasty, crazy slime" or otherwise describe him. Again, it will be your lawyer's job to characterize witnesses and make sense of everything for the jury, not yours. Your job is to provide the facts and tell what you witnessed, not to give interpretation or offer conclusions.

In a trial, the rules of evidence prevent you from being questioned about hearsay. This is not the rule in a deposition. If you are asked to repeat what someone else said, do not imitate their accent, voice, or personal characteristics. A client of mine who was suing his boss was able to do an excellent imitation of the boss, capturing his distinct inflection, accent, tone, even body language. After hearing his boss testify, I thought his imitation was a hilarious caricature. But I would never have let him do it anywhere near the case. Mocking other people will make you look bad. Just repeat, in your own voice, what you heard. If you're asked specific questions about tone, inflection, or accent, you can answer those questions.

Show respect for your adversary, even if you don't respect him. I usually advise my clients to refer to the defendant and many witnesses in their case as "Mr." or "Ms." Even if you've known the person you're suing for years, it makes you sound respectful; it can also help you put some needed distance between you and your adversary.

Table 3.   Objections Commonly Made in Depositions

TYPE OF OBJECTION	EXPLANATION
Objection to the form of the question	The question might be poorly worded or confusing. Often, if the questioner feels the objection is valid, he may simply clarify the question.
Objection on the grounds that the question seeks privileged information	When a question seeks information protected by privilege, your attorney will object and instruct you not to answer.
Objection because question is irrelevant and has nothing to do with case	While the parties have very wide latitude in fishing around for information, there are some limits, and there must be *some* bearing between the question and the case. If you are being deposed because you witnessed a car accident, and the questioner starts asking about your vacation plans in Hawaii, this is clearly irrelevant and should be stopped.
Objection for lack of foundation	This means the question contains assumptions that have not been established. For example: Q: What time did you arrive at the house? ATTORNEY: Objection! Lack of foundation—he never said he went to the house, and you've never established that he went to the house. The attorney may just withdraw that question and instead ask, "Did you go to the house that night?" Once that's established, he'll ask you his original question, and your lawyer won't object.
Objection because question is vague and ambiguous	As the objection implies, the question could be taken more than one way. For example: Q: Did you go to the house? ATTORNEY: Objection! Vague and ambiguous—what time frame are we talking about? Did he *ever* go to the house? Did he go to the house that year . . .?

Many people make an attempt at humor to lighten up a tense situation. Don't do that in your deposition. Don't tell jokes or be sarcastic. It may sound hilarious during the deposition, but read back at trial and out of context, it could make you sound cold and callous.

Remember What Your Case Is About

Why are you suing? Were you physically or emotionally injured? Financially damaged? Ripped off? Slandered? Discriminated against? Even if you're the defendant and are angry, you don't want to look as if you're going to blow your stack in front of a jury.

Prepare for Your Deposition

Before your deposition, go through any materials or evidence that might be relevant to your case. Try to anticipate what questions you might be asked, and think about how you can answer succinctly. Make notes, write out a chronology (but don't have it in front of you in your deposition). Do whatever you need to do to organize your thoughts so you can give the best testimony possible.

After you've done this, I strongly recommend you meet with your attorney a few days before your deposition and go through any questions you have. If there are some potential problem areas or areas you're worried someone might ask you about (and there generally are), discuss these with your attorney. Tell him your concerns, and discuss how to best to address these areas should they come up. You want to be as prepared as possible.

It May Go on and on and on and on

Depending on the size and scope of your case, your deposition may last a few hours, or it may last several days. Frequently, the deposition notice indicates that your deposition will continue "from day to day, excluding Sundays and holidays," until it's completed. This is standard. If you think you may be deposed for more than a day, it may be a good idea to have your lawyer clarify in advance whether the other side expects the deposition to continue the following day, if you don't finish in one day.

Some people may not want to go two or more days in a row; others may just want to get it over with, rather than be brought back again and again. The danger in not finishing the deposition in consecutive days, but taking one day of a deposition and returning a month or two later, is

that some attorneys will use the interval to investigate what you testified to in the first session, then come back with a ton of additional questions for you to answer based on whatever they unearthed. A witness or
party may be deposed only once. Getting it over with prevents the
other side from investigating testimony you gave and then dragging you
back in to ask many more questions on the same subject.

Be Prepared if You're Told to Bring Something

Some deposition notices and/or subpoenas require you to bring a document or other potential evidence to your deposition. You can expect
the other side to pick through that evidence and question you about it.
Before your deposition, study the document with your attorney and
anticipate any possible questions.

Reading the Transcript

Sometime after your deposition, you'll receive a copy of your deposition
transcript. You will have thirty days (or some other period of time
agreed upon by the parties) to read it, make any corrections, and sign it.
You want your deposition to be as accurate as possible. Often, when you
read what you said, you'll realize you may have misspoken or made a
mistake you wish to correct.

Before making corrections on the transcript itself, list them, complete with page and line numbers, and review your list with your lawyer.
Sometimes the corrections you wish to make are minor; sometimes
major. Whatever changes you make, be sure to present them in a way
that reflects best on you. Your lawyer may advise that a change you wish
to make is so minor it's better not to make it. Remember that trials are
won or lost on the credibility of the parties. If you prepared yourself
well for your deposition, you should not have many changes to make in
the transcript.

12

"Well, I *definitely* saw the defendant . . . Where'd you say he's sitting?"

Witnesses

I think one of the most fundamental responsibilities . . . is to give testimony in a court of law, to give it honestly and willingly.

—Adlai E. Stevenson,
American lawyer and diplomat

A witness can be anyone who has some knowledge, direct or indirect, about the facts and events in controversy. You don't always know who your witnesses will be; that's part of what the discovery process is for. In the simplest example, let's say you were in a car accident and the issue is whether or not the light was green when you went through the intersection. People who were near the accident will be potential witnesses as to the liability of the other party. The medical personnel who treated you may be witnesses as to the injuries you suffered (your damages). Another doctor may be a witness as to the reasonableness of the treatment you received and the treatment you will likely need in the future. The people who witnessed the car accident and the physicians who treated you are "fact witnesses"; they actually saw some portion of the event at controversy.

Getting to Know Your Witnesses

Friend, foe, or neutral party, you take your witnesses as you find them. It would be great if every witness recalled and testified to the facts and events exactly as you believe them to be, but that's not usually how it works. Memories may fade, circumstances can change, and people don't always turn out to be who you thought they were.

This is why it's critical for you to sit down as early as possible with your attorney and discuss potential witnesses in detail. It's important not to file suit first and figure out your witnesses later, because the strength or weakness of your case and settlement position may turn on the strengths or weaknesses of your witnesses.

At the outset you're concerned with who your fact witnesses are, what they know, how credible they are, what state of mind they might have toward you and the contemplated litigation, and what baggage they might bring. In the car accident example, perhaps you got the contact information of the witnesses at the scene of the accident and already know who they are. If you didn't, there are a number of ways you might try to locate them, ranging from advertising locally for "anyone who saw the accident at the intersection of Fifth and Main at 6:45 P.M. on May 14, please contact . . ." to retaining a professional investigative service to snoop around for additional information and witnesses. Also, a police report might include the names of certain witnesses.

Maybe you're in a breach of contract suit, and the question becomes an issue of going back and trying to figure out questions from a historical standpoint, such as, Who negotiated the contract? Who drafted it? Who was a party to the discussions that led up to the agreement? Who did or didn't do something that caused the breach? Who has documents in his files or computers that relate to the breach? Who wrote or received correspondence on the issue? All of these people can be important fact witnesses.

If you have an intellectual property case, there might be an issue of whether or not the producer you think stole your script had access to your script in the first place. After all, if you can't prove he saw it, how can you prove he ripped you off? In that case, the important fact witnesses could become an agent who submitted the script to a studio, an executive at the studio who received the script, people who know both the studio executive and the producer who might have heard about your script, and so on.

Regardless of your fact pattern, you need to sort through who your witnesses might be. If you're unsure, you'll have to use discovery and in some cases independent investigation to identify who these important witnesses are.

In nearly every case I've been involved in, I've wanted to talk to at least some of the primary witnesses right away. This is particularly true when I'm dealing with an individual who has individual claims; I always assume that my client has lost a certain sense of objectivity. A lawyer prosecuting a case needs to look at the case from all the angles, not just his client's passionate view of the facts. The lawyer has to look at it from the standpoint of what a jury or a third-party decision maker is likely to make of the situation.

More than Just the Facts, Mac

Fact witnesses may be either "party affiliate" witnesses or "percipient" or third-party witnesses. Party affiliate witnesses are essentially people who for all practical purposes are closely affiliated and aligned in some fashion with you (or the other side). If your company were suing, they would be the people who worked for you—your employees or your agents. If you're suing as an individual, they might be your spouse, children, or siblings. If you're suing as a partnership, they could be your partners.

The other important category of witnesses is what we refer to as percipient or third-party witnesses. These are the people who saw or heard what happened, wrote something, received something; they have firsthand knowledge about an event in question. (If they don't have firsthand knowledge, then they have hearsay information or are speculating, which, although it is discoverable, normally isn't admissible.)

The difference between discoverable and admissible information is important. Before going to trial you conduct "discovery." During this process you're allowed to ask any questions relevant to the trial. The information you collect is called "discoverable." However, at the trial, you may only introduce "admissible" facts, which are facts directly relevant to the issues in the case.

Many cases can rise or fall on a fact witness. It's not just an issue of what that fact witness saw or heard and is likely or not likely to say. It's an issue of how credible the witness is. If you have a case that's going to turn on the credibility and likability of your witnesses, it would be a mistake for your attorney to file suit and make a settlement demand without having met these witnesses. Their demeanor and how they're likely to come off at the time of trial can be critical. For example, let's say you're bringing suit for slander, and one of your primary witnesses heard the defamatory remark and is prepared to testify that he heard it and that the defendant said it. If, unbeknownst to you or your attorney, this person has a record for not telling the truth, you could have a huge problem. Perhaps your witness has a hidden agenda—like your case involves someone famous and your witness wants to sell his story to a newspaper. You might base your entire case on that witness, and he might get exposed at trial. Even if your case has tremendous merit, it could crumble.

I have seen many cases where a plaintiff has prepared diligently for trial, his testimony is solid, and the defense seems shaky. Then everything takes a turn. The plaintiff's star witness is not as solid as originally thought and the case goes up in flames as the suddenly shaky witness crumbles. As a result, the plaintiff, who may have been genuinely wronged, unjustly loses a substantial amount of time and money.

Many people felt that the prosecutors in the O. J. Simpson criminal case had an airtight case against Simpson. They purportedly had searched Simpson's house and found Simpson's blood samples, shoe prints, and other evidence from the crime scene. Initially, detective Mark Fuhrman looked like a star prosecution witness, but then the defense introduced evidence that Fuhrman had used racial slurs in the past. This powerful idea of Fuhrman's racism distracted the jury from the other evidence and introduced what jurors felt was reasonable doubt. In a criminal case, all you need to do is show there's some reasonable doubt, and the jury must then find for the defendant. If someone can plant the idea with the jury that a key prosecution witness may not be a truthful person, even if the jury thinks the witness is telling the truth about the issues at controversy, the fact that there's some question about the witness at all can be enough for the defense to prevail in a criminal case.

The same is true in a civil case, although the burden of proof is different (a preponderance of the evidence, rather than proof beyond a reasonable doubt). In either situation, jurors quickly begin a process of identifying who the important witnesses are, who might be biased, and who appears likely to be telling the truth. They'll focus on those key witnesses, so your lawyer should, too, as early as possible.

Unfortunately, too many litigants and lawyers begin and end the analysis of their case with an evaluation of the law based only on what the client has to say, using the client's perception, and not immediately examining potential witnesses. Often such litigants may be in for an unwelcome surprise at the end of the day. That surprise doesn't necessarily relate to the witness's account of what took place in the issues at controversy. The witness may have a perfectly clear memory of what happened and may sound convincing as to those facts. But he may be carrying into the courtroom some other baggage that somehow is brought out and used to impeach him.

If your attorney can spend the time doing so at the start of your case, have him make certain early on that your witnesses are going to be credible on the stand. A good lawyer should be able to at least anticipate where there will be a problem with a witness, or whether a witness may be biased.

Biased Witnesses

In a case where a husband testifies on behalf of a wife or an executive testifies in support of his company's position, the jury will clearly understand that bias exists. Is a biased witness unusable? Not necessarily. Jurors or fact finders will ascertain a witness's bias pretty quickly. Then they'll assess whether or not that bias is, in fact, a controlling factor in the testimony being given. If a person is credible, if he looks like someone who's telling the truth and is not impeached, then the fact that the witness is biased may not have a negative influence. This is because jurors or other fact finders may believe that this person is taking his oath seriously and is actually giving an accurate statement of what took place.

A problem, though, can be the biased witness who is overly zealous and basically tries to argue your case for you, beyond simply answering the questions. You don't want a witness in a deposition arguing your case; his entire testimony may be rejected. A good witness sounds as though he is simply doing what he's required to do, which is to tell the truth. He's under oath; that's all he needs to do.

There's a fine line, though, between a witness who might have bias but is telling the truth and a witness who is argumentative on every point. For example, say an employee sues a company for wrongful termination, and the employee's supervisor is being deposed. If the supervisor spends the entire deposition denying that the terminated employee had *any* positive attributes, then the supervisor may go too far. The jury may reject his testimony entirely on the theory that the supervisor isn't really being truthful; he's just telling a one-sided account. He's trying to score points for his company.

On the other hand, if the supervisor concedes, for example, that when the employee interviewed for the job, he had a solid background, that the employee did in fact do certain things well, and that the reason the employee was terminated wasn't because he did everything horribly, but because there were certain job requirements that the employee simply didn't satisfy, then the jury will give much more credence to the supervisor's testimony. Since he didn't entirely trash the employee, he is more believable and helpful to the company in the end than an overzealous supervisor wanting to take issue with everything to prove a point.

Contacting Your Witnesses

To establish who your witnesses will be and whether they will appear credible in court, you need to have contact and communication with your witnesses. What's the best way to do this?

There's no rule preventing you, as a party or potential party in a lawsuit, from calling a witness and talking with him. But should you? Generally I think it's a bad idea for the client to start contacting witnesses, unless they're close friends or family members. That's not to say clients should never contact witnesses; in some instances your attorney will advise you to contact a witness because of your relationship with an individual. But in most cases, as the case goes forward, your attorney should make contact with all prospective witnesses.

A lot of people will think that the minute you know who a witness is, the best thing to do is to just slap a subpoena on him, haul him in, and depose him. But as I've described, a deposition is a formal and daunting experience, so often people tend to clam up to some degree. They're intimidated and may not tell you things on the record that they might tell you if you met with them at their house or a similar informal setting. As a lawyer, I generally like to call a witness, be nice on the phone, and then maybe meet with him in an environment where he's comfortable and not on the record, having every word transcribed by a court reporter.

You shouldn't look at the formal discovery process as the sole, exclusive, or even optimal way to communicate with witnesses. In most instances it really isn't. Having said that, I don't advise that you go over the line. If a witness does not want to speak with you or your lawyer, if he is intimidated by your attempts to communicate, then you want to retreat to a more formal process. This is the time when your lawyer *should* subpoena him to come in for a deposition, because you could get into a situation where a potential witness believes he's being harassed. I have seen instances where a party in a lawsuit has tried to contact and discuss the case with a witness, and the witness has ended up going to court to get a restraining order to prevent that party from further "harassing" him. You don't want a situation where talking to a witness blows up in your face because the witness takes a position that you're intimidating or harassing him. In some instances, because they received a phone call, potential witnesses have even tried to dodge subpoenas or moved to an area outside the court's subpoena jurisdiction in order to avoid being deposed.

Some witnesses will be represented by their own attorneys at their deposition, especially if they're well-to-do or employees of a corporation. Your attorney will then have to negotiate with this lawyer about the availability of the witness, which documents the witness is going to turn over, and whether there are privilege or confidentiality issues that the witness wants addressed. Sometimes it's good that a witness has an attorney, because it makes it easier to set the deposition and to focus the inquiry. Other times it can make the situation more difficult, and a set of side issues can develop because the witness may not want to produce a set of documents, or he's claiming privilege.

Part of the process of evaluating witnesses is to determine how sophisticated your witness is. Is he the type who will secure representation? Will there be separate issues with that witness? Remember that in cases involving documents, you generally aren't just thinking about the witnesses; you're thinking about their files. You want to know where they keep their documents, how they keep them, how you would go about requesting and obtaining their documents. Do they save files in their computer? Where are the hard drive and backup drives? How do they save their E-mail? These are the kinds of things you may focus on in business-oriented cases—not simply the witnesses, but how they save their documents and store their data. All of these are potential sources of information that witnesses can help identify.

Naming Your Witnesses

Hard-fought, high-stakes cases with wealthy defendants often use what I refer to as the "scorched earth" style of litigation: they prevent you and the court from focusing on what is important by scorching you with their parade of witnesses, documents, and legal arguments. A potential client came to me once with a case that had been filed and begun by another attorney; he wanted me to take over and represent him midway through the case. He intended to have twenty-five different people as witnesses, and each had something negative to say about the defendant. My client obviously was hoping the defendant would see this and figure, "Uh-oh, I'd better settle. Look at all those people he's got lined up to testify. They all hate me." But no settlement was forthcoming at that point. Instead, the defendant's insurance company set out to take the depositions of all twenty-five witnesses. The first thing I did was withdraw ten witnesses, explaining to the other side that we didn't intend to call them at trial. But the defense didn't care. My client had named them, and now the defendant's lawyers were going to take all the depositions.

They were scheduling to take one deposition on Monday morning, another on Wednesday afternoon, the next on Friday morning—they were scheduling them in such a way as to inflict the maximum inconvenience on me and the maximum expense on my client by requiring me to drive back and forth across town to their office for numerous short, inconsequential depositions. And who was to blame for their ability to do this in the first place? My client, as well as his previous attorney, who had permitted the client to name so many people as witnesses—even though many were marginal.

It's your attorney's job to advise you to make judgment calls when you've been asked to identify witnesses. Most attorneys want to be overly cautious in identifying who the witnesses are and err on the side of being too thorough. This is appropriate because if you don't identify someone and that person turns out to be an important witness, you could be precluded from having that person testify at trial. However, in listing witnesses always keep in mind that the minute you name a witness, they become a part of the case. They can be deposed, and may end up speaking to the jury about things about *them* that have nothing to do with your case that could negatively impact them and your case. So, be prudent

One way to avoid throwing an overly wide witness net is for you and your attorney to spend some time early on asking some important questions: What are my claims? How am I going to prove these claims in a trial? Who do I need to testify about this case? Who might be carrying baggage? Who's essential, and who can we forget about? Ultimately, once you've decided who's an important witness, not just a potential witness, a more narrow list emerges.

Think from Your Witness's Perspective

As plaintiff or defendant, you're passionate about your case. You're willing to go the distance, and—consequences be damned—you want the truth to come out so you can get justice. The witnesses, however, even if they like you and are your friends, may not feel the same way.

You need to consider each person and how he might react to being brought in as a witness in your case. Just about all your witnesses will get cranky at one time or another, because they're getting dragged into a situation that they probably don't want to be in. They may have to miss work as a result of your case, answer questions they don't like, hand over files and personal documents to your lawyer and the other lawyers, or tell the truth about something that they wouldn't ordinarily want to testify about. Although they support you and have information helpful to you, they may come to see your case as an impediment to their own desires. Sometimes just bringing suit can be a tough call when you consider it from the perspective of how your important witnesses might react. Weigh this early on.

For example, let's say you're an employee who blew the whistle on a senior executive at the company. As a result you were fired, and you bring a whistle-blower wrongful termination suit. There seems to be no downside for you. You no longer work at the company, and you want to expose the senior executive for what he is and bring down the company that's trying to shield him. However, your witnesses may be good friends who still work at the company, and you have to decide whether you want to file suit and drag these people in as witnesses. You don't have to ask their permission to name them as witnesses. You may or may not legally have a duty to disclose their names as witnesses in your case, but you do have a choice of whether or not to bring suit.

How do you believe your friends will react if you file suit and name them as witnesses? After all, they're still working at the company. Yes, they may have also seen what the senior executive did, but will they testify to it in a forthright way, or will they downplay or spin it to seem more neutral? Is it, in whatever sense you want to consider it, worthwhile to bring suit and put these people in this position?

If your case is a witness-dependent case, before you go to a lawyer you may really want to stop and think about the ramifications of your case, the burden that it may impose on certain other people, and how this is all likely to play out.

A witness may not realize it at first, but he'll discover soon enough into his deposition that the standard for discovery is very broad, and this might steam him. As I mentioned in Chapter 9, the standard for discovery is not "Is a particular question or line of inquiry relevant to the case?" (and relevance itself is a gray area), but "Is it reasonably likely to lead to the discovery of admissible evidence?" The kinds of questions a witness can be asked during discovery and the kinds of issues about which he has to give truthful information during discovery do *not* have to be admissible at trial. They do not even have to bear on the case. They simply need to be reasonably likely to lead to the discovery of admissible evidence.

Talk about a loose standard! A creative lawyer who has a quick mind—and is hostile to a given witness—will be able to mow down a lot of people to get answers. He probably can even convince a judge to order a witness to give answers. Why? Because it's conceivable that almost anything is reasonably likely to lead to the discovery of admissible evidence.

Now, a good judge knows when somebody is clearly trying to harass a witness and where a question has no bearing in any way, shape, or form on the lawsuit. But the real wild card in these situations can be the issue of impeachment, of discovering evidence that could help show that the person is dishonest. A person can argue, "Well, this line of questioning isn't relevant to the case, but what it does go to is the credibility of the witness!" And almost anything can conceivably go to the credibility of the witness. A witness can be asked all about his education, job, and social security number, as well as the names, addresses, phone numbers, and information of many friends, relatives, and people with whom he has been involved in disputes in the past, and on and on.

Just about anyone could conceivably be hauled in if a hostile party wants to try to dig up dirt in order to impeach a witness. If you have a witness who can really do damage to the other side, the other side may decide to go find that former employer or ex-spouse living in another city who will jump at the chance to testify that the witness is actually a liar and a cheat.

You certainly don't want to be naive, and you don't want to think that because you're willing to go the extra mile and file the lawsuit, your witnesses are going to be pleased as punch to show up, sit in a conference room, be asked some tough questions, have to tell the truth about some things that maybe they'd rather not discuss, and expose themselves to a potential attack by the other side.

Getting Witness Statements

You can ask a witness at any time to give a signed statement, or witnesses might sometimes offer to give a statement of what they do or don't know, in the hope of avoiding being deposed. This is called "statementizing" or gaining a statement from a witness, and the idea is to anchor the witness to a position, get him to verify under oath, in a signed declaration or affidavit, swearing that this statement will be his testimony. Witnesses can be influenced, and sometimes they can be intimidated by one side or the other. In short, things can change. Statementizing is one way to lock someone into a position and make it harder for him to change later.

For example, maybe you have a coworker who was terminated at the same time you were, and he wants to be supportive in a sexual harassment suit you're bringing against your former employer. However, he is later hired by another company and decides that he doesn't really want to go on record in this kind of a lawsuit. In fact, at his new company he's now doing business with your old employer and has gotten cold feet about your lawsuit.

There are dozens of reasons why a witness who was originally supportive can suddenly develop amnesia and become unsupportive. And you can't arm wrestle him back into remembering a fact or being more forthcoming. When you or your lawyer first contact a witness to talk about your case, make a quick judgment call as to whether you should have him sign a sworn statement under oath then. If he changes his testimony, such a statement could be submitted to the court in support of a motion presented to the witness during a deposition, to "remind" them of their earlier statement, or used when that witness takes the stand at trial.

Frequently written or taped statements exist and are in the possession of other parties, and your attorney should attempt through discovery to obtain copies of any such statements. For example, after a car accident, typically your own insurance company or the other party's insurance company asks you and any other witnesses to make a statement, under penalty of perjury.

Out-of-State or "Unavailable" Witnesses

What if an important witness in your case is out of state? Can you force that witness to testify? Almost every jurisdiction has certain rules limiting your ability to call a witness at trial. If a witness resides out of state, generally you can't force him to appear at trial. For those witnesses outside the subpoena power of the jurisdiction where the case is going to be tried, you will have to take their deposition before trial.

Also, by the time your trial comes around, certain witnesses may have gotten sick, moved out of the state or country, forgotten key information, or destroyed certain records. If you believe you may have witnesses who will be unavailable at trial, you don't want to be left in a position where you don't have any testimony from them. You'll want to depose such witnesses early on, and you may even want to videotape their deposition, although that can be quite expensive. (Taping generally requires court-approved personnel to do the taping, in addition to the court reporter.) The benefit of videotaping a deposition is that you can later show the tape to the jury, who can see what they look like and how they're answering certain questions. That won't come across when a jury's just hearing a lawyer read a deposition transcript into evidence.

If you want to depose someone out of state, you usually obtain a court order called a commission, which authorizes someone to administer the oath in another jurisdiction. With a commission, you can have local counsel in the witness's state issue a subpoena.

Out-of-state depositions are expensive and can raise a number of issues, all of which are also expensive to address. If you subpoena a person in New York to testify for a case pending in California, you have to go to the California court, secure a commission, and then retain a New York law firm to issue a subpoena. If the witness in New York refuses to answer a question, you have to file a Motion to Compel in New York, which means you have to secure local New York counsel in order to bring the motion to secure the answer that you need. You may end up with a situation where you're before both a judge in California and a judge in New York about that particular deposition. Bring your wallet.

Having Your Lawyer Represent a Witness

Companies whose employees are brought into litigation or wealthy individuals usually can afford to hire an attorney to represent them when subpoenaed to testify in your suit. But in the real world where people have limited budgets, that's not generally the case. Sometimes a client will tell me, "I want you to go to the deposition of Joe Smith, a witness in my case, and protect this witness, because this witness is a friend of mine. He can't afford to hire his own attorney, and I don't want him left exposed to the wolves on the other side of the table." And so in certain cases I have represented witnesses in my client's case.

There are some potential problems with this. First, if you want a witness to appear completely independent, it may not be a good idea to have your own lawyer represent that witness in a deposition. Second, there is some gray area about whether conversations the witness has with your attorney are privileged. For example, say you've identified a witness, a business colleague of yours. He gets served a subpoena, can't afford his own lawyer, is very uptight, has to miss work, is concerned that he's going to be grilled by the other side, and wants to be protected. You ask your attorney to represent your friend in the deposition. Your attorney is all too willing; he meets with the friend and they discuss how a deposition works. The attorney advises the witness of his rights—what he does and doesn't have to answer—and instructs the witness not to speculate during the deposition, not to guess, not to slant the facts, and so on. They discuss what documents the witness will probably have to produce and which ones he won't, and they talk about the case and the probable areas of questioning the other side will go into.

If your attorney is truly representing the witness, much of what is said between the two of them is privileged and therefore protected. Unless the opposition makes a fuss about your lawyer's relationship with the witness. They may argue that your lawyer has a conflict in representing the witness and that you and your lawyer are controlling the witness; then what your lawyer and the witness discuss is not privileged, and can be discovered.

Your lawyer's representation of a witness is supposed to be independent and provided to the witness for the purposes and interest of the witness. That's where his relationship with the witness begins and ends. It does not give the attorney license to bring the witness into privileged strategizing on your case.

An attorney who comes into a deposition to represent a witness should be protective of the witness. The lawyer may decide that the deposition should end at a certain point, and he may decide certain questions are burdensome or harassing and instruct the witness not to answer. In contrast, you, the client, may want the witness to answer all the questions, agree to stay very late, and present his answers in your favor. So what's to your advantage as the client may differ from what's to the witness's advantage. This may present your attorney with a conflict of interest.

In addition, when the witness gets on the stand at trial, the jury will be told that your lawyer is his lawyer. Sometimes that doesn't look too good. For all these reasons, a big red flag should go up whenever the possibility exists that your attorney will also represent, for purposes of a deposition, your friend, the witness.

There are ways that your attorney can show up at the deposition and not technically represent the witness but still protect him. Your attorney can make objections and may also ask the witness questions in a friendly, neutral fashion.

13

Case dismissed!

Motion for Summary Judgment or Adjudication

The thing to fear is not the law but the judge.

—Russian proverb

A Motion for Summary Judgment is a motion in which one side or the other in a lawsuit argues that there are no issues that require a jury and that the court should rule in their favor before trial. Summary Judgment motions are typically filed by corporate defendants who want to take a shot at asking the judge to throw the case out before trial. Although it is less common, a plaintiff can also file a Motion for Summary Judgment asking the judge to grant judgment in his favor without the case ever going to a jury.

What the Summary Judgment Motion Means

When you file a Motion for Summary Judgment, in essence you're telling the judge, "We do not need to bring in a group of jurors and waste valuable taxpayer dollars, because even if we take as true everything that the other side says, the law makes it clear that I still win. Alternatively, in making this type motion, you could argue that there is such an overwhelming amount of evidence that if you take a look at the evidence and all relevant case law, you ultimately have to conclude that no reasonable juror could rule against you.

What does that really mean? You have to show the court that there is no genuine issue as to any material fact in dispute. Say, for example, your lawsuit is about a traffic accident, and there is a question of fact as to whether the light was red or green. You can't move for summary judgment on the issue of whether the light was green or red, because you can't establish that there is no genuine issue as to a material fact in dispute. The dispute centers on whether the light was red or green, and a trial will be required to decide this issue. Either the judge in a bench trial (one without a jury), or the jury will have to decide who they believe.

But let's say you own a car dealership and have been sued for fraud. By the definition of fraud, the plaintiff has to show that a "material misrepresentation" was made—not just any misrepresentation. *Material* means important, significant, something that would really go to the heart of the buyer's decision to buy. Maybe it turns out that months of discovery uncover no material misrepresentation; in fact, what your car salesman said was something called "puffery" (hype), not really a fact put on the table for the plaintiff to rely upon. If there is case law that says mere puffery isn't actionable, then your case is ripe for summary judgment. You can argue that, assuming your car salesman did make those comments, no law or statute has been broken and the case must be dismissed as a matter of law.

A judge may grant a summary judgment motion only if it shows that no material fact is at issue and that the moving party is entitled to judgment as a matter of law. The judge construes the evidence and factual inferences arising from the motion in the light most favorable to the nonmoving party. If you can interpret a piece of evidence or testimony in different ways, the judge must interpret it in the way most favorable to the side that is opposing the motion.

Timing for Filing a Summary Judgment Motion

When you get within about ninety days of trial, this is the time in most jurisdictions when a Motion for Summary Judgment is typically filed. The court generally dictates that a Motion for Summary Judgment can be brought and granted only after adequate time for discovery. Just what constitutes "adequate time" is subject to interpretation.

Jurisdictions have different time periods for hearing motions, but by and large in nearly every jurisdiction, the schedule for Motion for Summary Judgment is longer than for other motions. The non-moving party has a longer period of time to prepare the opposition, and then the moving party is given more time to file a reply brief. The hearing date usually provides for more time from when the motion was filed until the time it's scheduled to be heard. For example, in California most motions are heard fifteen days after they're filed. But a hearing on a summary judgment motion is scheduled at least twenty-one days from the time the motion is filed. So you get an extra week, in general.

If you're opposing a Motion for Summary Judgment, and in pulling together your opposition you realize that there are still people whose depositions you'd like to take or witnesses you'd like to interview, there is an alternative to filing an opposition. You can essentially ask the court to extend the time for you to file your opposition, to continue (delay) the hearing date, and to give you time to conduct certain additional discovery.

You have to be careful, though, because most of the time a party waits until almost the end of the normal discovery period to file a Motion for Summary Judgment. If you have had months and months to take discovery and now at the eleventh hour you tell the judge, "There are some important depositions and I need time to take them now before I oppose the Motion for Summary Judgment," more often than not, the judge will say, "Sorry. You've had enough time."

The Defendant's Strategy

Motions for Summary Judgment are a crucial turning point in a case. If you're the party moving for summary judgment, you usually have to prepare what's called a Statement of Material Facts Not in Genuine Dispute. This means that for every fact that would be important to your lawsuit, you must cite evidence that conclusively resolves that fact— either an admission by the other side or some other conclusive evidence that no one could rightfully challenge. If your statement of undisputed facts contains the fact that the light at the intersection was green, you need to list the evidence showing that there is no way a reasonable juror could arrive at any other conclusion. Maybe you'd list a surveyor who was on the location and happened to videotape that the light was green at the time in question; maybe you'd have declarations of deposition testimony from twelve witnesses who all said the light was green. The court will be inclined to grant a Motion for Summary Judgment when you present evidence that can't be disputed by the other side.

If you are a deep-pocket defendant, you almost always look for a ground, a reasoning—a hook, if you will—for filing a Motion for Summary Judgment. If you can afford to pay for a summary judgment motion, not only might you have an outside shot of winning, but it adds the burden to the other side of mounting a significant defense on paper. The plaintiff might run out of cash and energy at this time, and there are many potential upsides for a defendant in bringing a Motion for Summary Judgment.

The judge holds a tremendous amount of power when he is sitting on and hearing a Motion for Summary Judgment, because what hangs in the balance is a party's right to present his claim to a jury of his peers. It used to be the exception rather than the rule for judges to grant summary judgment motions. Judges are now more willing to grant a Motion for Summary Judgment on cases where it's a close call. That's not to say that judges inappropriately grant such motions, but many courts in our major cities are so overcrowded that judges have huge workloads. At a certain point in time, it becomes an issue of fact as to whether a question of fact does exist. This can sometimes get into a little bit of a gray area, where a judge gets to exercise his own discretion. I've seen judges deny Motions for Summary Judgment that had no right being denied, and I've seen judges grant motions that had no right being granted. Because of overcrowded dockets and the enormous pressure on judges to dispose of cases that don't have any merit, getting a ruling has elements of a roll of the dice.

Many defendants will research the background of the judge and may discover that their judge tends to be more active in granting Motions for Summary Judgment. You may have a case that screams out for a Motion for Summary Judgment, but even if you don't, you may look at the judge's background or the fact that you're in an overcrowded court system and decide that it's worth a try.

If you're a defendant, the best part of filing a Motion for Summary Judgment is that it tests the other side's commitment to its case and the case itself. To oppose a Motion for Summary Judgment, the plaintiff's lawyers have to explain on paper the entire theory of their case. They have to put together declarations, recall important testimony from depositions, and organize it into a written statement of their case. This can be a very big job. They must obtain sworn statements from important witnesses and copies of important documents in order to support their argument that there is an issue of fact—that there is a real question as to how to resolve a certain question of fact—and that it does make sense to have a jury put in the box to decide this case.

Of course, preparing this response will be very costly to the plaintiff. Opposing a Motion for Summary Judgment probably takes the plaintiff's attorney two or three times longer than researching and drafting the complaint. The lawyer must provide a full overview of the history of the case, discuss any relevant case law and legal standards, and then put together the facts, documents, and testimony that will support the plaintiff's position. The client may have to personally provide answers to his counsel, perhaps help his counsel locate witnesses who will give statements in opposition to the motion, and go over the statements himself. In addition to being costly for the plaintiff, it's very time-intensive, like a minitrial. The plaintiff may have gone through a period of months where all he had to do was be generally aware of depositions that are taking place. Now, all of a sudden, he has to work with his attorney around the clock on sworn statements and on how this opposition will shape up.

If you are a plaintiff who is not litigating on a contingency fee basis, your attorney should have anticipated the possibility of a Motion for

Summary Judgment and built it into your budget. If not, you could have a problem. When you get to within ninety days of trial, you are beginning to look at questions like, How much money do I have? How best do I use it to prepare for trial? To bring witnesses into town? To subpoena witnesses? To pay for exhibits? To pay my expert? A Motion for Summary Judgment can be an unexpected twist financially; now some of your financial resources have to be diverted to paying your attorney to oppose this very important motion and interviewing a few more witnesses and getting statements. These statements, by the way, are not themselves admissible at trial, so you're not paying for trial preparation, but only to oppose this motion.

If you hired your attorneys on a contingency fee basis, a summary judgment motion might be a cause for concern. Some lawyers are fantastic in the courtroom; they file their complaint and look for what is called a quick settlement, but their strong suit might not be "motions practice." If you have this kind of attorney, you might lose your whole case in a summary judgment motion. A judge might feel that maybe it was a close call on whether he should have dismissed the case in the first place, but he gave you the opportunity to proceed and take nine months' worth of discovery. In the context of a carefully, fully briefed Motion for Summary Judgment by the defendant, the judge may feel that you, the plaintiff, haven't sustained your burden of proof. You haven't given him a full overview of how the case law supports your position; you haven't provided a well-written brief. In fact, some plaintiffs' counsel who are contingency fee lawyers are so overworked that sometimes they don't fully oppose the Motion for Summary Judgment or don't oppose it in a timely fashion. Case dismissed!

Many defendants also use a summary judgment motion to do one more thing: to get a blueprint for how the plaintiff is going to try the case. Even if the defendant's motion doesn't get granted, it forces you, the plaintiff, to show your hand, to put together your whole case and put forth declarations from your key witnesses. Those witnesses will have committed in writing to a certain position; you'll have explained your theories of the case and put forth your best evidence in support of each claim. The defendant will learn what your case is all about through a summary judgment motion and use it to see how you intend to put your case on at trial.

The Plaintiff's Strategy

Opposing a Motion for Summary Judgment is not something your lawyer can do quick and dirty. If you lose, your entire case is thrown out before ever reaching a jury. You should anticipate that a Motion for Summary Judgment is likely to be filed in any case where there's a substantial recovery at issue and the case is not settled early on. A defendant with a lot to lose will probably move for summary judgment.

Plot well how you're going to overcome that inevitable Motion for Summary Judgment. It is one big reason why you need to be careful deposing people and securing deposition testimony that at least raises an issue of fact that would warrant the case going to a jury. Maybe you'll get a witness who says, "I'm not sure whether the light was red or green." That would certainly be helpful in opposing a motion where the other side is trying to establish that no reasonable juror could find that the light was red.

All through the discovery phase, think about putting together your arsenal of evidence, which will not only win at trial but will defeat a Motion for Summary Judgment. If your attorney tells you, "Oh my gosh, they filed a Motion for Summary Judgment," and you're surprised that he's surprised, then someone's not doing his job.

Make sure your attorney tells you about the Motion for Summary Judgment. Ask about this particular process in your initial interview with the attorney. Ask whether the other side is likely to file this type of motion; how much it will cost to oppose and defect the motion; and how good your chances are for overcoming a Motion for Summary Judgment. Some attorneys believe that the client only needs to be updated about major events in a case as they unfold. But if you're going to manage your case, you must know important events in your case—like a motion for summary judgment—well before it happens.

In some circumstances, though, especially in the personal injury field, the case is sort of "turned over" to the lawyer. I know of unfortunate instances where the lawyer suddenly informs his client that the case is over. The client's case was dismissed, and he didn't even know that a summary judgment motion was on file, much less know what one was. Finding out about a Motion for Summary Judgment after the fact, or shortly before your opposition is due to be filed, is a clear indication that you failed to manage your own case well.

If you're a plaintiff trying to litigate your case within a budget, or if you have a contingency fee agreement and your attorney is trying to invest just the minimum amount to win your case, you know that the name of the game is to make it to that trial court. You want to stand in the courtroom before a jury and get a verdict in your favor.

The Motion for Summary Judgment is the last substantial hurdle for you as the plaintiff before you advance to trial. If you've made it that far, you've made it past a preliminary Motion to Dismiss or a demurrer; you've probably survived some kind of technical challenge, either jurisdiction or an attempt to force you to arbitrate; you've probably dealt with all of the discovery battles; and now you've survived a Motion for Summary Judgment. If you beat a Motion for Summary Judgment made by a desperate defendant, usually you'll be in a position to be more aggressive at the settlement table because the Motion for Summary Judgment may be that defendant's last chance to get rid of the case before facing the firing squad—the jury.

Just as the momentum can change at a certain point in a football game, the momentum changes at a certain point in litigation, too. It almost invariably changes in favor of the plaintiff if he successfully opposes a Motion for Summary Judgment. Now the plaintiff can look the defendant in the eye and say, "There's nothing standing between me and picking a jury." A lot of large corporations with exposure, or the insurance companies that are insuring those large corporations, may suddenly become nervous and a little more serious about settlement.

As plaintiff, you have every incentive to dump all your ammo into the opposition to the Motion for Summary Judgment, not just because you must do so to win the motion to prevent your case from being thrown out, but because by winning this battle, you gain the momentum heading into trial. If your papers look solid enough and your evidence looks well prepared, organized, complete, and comprehensive, and if your discussion of the law makes it clear that your lawyers know what they're talking about, maybe the defendant will finally realize that you have a sharp lawyer and a well-prepared case. Maybe the judge comments during the hearing that he feels your case has a lot of merit. Even if the defendant previously hasn't made a significant settlement offer, now perhaps you'll get one.

Another piece of potential good news for the plaintiff is that certain judges almost never grant summary judgment motions. Granting a Motion for Summary Judgment often requires making findings of fact and possibly preparing a written decision. I hate to say it, but some judges just don't have the time to sink their teeth into a case, read all the underlying cases, read all the deposition testimony submitted, and write up a decision. If a judge can't do that, then he may just deny the Motion for Summary Judgment. This can happen even if the motion has great merit. This hardly ever happens in federal court, but some judges in some state courts just don't have the resources they need. They may not have a clerk who's ready, willing, and able to work with the judge on the summary judgment motion, and they'd rather the case go to a jury so the jury will do the work in getting to the bottom of the case.

For a judge to allow a jury to decide a case is easy. The judge can usually direct courtroom traffic in his sleep. He can let the lawyers do the work, and when they're done, he'll read the instructions to the jury. Often he'll just get that out of a form book. Then he lets the jurors go to work, make a decision, and fill out a verdict form. Hence, some judges are inclined to deny summary judgment motions so as to delegate the hard job of getting to the bottom of a case to the jury.

Also, there are some judges who are extremely protective of the right to trial, so they rarely, if ever, grant a motion for summary judgment.

Motion for Summary Adjudication

A common mistake that even experienced attorneys make is moving to dismiss a portion of the case and calling it a Motion for Summary Judgment rather than a Motion for Summary Adjudication. Watch out—a motion can be denied simply because your lawyer titled it the wrong way! There's an important distinction between the two motions. In a Motion for Summary Judgment, you're asking the court to throw out the entire case filed by the other side—all of the causes of action, all of the claims (or defenses). If you want something less than that—if you want to pick, say, one cause of action among several and have that particular cause of action dismissed—then that's called a Motion for Summary Adjudication.

Your attorney may believe that there are one, two, or three causes of action that should be dismissed and do not really present a situation where a jury is required. Therefore, you might file a Motion for Summary Adjudication to dismiss a portion of the case.

Filing a Motion for Summary Adjudication can provide certain advantages. For example, you might file a motion to dismiss the claim for punitive damages. If your motion is granted, the other side may see the case in a different light; without the possibility of obtaining punitive damages, it's not as valuable. If the case is now just about compensatory damages, the plaintiff may be more willing to accept a lower settlement. Or say you're the plaintiff, and the defendant thought that your punitive damages claim had no merit and filed a Motion for Summary Adjudication. If the defendant lost, he would realize that the issue will be presented to a jury, so maybe he'll be willing to pay more to settle.

In a case where I represented the plaintiff, we alleged a number of causes of action against two defendants, including an action for a civil conspiracy between them. We alleged that Defendant "A" had deliberately harassed the plaintiff, and that he had done so at the behest of Defendant "B." As we got close to trial, Defendant "B" filed a Motion for Summary Adjudication on the cause of action for conspiracy. In the motion, Defendant "B" argued that, assuming that Defendant "A" *had* harassed the plaintiff, there was absolutely no credible evidence to show that Defendant "B" had any knowledge or involvement in the harassment, either direct or indirect. Defendant "B" argued that the only evidence against him was circumstantial, and that no reasonable juror could find him liable for conspiracy based on this evidence, so the cause of action for conspiracy should be dismissed. The judge denied the motion and, during the hearing, opined that the evidence against Defendant "B" was good enough, and a reasonable juror *could* use it to find Defendant "B" liable of conspiracy. Shortly thereafter, Defendant "B's" insurance company called me and began making substantial settlement offers for the first time.

You don't have to think in terms of dismissing the entire case. There are strategic reasons for why you might want to test the sufficiency of evidence or the legal sufficiency of a claim or part of a claim. That's what a summary adjudication motion is for.

Final Thoughts

I definitely recommend that the client go to the hearing on a Motion for Summary Judgment or Summary Adjudication. It's important to show the court that you really care about your case. If you're a plaintiff and a judge is about to enter an order granting Motion for Summary Judgment against you, your presence in the courthouse may have no impact on the ultimate outcome; the judge in all likelihood made up his mind before he took the bench that day. But sometimes your attorney will point out to the judge that he overlooked a key factor, a key piece of evidence, a key case in the legal argument. There may be some dialogue. It's helpful for a judge to look over your attorney's shoulder and see you, the party, sitting there, interested. It's a lot more difficult for a judge to look a client in the eye and let that client know that he's never going to have his day in court than it is to look at an attorney, who may be appearing before that judge on six different cases, and tell the lawyer that this particular case is being dismissed.

Lastly, if the court grants a Motion for Summary Judgment and your case is dismissed, you have the option of appealing that ruling and attempting to get your case reinstated (see Chapter 18).

14

Tell me about your relationship with your sister's dog.

Experts and Expert Exams

"Is that your conclusion, that this man is a malingerer?"
Dr. Unsworth responded: "I wouldn't be testifying
if I didn't think so, unless I was on the other side,
then it would be a post-traumatic condition."

—Ladner v. Higgins, 1954 Louisiana Court of Appeal

Some issues in a case are very basic. Was the light red or green? Did the buyer of goods make a timely payment? Was the pavement wet or dry? A jury can resolve these cases using common sense. However, there are often more complex issues presented by a case. What surgical procedure was required? Was the artificial-heart valve design defective? Did the company's software design originate from a competitor's protected ideas and technology?

Left alone to resolve these questions, a jury could make an uneducated guess resulting in a horribly wrong decision. For this reason, the rules of trial allow each side in a case with complex issues the opportunity to have experts explain the issues to the jury. For example, a doctor might testify about the appropriate surgical procedure; a scientist might testify about the design of an artificial-heart valve; or an engineer or programmer might testify about a software design.

Therefore, in certain cases, expert witnesses play a key role. However, be assured that experts do not come cheaply—and like any other witness, they can either save the day or backfire.

What Does an Expert Do?

The role of an expert in a lawsuit is to assist the finder of fact in interpreting and understanding certain complex evidence. It's very important to start at that premise. In theory, an expert is supposed to act as an impartial third party to help the jury members or judge with an issue that the average person would have difficulty understanding or deciding.

In truth, the parties to a lawsuit hire experts as advocates for their side. No one knowingly calls an expert who doesn't agree with and support his side's theory of the case. I don't mean to imply that many experts are simply "for hire" to whomever will pay their rate (although some are), but if a dispute centers on whether Uncle Joe signed the will or it's a forgery, one side's handwriting expert will say the signature is authentic, while the other's will say it's a fake. (It's possible that the experts might agree.)

Talented expert witnesses can simplify for the jury a bunch of complex evidence. The jury will then evaluate the experts' reasoning and credibility to decide if one's position seems to make more sense than the other's.

For just about every type of non-routine case, there are generally established guidelines as to what experts you'll need. An expert will be mandatory at some times and optional at others. For example, in a medical malpractice case, it's unlikely that you'd be able to prove your case without an outside doctor testifying at trial. Likewise, it would be impossible to prove a music infringement suit without a musicologist. Or in a contract suit where damages are complex and not easily understood, you might need an accountant to come in and explain to the jury how certain numbers were arrived at.

Experts are available for just about every subject area imaginable: safety and construction, medicine, emotions, voice, handwriting, fingerprints, DNA, sex, dust, shoe prints, car accidents, sleep, food, you name it. If you have a case involving an airplane crash, you probably would have numerous experts testify about the plane's design; you'd also have engineers, people in the airline industry, perhaps an expert on weather conditions, etc.

Experts Versus Consultants

There is an important distinction between experts and consultants. A consultant can essentially be anyone with some particular expertise whom your lawyer might bring in to help evaluate some aspect of your case, but consultants will not necessarily testify at trial. You can have endless numbers of consultants, and their job is just to help you, for example, add numbers, analyze evidence or facts, or help you put together your case.

Specific rules determine whether or not the information of a consultant or an expert can be discovered by the other side in a lawsuit. Generally, though, a consultant's information and work product is protected by the attorney work product privilege, so the other side isn't entitled to find out about it.

You may want to use a consultant early on if, for example, you're doing an audit of what certain numbers look like and whether you owe or are owed money. Or maybe a consultant gives an opinion on what a soil survey study reveals. You may want to use a consultant because if adverse information comes back or the consultant finds some damaging facts, then that information isn't automatically discoverable by your opponent. On the other hand, if you hire an "expert," his findings and conclusions are discoverable, as is every communication he's had with you or your attorney.

Often, you may hire someone to do preliminary work on your case as a consultant, then later decide to designate him as your expert once you're comfortable that he would be effective in your case. Of course, when you designate him, most of the work he has already done will be discoverable.

Do You Need an Expert?

Even when clients dog their attorney about his bills to make sure he stays within the budget, they can forget to focus on expenses when the expert arrives. As some clients do when they start out with the attorney, the client falls in love with the expert's expertise and doesn't see what it's costing to engage the expert. Because this expert can talk metal fatigue or foreign distribution or voice identification in a way that neither the client nor the attorney is able to, the client signs him right up—only to later get a rude wake-up call in the form of the expert's bill.

Experts are frequently brought in when the trial nears and everyone's getting nervous. When the expert comes into the picture, many elect to give him carte blanche in order to appear in court and sound as eloquent as possible. But experts can charge as much as or more than your hourly attorney. Many experts charge $200, $300, or $400 an hour and ask for substantial retainers.

Before you leap on board and tell your attorney to sign up the expert, ask some questions. What are the expert's qualifications? Why are we using this expert? Do we really need the expert? Some attorneys use experts like crutches, and they have the expert help them put on the case. You don't want your lawyer to be expert-happy, using experts when they aren't necessary or bringing in two experts to say what one could say. In some instances, however, not having an expert can be fatal to your case; your case could get dismissed if you don't have the proper expertise to help the judge or jury make a decision.

A lot of people believe that experts simply cancel each other out in a trial. That is true in some situations. The need to rebut and cancel out the other side's expert could be reason enough to necessitate your having an expert testify.

If you have a case that is not simple and straightforward—not a simple landlord-tenant dispute or a simple breach of contract action—but an intricate case that involves issues the average person is not very well versed on, then your attorney may feel you need an expert. You may want to discuss the issue of experts in your initial consultation with your attorney. One of the factors you may want to look at is whether the attorney is experienced in working with experts.

As the client, you can and should play an active role in selecting the expert. Maybe you have some background in the subject matter of the litigation and are in a better position than your lawyer to seek out and find a good, honest, cost-effective expert.

Bench Versus Jury Trial

Whether your case is to be decided by a judge (a bench trial) or a jury can affect the selection of an expert witness and how the expert makes his presentation. It's important to understand that a judge will not be moved by theatrics or rhetoric. If you're trying your case to a judge instead of a jury, your expert will not need to simplify things quite as much, and his testimony can be more to the point. A judge is also likely to become upset if you use an expert whose testimony is unnecessary or overreaches, because that wastes the judge's time and insults his intelligence.

If you're in a jury trial, you'll want an expert who is personable, charming, and can simplify things for the average juror. Think about television. Many (but not all) jurors are big TV watchers, and there is a school of thought that if you keep your presentation on a par with network TV programming—short sound bites, simple concepts repeated over and over again—you can succeed better with the average juror. If you follow this school of thought about jury trials, then you want your expert to take a complex subject and present it in a "made for television" style and manner. You don't want an expert who puts the jury to sleep or talks over their head. Also, you certainly don't want an expert who will wilt in front of the jury upon a tough cross-examination, or seem defensive or overly biased.

Designating Your Expert

You must formally notify the other side of any expert or experts you plan to call at trial. This litigation process is called designating the experts. By designating them, you're identifying each of them as an expert witness who has information and testimony relevant to the controversy at issue. Designation allows your opponent to conduct discovery of your expert before the trial.

Each jurisdiction has its own rules for how and when designation takes place, and you should make sure your attorney knows what those are. Some jurisdictions have a deadline by which you must designate your experts, a set number of days before trial. In other jurisdictions, such as California, either side can make a demand for the exchange of expert information sufficiently after the inception of the case. Sometimes the parties exchange this information simultaneously; sometimes it's done in a staggered fashion.

Qualifying Your Expert

Before your expert can testify at trial, he must prove to the court that he is, in fact, qualified to give testimony on the evidence at issue. There are strict rules for this process of qualifying an expert. Your lawyer must follow certain steps to proffer the person as an expert and then qualify him. Essentially, this entails showing that the person has had enough experience, either in terms of classroom study, degrees, or practice, to have developed the required expertise in a particular area.

Different courts use different guidelines to determine whether somebody qualifies as an expert. It's conceivable that you could spend a lot of money for an expert who doesn't qualify and can't testify. This can happen if an expert doesn't have the specific expertise that you need for the specific area at issue.

Budgeting for an Expert

Experts don't and shouldn't work for a contingency fee. In fact, it's improper for an expert witness, who wishes to preserve at least the appearance of independence, to have a financial stake in the outcome of the case. It would look horrendous at trial.

Expert witnesses will be paid by you or, in some contingency agreements, by your contingency lawyer. Experts can be expensive, so you shouldn't ignore this part of the case when trying to decide whether you can even afford the lawsuit. When you're first discussing a budget with your attorney, the question of an expert and expert costs may not come up. Perhaps an attorney is already concerned about overwhelming you with just the cost of the litigation, so he may feel it's poor salesmanship to bring up how much more an expert will add. A more common reason an expert isn't figured into an initial budget is that in the early stages, your attorney may not really have had the chance to develop sufficiently a theory of your case so as to focus on whether experts will be necessary.

Sometimes discovery uncovers evidence that requires some form of expert analysis and testimony. Maybe you find a financial record you didn't know about. Maybe a recording of a phone call comes out, so you need to have an expert analyze a tape and a tape-recording device. The expert may have to age the tape in order to determine whether it was compromised or dummied, and issue a detailed report on voice comparisons. Now you have an unexpected wrinkle that is going to cost you a lot of money, maybe another ten thousand dollars on top of everything else, just for one expert on one point.

After the costs for your trial and for depositions, experts can be the third largest expense in your litigation. I've seen clients get an expert bill right before or shortly after trial, and it's for $5,000—or $20,000—and they're shocked. They didn't quite realize that there was this expert who was poring over every sheet of paper that the lawyers had pored over, and reinventing the wheel in some way so he could come to his own independent conclusion.

Before hiring an expert, your lawyer should get a budget from the expert for his projected services. But the expert's bill is only part of the cost of having an expert in your case. The other, hidden cost is that if you have an hourly attorney, he'll spend many hours with the expert, being tutored on the discipline at issue, preparing the expert for trial, and generally working on the case with the expert. The attorney bills you for being tutored; he's learning this issue not because he wants to go home and impress his kids at the dinner table, but because it's necessary to present your case at trial.

So now you're really paying two professionals, an accountant and a lawyer. Or a doctor and a lawyer. Or a construction safety expert and a lawyer. Imagine paying for a $250-an-hour lawyer and a $250-

an-hour heart surgeon who, for four weekends in a row, spend ten hours together every Saturday working on your case. It adds up very fast.

At this point you have to be really alert. You have to have put in place a budget that takes into account the expert's anticipated time researching, meeting with your lawyer, possibly preparing a report, being deposed by the other side, preparing for trial, and testifying at trial. You had better also take into account the considerable additional time your lawyer will bill to work with that expert. Make it very clear that both the expert and the lawyer are not to go beyond that budget without your express authorization.

Before an expert is brought in, your lawyer should tell you the specific goal he has for this person. The goal may be, for example, to have someone compare the handwriting on this document with those documents, then to explain what aspects are similar or dissimilar, how this should best be presented to the jury, and what further work needs to be done to accomplish that. Whatever the lawyer lays out as the goal or goals, you should know how long it will take the lawyer and the expert to accomplish the goal and what the budget is to do that.

The lawyer should keep you posted on whether they're on track for the goal and whether they're on budget. That requires a lot of oversight. If your budget is important to you, don't allow yourself to fall asleep at the switch when experts are brought into the picture.

Who Talks to Experts?

Everything that you or your attorney say to an expert is discoverable; the other side's lawyers can ask about it in a deposition or when the expert is on the stand. A lot of plaintiffs or defendants feel that because the expert is "on the team," they can be very open and talk casually to the expert about their case. They may even talk openly to their own attorney in the presence of their expert, thinking that attorney-client privilege is in force. But there are issues relating to where that privilege line begins and ends, how it affects the expert, and what the expert can be asked about concerning client contacts. The safest thing to do is to let your lawyer deal with the expert as much as possible. As the client, you probably shouldn't have very much contact with the expert at all.

In addition, if people on the other side were to find out in your expert's deposition that you were talking with him about the case and expressing your perspectives on it, they could make a good argument that the expert's integrity and independence have been compromised. They might argue to the jury that your expert's opinions don't truly reflect an independent review of the evidence, but are colored by prejudicial statements you made to him.

Experts Help Rich Defendants Most

Top experts often have busy schedules, and large corporations often hire two experts. If one can't make it to trial because he is too busy, then they have a backup. Often they'll see how each one does in his deposition, then go with the most effective one at trial. That's what you, as a plaintiff, are up against, among other things.

An insurance company or other corporate defendant can pay experts a lot of money. Sometimes corporations even have certain types of experts on retainer. They can also pay their lawyers a lot of money to work with the experts. In a case where the testimony turns a great deal on expertise, such as understanding the health consequences of second-hand smoke, a rich defendant can have a big advantage.

A lawyer trying a case with expert issues needs to immerse himself in the subject matter and learn everything necessary from the experts to make a clear and compelling presentation. You're talking about an expensive, elaborate process that necessarily gives the advantage to the big corporate or insurance company defendants, because they can pay to have their lawyers spend more time learning. If you're the plaintiff in that kind of case, unless you have a lawyer who's handling the lawsuit on a contingency fee and has decided to bet the ranch on your case, then the wealthy defendant has a built-in advantage of being able to tutor his lawyers around the clock.

What Makes a Good Expert?

The best expert strikes a balance between knowing the technical aspects of an issue and being a good communicator. You want your expert to be interesting and keep the jury alert. Some of the best experts you can put on the stand are teachers. An ideal expert might teach a business course at a university by night and testify for you by day on a business management issue. Those types are used to being on their feet in front of a group of people, and they can take a complex body of material and break it down in an organized, understandable fashion.

Whenever information is communicated, it has to be communicated in a structured way. No matter how thorough and prepared your expert is, and no matter how brilliant his theory of the case, if he speaks at a level that's above the comprehension of the jury, it's useless. In a classroom setting, people can raise their hand if they have a question, and you can often gauge from their questions whether or not they understand. Jurors can't ask questions. Courts are formal and sometimes stuffy, and jurors may not even register reactions. You want an expert who's not only a good communicator but can read a jury.

Experts often have charts and blowups and computers and diagrams and laser pointers. On a very complicated case they may waltz around in front of a jury for days. Sometimes an expert may be on his feet in front of the jury for a quarter of the time your attorney is. If you think about it that way—that maybe a quarter of your case will be explained by someone who's going to walk around the courtroom with a pointer talking to the jury—you begin to grasp that expert's importance to your case. If you take the time to hire a really charismatic, articulate, successful trial lawyer who can keep a jury awake and focused, you sure don't want an expert who drones on and is totally uninteresting. With such an expert, the jury might tune out a significant portion of your case.

You also want to avoid an expert who's going to have little or no impact because he appears too biased. He's your friend or works for your company, or he's so overly zealous that the jurors realize that he's not being objective or independent. He's not an expert; he's a paid cheerleader.

Also avoid an expert who is overly detailed or so in love with the science of his discipline that he forgets that there's a group of people in that jury box who have to understand what he's saying on the stand.

You need to strike a balance between an expert who has testified enough that he doesn't get on the stand and freeze up or make a mistake and an expert who has testified too much. There's a danger in an expert appearing as if everything he does and says on the stand is overly polished, and he has an answer for everything. You don't want your expert to look as if he's reading from a script. And you don't want somebody who has done this so much that he's lost all sense of anxiety when he gets on the stand. It's a good thing for the jury to see that your expert is a little nervous but confident enough to make a good, solid, understandable presentation.

Experts are allowed to testify about all the things that they relied on in forming their opinion. Therefore, unlike any other witness, an expert can even refer to hearsay statements. They have a powerful ability to get information before a jury that no other witnesses can; they can draw inferences, make conclusions, and repeat otherwise inadmissible hearsay testimony. The judge will tell jurors in a cautionary jury instruction that the expert's testimony of hearsay is not admissible, and that the jurors may only focus on the opinion given by the expert. But once jurors have heard the expert testify that he spoke to so-and-so, who said this, and that's part of the basis of his opinion, the jurors will be hard-pressed to forget about it.

Common Mistakes and Problems

If you or your contingency fee lawyer are litigating your case on a shoestring, don't make the mistake of skimping on expert preparation. Maybe you or the lawyer can't afford the expert's rate to prepare adequately, or maybe the lawyer just doesn't have time. If the expert is asked a question that he and the attorney have never discussed, the expert could give an answer that damages your case. You can't imagine how many times I've seen this happen. A lawyer who hasn't spent enough time with his expert puts the expert up on the stand, asks for the first time a question that's critical to the case, and assumes that just because the expert is "his expert," the expert will give the answer the lawyer wants. The expert is under oath and very often gives the "wrong" answer, and the case is over, or part of the lawyer's case has been hurt.

There are parts of your case where you, as the client, should spend the money, if you have it to spend. Make sure your lawyer allocates adequate time to get in sync with your expert. Again, this is an area that is hard for clients to police, and you don't want the lawyer to spend one hour more than necessary. Keep close tabs on this through your attorney.

If your expert is too technical or is on the stand for too long, there can be problems. I had a case in which the other side's expert was intellectually stronger than our expert. He knew more, his analysis was more sophisticated, and you could tell from listening to him that he was simply more intelligent and better informed. However, he used too many charts and was too technical. Some jurors were literally fighting off sleep during part of his presentation. Our expert may not have had as many charts, but he spoke in simple terms, was very comfortable in front of the jury, and kept his presentation pretty much to the point.

We won the case. And afterward, a few jurors said that our expert had helped them to rule in my client's favor because the expert's explanation was so clear and simple. So while the lawyers and some of the people involved in the case had walked out thinking that the more intelligent expert had won the day, in fact most of what he had said had gone over the jurors' heads.

Expert Reports

Any reports prepared by an expert are discoverable, and anything your lawyer has put in writing and sent to the expert is discoverable, so your lawyer should be careful. Don't put much in writing with your expert, because often the other side will latch onto a comment made in writing and use it to try to undermine something the expert said or wrote elsewhere, especially if it could be construed as a contradiction.

If the expert provides a report, he should talk to your lawyer about what that report will say before he puts anything in writing. If the expert has some opinion that could be construed against you, why have it sitting there on paper? Why bring it up at all, if the question isn't asked?

Cross-Examining the Expert: Things to Keep in Mind

Assume that the other side is going to spend hours preparing to cross-examine your expert. The other side's expert will work with the lawyers to show how they can string up your expert. Experts love to team with lawyers to try to trip up the other side. It's like a chess game for a lot of them.

The problem with this is that the experts start to get hypertechnical, and what they believe will be a really interesting point for impeachment purposes is not the kind of detail that's going to play well in front of a jury. For example, experts have urged me to confront the other expert with something like, "Isn't it true that on page 12, column number 14, you forgot to put the decimal point in front of the two zeros, and the footnote doesn't match?" Your own expert might be thinking, "Oooh, we got 'em!" but the jury won't know what the heck you're talking about. Don't lose sight of the fact that your presentation is for the finder of fact—not to have fun or to stage a duel between the experts.

The experts will be asked on the stand about their hourly rate, so you should be sensitive to the fact that whatever they are paid will be disclosed to the jury or judge. If one side paid $5,000 for an expert and the other side paid $30,000, the jury will take this into account when evaluating the experts' testimony. Also, it does not look good if an expert says he has an outstanding invoice with you and groans a bit. Keep your expert's invoices current.

Often, you can make progress on your own case through cross-examination of the other side's expert. Sometimes your lawyer won't designate an expert because he feels you don't need to. Your lawyer will learn the relevant part of the necessary science or the discipline from a consultant—who won't be designated, who won't testify, and about whom the other side may never know. Then your attorney will do battle with the other side's expert on the stand. As long as the jury understands the points your attorney is making, you could actually advance your cause by an effective cross-examination of the other side's expert. When done by a skilled attorney, this tactic can devastate the other side's case.

When an Expert Examines You

Experts examine evidence like tape recordings, fingerprints, handwriting samples, and buildings. The other side is entitled to have an expert scrutinize and form an opinion about any facts or objects that may have a bearing on the case. If part of what is at issue has to do with you physically or emotionally, you may be subject to an exam yourself. If you're suing because you broke your leg, got whiplash, or suffered some other kind of injury as a result of the defendant's conduct, the other side is entitled to have a doctor examine your injury, assess your general physical health and condition, and look at your medical history.

Before any exam, the defense will probably send over interrogatories asking you to identify the names and addresses of every doctor, medical provider, and other health practitioner you have seen during the past ten years. They may also subpoena your health insurance carrier to obtain a list of providers who have submitted claims on your behalf. Once the lawyer for the other side has this information, he'll issue subpoenas to collect your records from your doctors' offices and, if he desires, he may take depositions of one or more of your doctors. The defense may then set up a time for you to be personally examined by their own medical expert.

This is often referred to as an "independent medical exam" (IME), but the truth is the experts are rarely completely independent, and the exams are sometimes more like an interrogation. If you're subjected to an IME, you will probably find that it's not like any medical exam you've ever had.

Here's what often takes place. The defendant's lawyer or insurance company retains a doctor, supplies him with copies of your medical records, and confers with him to explain the defense's theory of the case. For example, the defense team may tell the doctor that they believe you're a liar or are faking, and that if you do have any injury it was probably due to a preexisting condition. (Sometimes insurance companies leave a written trail showing their attempt to bias their examiner, but more often discussions like this take place in phone calls or face-to-face meetings, so they are difficult for your lawyer to prove.) The doctor understands that his mission is to try to confirm these theories and to help provide the defense with ammunition to use against you in the widest possible way.

When you go into the "independent" exam, the doctor may have spent hours poring through your medical records, and he interviews you about your history in the same way a lawyer would at a deposition. Although he has your entire medical history file and already knows a great deal about you, he probably takes you step by step through each doctor and medical issue or incident in your files, and questions you in detail about them. At least part of the reason the doctor interviews you this way is that he hopes you will give an answer that contradicts something written in your file, so the doctor will have evidence to help establish that you're not credible. (Remember, many doctors who do IMEs want to please their employer and work again, so they'll do what they can to help string you up.) The doctor may ask that you permit him to perform certain tests that he may not be legally entitled to conduct. If you don't know that he's not entitled to do a test, you might consent.

After the exam, the doctor probably prepares a written report that agrees with the defense's position. When you read his report, you may be shocked and angered, and you may find several misstatements, twistings of things you said, and in some cases outright lies. This defense expert will be called at trial and may attempt to impugn your character and prove that you're exaggerating or faking your injury or otherwise complaining about what is actually, in his opinion, a preexisting condition that had little or nothing to do with the defendant.

Am I exaggerating the description of doctors who give IMEs and act as expert medical witnesses? By no means are all IME doctors so biased, but some actually are. And while not all independent medical exams are conducted as in this example, some certainly are. For this reason, you would be well served to brace yourself to be examined by this kind of doctor, so that if he turns out to be the expert the other side hired in your case, you'll be prepared.

What should you do, if you're going to undergo an "independent" medical exam? First, get copies of all of the medical records that the defense has obtained. Read those records before the exam to refresh your memory and become familiar with the same documents the doctor has reviewed. Some experts will tell the jury you "lied" to them, just because you didn't recall something in your medical file. "Were you ever treated for dizziness?" the IME doctor may ask. And if you say "No," because you forgot that five years ago when pregnant you felt dizzy one day, and your OB-GYN wrote it in your file, you may have just given the expert an opening he's looking for. Now he can offer an expert conclusion to the jury that you're not credible.

Next, take a pad with you and make notes of how long you were at the doctor's office and how long you spent on each activity. You might note that you arrived at his office at 1:15, signed in at 1:20, sat in the waiting room until 1:45, sat alone in the exam room until 1:55, were examined from 1:55 to 2:30, got dressed, and left at 2:40. How would this information benefit you? Well, if later the expert has drawn all sorts of damaging conclusions about you based on his exam, you will be able to show that, in fact, he spent a total of only thirty-five minutes with you, whereas your own expert (whose opinion differs) examined you for two and a half hours.

Take a tape recorder with you and record the entire interview and interaction with the doctor. If this sounds paranoid, believe me, it's not. I have seen cases where the doctor has written up a report that says the plaintiff said x and denied y and asserted z. But listening to the tape showed that this was just plain wrong. Because we had a tape, we could destroy this expert's credibility on the witness stand by letting the jury hear how he had totally misstated many important facts. Without that tape, it's just the doctor's word against the plaintiff's.

Some people take a video camera to their IME. I think that's a great idea. Tape-recording or videotaping an IME can be a huge weapon in a trial. In cases I have seen, the expert's questions and the way he asks them reveal that he drew his conclusions before the exam. Playing portions of the exam at trial and allowing the jury to see or hear that there was nothing independent about the exam can really incense a jury. That can translate into a bigger award to you. Juries don't like to see people treated unfairly.

If your lawyer can attend your IME or send an associate to be with you, so much the better. Now you have a witness to what was said and someone to counsel you on whether you have to answer certain questions or submit to certain tests. For example, when you are being examined for a physical injury, the expert has no right to question you about any emotional or psychological treatment you may have received. Yet if an expert has obtained a copy of insurance billings and sees that you saw a therapist or counselor, he may attempt to ask you about this and draw out information to pass along to the defense to try to use against you.

Think of the defense IME doctor as just another lawyer on the defense's team, except that he has tremendous latitude and can employ tactics that would never be permitted in a deposition. He might attempt to get a free deposition when you come in for an exam. He may ask many questions that don't bear at all on your health, planning to pass the answers along to his employer, that is, the defendant or the defendant's insurance carrier.

If you assert a claim for emotional distress or some form of psychiatric injury or illness, then your entire psychiatric history will be investigated, and there will probably be requests to take discovery of any psychologists or psychiatrists or church counselor you've ever seen. The other side will ask for an opportunity to have its psychiatrist sit down with you in a room and interview, evaluate, and test you. Again, you want to take the same precautions as you do for the IME. Tape-record the session, and have your lawyer or someone come with you, if possible. These kinds of exams can be very intrusive and very difficult.

Remember that the damages you have put at issue invite the other side to bring in experts. How public do you want your private life to be? If you claim lost profits, for example, don't be surprised when the other side brings in accountants and bookkeepers to start crawling all over your financial statements and tax returns to verify whether you have lost profits.

15

Alternative Dispute Resolution

A lean compromise is better than a fat lawsuit.

—English proverb

In fourteen years of litigating, I have yet to come across a problem that didn't have a practical solution. Often it isn't a solution everyone will be crazy about, but it will be practical and cost effective.

The problem with many litigants is they become entrenched and cannot see their way clear to a compromise. Instead, they use an expensive and blunt process called a lawsuit to try to impose their solution on the other party. But there's a roulette wheel element to litigation, and it can be counterproductive: "Hey, baby, will the ball land on number 14 red? If it does, I'm a winner, and I get to go to town on you!"

While I'm being a bit harsh, this is a harsh reality to litigation, and as such, it is becoming most important to consider alternative forms of dispute resolution.

In short, before you set the wheel of litigation roulette in motion, think about alternative dispute resolution. There are all sorts of alternatives to the time and expense of a lawsuit. Your situation may be as simple as "I've got a dispute with my neighbor over whether his fence is on his property or mine." Rather than tearing into court, perhaps you and your neighbor could go to a homeowners' association and find someone you both respect to help resolve the matter. More formally, there are mediation firms, arbitration processes, and retired judges available to hear and help decide controversies.

The Mediation Process

In mediation the parties to a dispute consult with an impartial third party to analyze and help settle the matter. Both parties present their case and ask that third party to help them and possibly try to reach a settlement. Typically, mediation is nonbinding, meaning that the mediator cannot force a resolution upon the parties. Rather, the mediator is left to use reason and logic to help each side see the other side's perspective and the value of a compromise.

If you and the other party agree to mediate, you must agree on a format for handling the mediation. The process usually begins with an agreement on who pays for the mediation. The parties may agree to split the cost of a mediator, or one party may propose paying for it. Next, the parties settle on who the mediator should be; this may be a retired judge, a mediation service, a company specializing in providing mediation, or a lawyer who mediates in his spare time.

When a lawyer represents you in a mediation process—and I strongly urge you to have a lawyer represent you for any sizable dispute—the parties agree on a schedule for briefing their respective positions in writing. Mediation does not require that the parties submit written briefs ahead of time, but often both sides will want the opportunity to submit their case in writing and to note the legal basis they contend supports their right to a judgment in their favor. The parties usually agree that on a given day they will exchange briefs and that the briefs should not exceed a given page length. Then, after another established time period, each party exchanges a reply brief with the other, responding to the arguments in the opponent's brief. I should note that some mediations are far less formal and involve no briefs or papers being filed in advance. Copies of the briefs, the complaint itself (if a complaint has been filed), and any other materials the parties have agreed on are then delivered to the mediator for review.

On the day of the mediation, the lawyers meet with the mediator and present their case, which can be anything from the lawyer just talking and answering the mediator's questions to putting on evidence, showing documents, and having witnesses and/or parties give testimony in front of the mediator. The amount of evidence put before the mediator depends on the parties' agreement. After the mediator hears from both sides, he usually meets privately with each side for what is called a caucus with each party and his attorney. This can be an important part of the process because it can help a party to see weaknesses in his position and hence be more open to accepting the idea of negotiating a resolution. After the caucuses, the mediator usually meets with all involved parties again. This process can continue if the parties so desire. The key to a successful mediation lies in what the mediator says to each side during the caucus (the mediator's one-on-one meeting with each party and his lawyer). A good mediator will make you feel comfortable and will be quick to acknowledge the obvious—and even not-so-obvious—strengths of your position. However, an effective mediator will also look you straight in the eye and tell you the plain and simple truth about the flaws in your case—something your lawyer may be afraid to do.

Your role in mediation is to keep an open mind. Don't be afraid to hear the truth about your case, or at least what someone experienced in resolving litigation disputes thinks about the case. However, don't feel the mediator is all-knowing either. Sometimes, in fact, the mediator just "doesn't get it" or there is too big a gap to bridge. In most states, what is said during mediation is confidential and cannot be used at trial. To ensure this, sometimes parties to a mediation agree in writing to prohibit disclosure of what was said in the mediation. This allows for open and honest dialogue.

If the parties *do* reach a compromise, the mediator may work with the parties to prepare a settlement. If the parties have not yet reached a settlement but are close, the mediator may schedule a follow-up session. If the parties simply will not agree, then the mediator will adjourn the mediation and you will resume with the litigation. If the parties agree to a "binding" mediation, then the mediator will in fact impose a binding resolution upon the parties if one is not voluntarily reached, but only after trying very hard to reach an acceptable compromise. If the mediation is binding, then the parties are bound by his decision. However, more often mediation is nonbinding. Thus, if one of the parties doesn't want to accept the mediator's recommendation, he doesn't have to.

Why You Might Want to Mediate

Mediation is generally an informal process, and a number of law firms specialize in it. There is a real art to dispute resolution. Few hard-nosed litigators are adept at it because in order to settle a dispute, you have to know how to convince angry parties to compromise. You must be able to persuade them to put aside their rancor and look at their dispute objectively. A good mediator can lead parties to understand and acknowledge weaknesses or flaws in their positions. People don't like to admit they're wrong. They don't want to concede that they didn't consider the full picture when they got embroiled in a fight. The artful part of mediation is telling someone he is wrong in such a way that he will believe, agree with, and accept your opinions.

A case where mediation was successful was one between an oil company and a public utility, involving some leaky oil tanks located on property the public utility leased from the oil company. After the lease expired, the oil company sold the property to a developer, which discovered that the oil tanks had leaked and demanded the oil company pay for the expensive cleanup. The lease between the oil company and the public utility said the utility was to return the premises in essentially the same condition it leased them, absent normal wear and tear. So one big issue was, if you're running a tank farm with petroleum products, what constitutes "normal wear and tear"? Another dispute involved who actually caused the spills. The litigation had become very complicated, and all sorts of chemists and other sophisticated experts were probing the soil, peering at the pipe erosion, and trying to determine scientifically at what point the leak occurred and who, therefore, should get the blame.

Beyond these issues, there was what I would call a political issue that went all the way up to the heads of both companies. This dispute was contentious, and the two businesses were millions of dollars apart in their notions of settlement. The utility had taken a firm position: "This is a tank farm, leaks happen, and you guys have sold the property to a developer and made a lot of money. We'll give you a modest amount of money, but that's it."

Eventually both sides agreed to submit this case to nonbinding mediation. To my disbelief, we settled it. Mediation worked because the mediator was able to articulate in a courteous, diplomatic, dispassionate, and intelligent manner precisely the strengths and weaknesses of both sides. He illuminated how a jury would probably evaluate the evidence of both positions, and described how the jurors would likely arrive at a particular result. The parties on both sides were impressed and decided to accept the mediator's recommendation.

I'm a big believer in trying alternative dispute resolutions before or immediately after a lawsuit is filed. A good mediator can help take off the rose-colored glasses that both litigants are wearing. But this works only if it's done correctly by someone who knows what he's doing.

If you can mediate early on, do it. Your costs will be much less than to litigate your case from start to finish, because it happens quickly and when you reach a result that's accepted by both sides, it's over.

The parameters imposed by mediators can also be beneficial. Before beginning mediation, a good mediation firm I know requires the parties to prepare a ten-page statement presenting their positions. The firm's mediators won't read more than ten pages, period. Even if you have intricate legal issues, you can only present ten pages. This requirement forces lawyers to choose their words and points carefully, and to focus on facts and minimize the rhetoric. This translates to far fewer dollars for you to pay than if you went to trial. (There's a correlation between the weight of your litigation file and the amount of legal fees you incur.) Less is always better.

Ninety percent of the people in this country can't afford our modern litigation process. Taking this into consideration, wouldn't it be preferable to go to some third party and walk away with a result that resolves the problem through a compromise? Isn't the act of compromise something we teach our children? You may not be thrilled with the solution, but you can get on with your life.

If you don't try to resolve your dispute early on but decide to proceed with a lawsuit, you'll be experiencing "fight or flight" in your stomach for two years and paying a fortune in legal fees. Maybe you'll win. Then there could be an appeal, which can take another year and a half. Even if you do eventually win, you might be left so bitter, angry, and broke, you won't even remember why you got into the lawsuit in the first place. The solution may not even be half as good as what you could have gotten up front if you had the right mediation firm lending a hand.

Why You Might Not Want to Mediate

A good mediator can save the day; a bad one can ruin it. Mediation has some pitfalls. One of the biggest is that some retired judges and groups that call themselves mediators are good at quoting words of wisdom and telling war stories about courtroom drama, but simply lack the skill to move the parties through logic and analysis to an acceptable compromise. Beware of the retired judge who is now past his prime. He may have been a great judge, but that doesn't mean that he'll be a good mediator.

An effective mediator is shrewd, grasps quickly the facts of a variety of different disputes, and can communicate well and make people trust him. He should understand the legal system and how it works in the particular area where the dispute would be heard. Go to a mediator who is familiar with the rules in the city where your case would be tried. Otherwise, the mediator can't tell you about some of the dangers that may lie ahead for you in your lawsuit. Parties to a mediation will walk away from the table in a second if they find themselves before a mediator they don't respect. That's a big waste of time.

In my experience, 20 percent of mediators are helpful, and 80 percent are not. One type of beast to look out for in mediation is lawyers who may not have enough of a practice to keep themselves afloat, so they volunteer to be mediators. If they lack experience or insight, they'll be of little use. (However, some lawyers, who have been trained to mediate are outstanding.) Also, as noted, the other kind of creature to avoid is retired judges who love to sit around and tell war stories. They spend most of their time on the golf course, and they squeeze cases between rounds. Some of these guys may have been great at settling cases when they were judges, because they had the authority to say, "Look, if you don't settle, I'll throw out half your case . . ." If that's the way they operated as a judge—if they didn't use cogent, careful, intellectual analysis to expose weaknesses and flaws in one side's thinking— then they probably never developed the ability to loosen the parties up and get them to take off those glasses that distort a party's vision.

With this kind of retired-judge mediator, you may walk into a room and think, "Oh, great, this is Judge So-and-So!" Well, Judge So-and-So is seventy-six years old, takes four medications, can't hear out of his left ear, and is going to spend a half hour recounting his favorite cases: "Did I tell you about the case where we had the dry cleaners and this guy with the gimpy leg . . .?" You'll end up wondering why you're wasting an afternoon and $400 an hour on this guy. At the end of the mediation, old Judge So-and-So is going to say, "Why don't we just split it down the middle? Whattaya say, fellas?" And you'll be thinking, "Hey! This has never been a case where we even contemplated splitting it in half! Even the other side agreed it shouldn't be any more than 30 percent! Come on, Judge, was your hearing aid on?"

The unfortunate tendency of bad mediators is that they're always looking for a way to split the baby down the middle. They interpret compromise as meeting in the middle, and that's an unreasonable solution for most cases. Perhaps some mediators think they stand the best chance of being hired again if they "make everyone happy."

The courts have their own mediation processes, and you should be wary of them as well. In courts in major metropolitan areas, alternative dispute resolution has become popular, so the courts throw something together with whatever resources are at hand. The best resources of the court system are rarely devoted to mediation. You get stuck with retired judges or part-time lawyers, and most of the parties who go through that process are dissatisfied. Yet, there is always the exception to the rule. Ask your attorney about your court's mediation program. Also, as mediation becomes more and more of the future trend, look for even the weakest program to improve.

Find out what a mediator's pass/fail rate is. How many matters that go before him actually get settled? How often do one or both parties say, "Forget this! This mediator is nuts!" On the other hand, it's probably a good sign to see parties running in droves to a certain mediator, saying, "Can you help us decide this dispute?" You want people who have previously worked with a mediator to say, "We didn't get everything we wanted, but we really respect that person."

You also need to find out what relationship, if any, a potential mediator may have with the other side. Has the mediator worked with the other law firm before? Does he know any of the lawyers or parties involved? Was the mediator's spouse once represented by the lawyer on the other side? (It happens.) Your lawyer should confer with his colleagues and other lawyers with experience, then cross off his list any mediators who look questionable. Before agreeing to retain any mediator, he should insist on getting a written statement from the mediator disclosing any relationship with the parties, their lawyers, or any significant witnesses. A plaintiff's lawyer once agreed to a certain mediator, and two days before the scheduled mediation, the mediator disclosed that he was applying for a job with the defendant's law firm. Because the mediation was only two days away and the attorney had a contingency arrangement and a heavy caseload, the attorney didn't have time to file the required objection to knock out this mediator. He took his client's case before the questionable mediator anyway. As you might expect, this mediation was a disaster.

Another downside of mediation is that if the other side isn't that interested in settling, you can get ambushed because your opponent may be using mediation as a form of cheap discovery. He'll invite you to mediate mainly to have an opportunity to hear you present your case, and then he won't settle. You'll spend money having your lawyer put on your case simply to give the defendant a better opportunity to beat you. Beware of a situation where the defendant has refused to make a reasonable settlement offer, his lawyer keeps telling you you're full of it, and then a short time before trial he's suddenly eager to mediate.

If you're concerned about this and are confident in the person you select to mediate, you can insist on setting a minimum award you're guaranteed to receive. Make it a condition of the mediation that not only will it be binding, but that all parties will waive the right of appeal, regardless of the decision. If your opponent hasn't shown any good faith or any willingness to enter into a binding mediation where you can set some kind of floor for the award you'll receive, watch out for a maneuver.

The Arbitration Process

Arbitration is similar to mediation, except that usually arbitration is binding. One or more arbitrators hear the evidence, but rather than simply making a recommendation or giving advice, an arbitrator issues a ruling and makes an award of who gets what. Sometimes the arbitrator issues a written opinion, but not always.

Not only are arbitration decisions binding, they cannot be easily appealed (unless the parties have agreed otherwise). There is a process by which the loser in an arbitration can oppose the confirmation of the judgment at court, but it's very difficult to get an arbitration award overturned. (See Chapter 18 for more on the appeals process.)

Frequently, business contracts or agreements with doctors, hospitals, or insurance companies provide that any future disputes arising from the agreement must be submitted to and resolved by arbitration. If you ever have a problem, you may not sue the other party but are bound by an agreement to arbitrate. If something has gone so wrong that you really don't want to arbitrate, but prefer to sue and get a jury to deliver a strong verdict against the other side, you'll have a tough time doing so if you have agreed to arbitrate. Your attorney might make a case that the issue falls outside the scope of the agreement, so you should be able to sue rather than arbitrate. It might work, but judges tend to interpret arbitration clauses broadly, so they're not easy to escape. When plaintiffs ask judges to rule on whether or not an issue falls outside a contractual arbitration clause, the judge often forces them to go to an arbitrator just to decide that issue.

Sometimes the parties who are already involved in litigation agree at some point to submit the dispute to arbitration, in order to resolve it without going to trial. Before agreeing to arbitrate, the parties may agree to a floor and/or ceiling for the amount the arbitrator will award. This way, the plaintiff knows he'll at least get a given amount by going into arbitration, and the defendant knows his exposure is limited to the top number.

Unlike mediation, which is less formal and typically involves informal dialogue, arbitrations are more formal and present witnesses and evidence. However, compared to a trial, an arbitration hearing has more relaxed rules of evidence and moves much more quickly.

Also, arbiters generally have very solid experience in the field of law or the business trade involved in your dispute. They are much more likely to understand the issues at hand than a jury would. Arbiters are also far less likely to allow their emotions to govern, which may happen with juries. In short, an arbitration—while having elements of a mini-trial—is almost always quicker, more cost-effective, and more likely to serve a fair resolution than a traditional lawsuit that ends in a jury trial.

Creative Settlements

Your goal as plaintiff should be to get an acceptable settlement, if possible, rather than to litigate. Lots of deep-pocket defendants, after jerking you around and forcing you to pursue them vigorously, say shortly before trial, "Ok, let's sit down and work out something reasonable." Unfortunately, because they've made you spend many tens of thousands in legal fees, settling will take more money than if they'd taken that attitude two years earlier.

In a long, bitter, hard-fought case where I represented the plaintiff, as the trial date approached, the defendant's insurance company said, "Hey, let's mediate; it's the only way." We had tried to settle the case early on, but parties for the other side had told us, "Get bent. We'll see you in court." Now they wanted in the worst way to get a mediator to come in and settle it.

When we discussed the range that my client felt he deserved, the defense lawyer just laughed, saying, "What are you guys smoking anyway?" The problem was that my client had been forced to spend around $175,000 in legal fees to keep up with a deep-pocket insurance company. He wanted to recoup his legal expenses and get a reasonable settlement for his case. Fortunately, he had a contract with the defendant that said the prevailing party in any lawsuit would be entitled to be reimbursed for reasonable attorney's fees by the loser. The insurance company said that my client had spent an inordinate and unreasonable amount on attorney's fees, and that even if we went to trial and won, no judge would award to my client anything approaching those fees.

We were stuck. They offered $200,000 to settle, but my client insisted on $300,000. He felt that he had been wronged not only by the defendant as to those issues he'd sued over, but in the way the defense had handled the litigation, refusing to discuss settlement until the final moment, thereby forcing him to spend a huge sum on the lawsuit.

I suggested a compromise: my client would accept $175,000 now and dismiss the lawsuit, and then we would go into an arbitration where my client would be regarded as the "prevailing party" for the purpose of determining how much of his legal fees the defendant should reimburse under the contract provision. My client agreed, and so did the defendant's insurance company. As part of the arbitration, we were permitted to see the defendant's legal bills so we could argue that, in relation, ours were reasonable.

The outcome of the legal fees arbitration was that the arbitrator awarded my client a $175,000 reimbursement for his attorney's fees. Thus, my client received a total of $350,000 as a settlement— $50,000 more than he had asked for only a short time earlier.

It's easy to get locked into a mind-set, a given goal, a number, or a result that you feel you absolutely want. But keep an open mind as much as possible. Consider creative ways to resolve your matter, and you might find one. Arbitration and mediation can work. But only use them under the right circumstances.

Where to Find Mediators and Arbitrators

Your lawyer is the best place to start the search for a mediator or arbitrator. I would never recommend you go into an arbitration or mediation without representation, unless only a minor sum was in controversy and the issue was very simple. A lawyer should be able to find a good mediator through referrals from other attorneys he knows and works with. He must check out the types of cases any potential mediator has been involved in, ask how he works, and get some references. He should call those references and hear their opinions of that mediator.

Agreements with arbitration clauses frequently spell out how the arbitrator will be selected. The American Arbitration Association (AAA) can provide you with a list of arbitrators and arbitration procedures. In fact, many contracts require that you submit your dispute for arbitration before AAA. You can visit their website on the Internet at www.adt.org and find a great deal of information.

Anyone, not just a lawyer or judge, can be an arbitrator. Often arbitrators have some specialty in the area of the issued being arbitrated.

By the way, even if the other side has worked with a mediator or arbitrator in the past, it doesn't mean the individual will be biased in the other side's favor. I have worked repeatedly with a certain mediation firm because I trust and respect the firm's people, not because they give any deference to cases I bring. The key is to research the mediator's reputation.

"Photos, witnesses, videotape . . .
everything but the smoking gun!"

Trial Preparation

Extemporaneous speaking should be practiced and
cultivated. It is the lawyer's avenue to the public.

—Abraham Lincoln

If you've watched *Perry Mason, Court TV,* or the O. J. Simpson trial,
you know that a dramatic presentation and a good orator certainly
help your case. But many people fail to appreciate that if their lawyer
is not adequately prepared and doesn't have command of the facts,
then he probably won't do very well. Everyone respects a prepared
lawyer. The presentation comes off more smoothly and without gaps.
The lawyer gains credibility with the jury if he knows the dates, medical charts, music, exhibits, and witnesses.

Just as important as the lawyer's preparation—and part of his job
in preparing the case—is preparing the exhibits to be entered and the
witnesses who will appear at trial, including, of course, you, the party.

A month or two before trial, you really need to know and understand what your trial attorney is doing to prepare for the trial. As the

235

trial grows near, the lawyer possibly has various assistants take care of a number of activities, such as preparing his opening argument, making blowups of exhibits, and talking to witnesses. You can do some of these yourself, if you have the time. You'll certainly save yourself some money if you can help out with various tasks.

Exhibits

The exhibits are your documented proof of a case. By the time you go to trial, you should have all the documents that need to be presented to the jury. Remember, documents can include videos, audiotapes, photographs—a lot more than what most people commonly think of as a document.

Jurisdictions vary, but you're usually required to provide the court ahead of trial a copy of the exhibits that you will be using at trial. They're usually organized and placed in a notebook. Jurisdictions have different numbering systems for these exhibits.

Ask to see the exhibit notebook well before you go to trial. Get some sandwiches, go into a conference room with your lawyer, and spend an hour or two having your lawyer explain to you why he wants to introduce each of those documents before a judge and jury. One common error of some trial lawyers is that they overdose the jury with documents. Jurors can only be expected to read so much. If you give them 200 exhibits, it might be fun admitting them all into evidence, but the jury is unlikely to actually examine, break down, and understand those 200 exhibits. This is an area where less is more.

If you delegate to your attorney the process of identifying exhibits for trial, you're making a huge mistake. Your attorney might forget something important. Moreover, *you're* going to trial; it's *your* case. You should know what's being presented to the jury. If you get a notebook containing 200 exhibits but your case is about a single contract and a few letters, ask your lawyer why the other 180 exhibits are there. If he doesn't have a good answer, tell him to get rid of them. You don't want to annoy the judge and jury by giving them a huge notebook to sort through if there's not a good reason for it. The other benefit to reviewing exhibits in advance with your lawyer is that you'll get a sense of how your lawyer intends to present your case at trial.

I am a big believer that the visual sense is one of the strongest in a courtroom. In preparing exhibits, your attorney will probably want to make some charts, perhaps one or two that underscore conflicts in testimony, or perhaps he'll want to blow up a crucial line or paragraph in a contract at issue. Blowups can be extremely useful and have a substantial impact on the jury.

In a bench trial where a contract clause was at issue, the location of a comma was important to the way each side interpreted the clause. We made a blowup with huge words and put the comma in bright, fluorescent yellow. Throughout the whole trial, the judge kept looking at that fluorescent yellow comma. When he made his decision, ruling in our side's favor, he talked quite a bit about that comma. Now, had I not blown that up but only kept referring to it in my oral presentation, then maybe the judge would have just looked at some small-print copy in the exhibit notebook, and maybe that comma would not have been as present in his mind.

Some parties spend tons of money using computers, graphics, videos, models, re-creations of events. These can be useful and really get the jury's attention—or they can just be gimmicky. At trial, your attorney should think visual.

Giving a juror a few handouts of items that were also replicated in a blowup can be much more effective than giving him three full three-ring binders of documents that are tabbed "1 through 75," "76 through 150," and "151 through 225." It's far more likely a juror will carefully study a few select documents and a blowup than to wade through hundreds of pages of small type.

On a cost front, you should know that your lawyer needs to make multiple copies of that exhibit notebook. Usually you need a copy for the judge, one for opposing counsel, maybe one for the witness, one for yourself, and one or two backup sets for other witnesses. So you'll need about six copies of these notebooks. Lawyers are generally paper-happy and will err in the direction of having too many extra copies made. If your attorney is working with exhibit notebooks that contain 250 exhibits when you only want 50, and he's making six copies of those three-ring notebooks and sending them to an outside copying service on a rush basis, the expense could be significant.

To be fair, some cases require admitting hundreds of documents into evidence. You just need to know why, and what documents they are.

Witness Preparation

A lawyer preparing witnesses in an involved case will spend hours with them. He may have a colleague stage a mock examination with the witness, and then the witness will discuss the case with the trial lawyer. This is how a large firm might handle an elaborate case with a sizable budget.

But if you're a small-business owner or an individual on a limited budget and don't have a contingency fee case, you will want to know how many witnesses your lawyer is going to prep, how much time he expects to spend, and what topics will be covered. You need to know this to understand the trial preparation itself, as well as to keep track of the budget.

My typical approach to witness preparation is to meet with each witness, probably early in the case, and learn what he knows that's relevant. I review his documents, interview him, perhaps take a statement. If he has been deposed and I'm preparing him for trial, I may have an unstructured session where I go over his deposition with him, alert him to areas where he could be asked tough questions on cross-examination, and explain my goals as the trial attorney in terms of his testimony.

For my first trial preparation session with a witness, I prepare what I call the case's themes outline. Witnesses and jurors sometimes have a hard time grasping the legal issues, so I reduce issues to themes I want to bring out again and again at trial. The themes depend on the particulars and individuals involved in the case, but examples might be statements like these: "The corporate defendant is very untruthful," "We are a small company that pays our bills," and, "We're not in this lawsuit for a windfall profit." I usually call the witnesses in individually (or sometimes together) and go over the themes in the case.

Your witnesses need to understand these themes, not just the facts. They have to understand that when your attorney is submitting a closing argument to the jury, he's going to be harping on the themes, as the defense did in the O. J. Simpson case: "If the glove doesn't fit, you must acquit." Well, the glove was such a small portion of that case, but it became a theme. The outcome of that case shows the importance of having basic themes that you can submit to the jury. Your witnesses should hear your themes before they're in the courtroom hearing your opening or closing statement. Once you know your witnesses and they know your lawyer, and once you've identified your themes, then your lawyer can gauge how to break up the testimony.

A large part of the prep session, then, will be devoted to exploring the testimony the witnesses will give at trial. I'll say, "If I asked you this question, how would you answer?" I let them answer in their own words, then I might suggest that there's a better way of saying it.

In the end, your witnesses should always tell the truth, but let's talk about the truth. In our society the answers to certain questions involve shades of gray. If your spouse asks you, "Do I look tired and haggard?" you can say, "Yes," in which case you're dead. You can say, "No," in which case you're lying. But maybe you could say, "Well, you look like you have had a long day." Is that a lie? No, it isn't. So sometimes a trial can be about the difference between saying, "Yes, you look tired and haggard," and, "Well, you look like you had a long day."

There's a fine line. It is entirely unethical to suggest to a witness that he lie. Any lawyer who does that deserves to have his license taken away. But, for example, I had a case in which a client was invited to someone's house to sign a contract; when he got there, a party was in full swing, and my client was given alcohol in a social atmosphere. After the party was over, he was given the contract and asked to sign. Let's say my client went to trial unprepared and was asked, "At the time you signed the agreement, were you sober? Were you able to understand what you read?"

In a prep session with me, my client might say, "Look, I wasn't drunk, not past the point of legal intoxication. I do think I recall reading it . . ." That may not be the best way to answer that question, so I might say, "Well, wait a second. How many drinks had you had? Was there loud music in the background? Did you read every line? Were the words a *little* blurry? Was your state of mind different than it would have been if you had been sitting in an office?"

If the client says, "Yes," I could suggest a different way to phrase his answer: "I was distracted, the music was loud, and I had had two drinks. I really wasn't completely focused, and I was slightly under the influence of alcohol. It did affect me." This answer is different but not untruthful. It's the same basic fact pattern, but I've given some guidance with the wording. If you don't choose your words carefully in a trial and you say the wrong thing, you could lose your case. There could be a directed verdict (see Chapter 17), or the jury might focus on that one, lone line and decide differently than if you had answered that question differently.

A witness prep session should never be a cram session where the lawyer tells the witness what he'll testify to. It should be a discussion of what the witness knows and how he'll answer questions at trial. More importantly, witness preparation shouldn't stop at saying, "Here are the questions I'm going to ask you." It should also include a sample of what it might be like to be involved in a cross-examination.

Preparing for Cross-Examination

In court, your lawyer will gently question your witnesses on the stand, and the witness will tell his side of the story without interruption. Then the judge will say, "Are you done with your examination of this witness?" and your lawyer will say, "Yes, your honor." The judge says, "Cross?" and suddenly this big mean attorney is standing above the witness, saying, "Isn't it true that you've lied about exactly where you were standing at the time of the incident?"

The whole temperature in the courtroom changes dramatically between direct examination by your attorney and cross-examination by the other side. When your lawyer is questioning you or your witness, it's a positive situation. Your lawyer is lobbing up questions you know are going to be asked, and you're giving answers that are entirely helpful to your case. There's no friction, the lawyer is pleasant, you're making eye contact with the jury, and it's not as hard as you thought. But when opposing counsel stands up, you don't know the script. He's asking you about whether you file your tax returns on time, whether you lied in another case, whether you had an issue with another employer. This can be the scariest event in the world, because the other side has quite a broad latitude of questions. Suddenly you're racing through your past: "Did I ever do anything that could be embarrassing? Oh my goodness, where are they heading?"

Simply preparing a witness to take the stand and answer your own lawyer's questions is like showing a person how to start a fight by throwing the first punch but not how to defend himself. Your lawyer should anticipate how you and your witnesses are going to be cross-examined. He should walk each of you through a tough cross and predict questions that might be asked. The best thing that can happen in your case— better than a well-presented direct examination—is for the opposing lawyer to bear down, thinking he's going to draw blood through a tough cross, and you and your witnesses are prepared. Your answers are tough, on the money, and correct. The jurors look at you and think, "Wow! That's *really* credible because those aren't puffball questions being asked by your own attorney. You stood up to some tough examination, and you didn't waver!"

If your lawyer meets with a witness over coffee and says, "Look, I'm going to put you on the stand, and these are the few things I'm going to ask you. Are you OK with that?" and your witness is glad because it didn't take long and he can get back to work, stop and realize something's missing. Where's the other part of this? What tough questions is the witness going to be asked by the other side? Insist that your attorney also run though some of those—and not simply by outlining the possible areas for cross-examination, but by actually practicing the question and answers.

I take my clients into a conference room, put them in a chair over in a corner, and ask them some extremely tough questions. To make it more effective, I'm standing up and they're sitting. I interrogate them while I bore in their eyes. They'll suddenly realize, "Wow! This is uncomfortable! I'm in this chair, I'm stuck, I've got to answer this guy's questions. And he's looking aggressively at me."

No witness should feel those sensations for the first time in a courtroom. A lot of lawyers think, "If I'm too tough on my own client, I'll shake him up before trial or piss him off."

I definitely think you and your witnesses should feel the hot water before you're in the courtroom. Letting a witness know what a good cross is like helps prepare him to give solid answers. Sometimes I'll have my partner come down the hallway and cross-examine my client or an important witness. The client may decide that he hates that partner forever. When the trial is over, however, the client wants to go hug that partner. He realizes that the opposing counsel was very tough, but the partner was just as tough, and the partner prepared him for those difficult questions, which were asked in a fast, heated way.

Cross-examination is something few lawyers do well. Some use cross-examination as a way of discovery: they ask questions they don't really know the answer to and get burned, or they try to create a *Perry Mason* moment in court that doesn't quite come off right. If it's done correctly, your lawyer will be able to use cross-examination to get the other side to admit the weakness of its case on the stand. A good cross is usually short and succinct, and short, quick answers are given. The lawyer knows exactly what the answers will be. In fact, it can sound like the lawyer is testifying:

ATTORNEY: You *admitted* that you didn't stop at the red light, isn't that correct?

WITNESS: Yes.

ATTORNEY: And you *were* drinking on that particular evening, isn't *that* right?

WITNESS: Yes.

In a bad cross-examination, you can almost hear the tentative tone in the lawyer's voice; "Well, did you have something to drink on the night of the, uh, accident?" And he timidly waits for the answer. A lawyer who's conducting cross-examination correctly usually leaves very little room for the witness to testify, because at this point, the lawyer is telling the jury what the admissions are.

In some cases, cross-examination is used to show that the party on the other side is a hothead. It affects the likability factor of the other party, and it also might affect his credibility. When someone gets angry, he may forget his themes, his case, and he might blurt out something that undermines his case.

Lawyers are looking for hot buttons. It starts as early as the depositions, when they're testing to see how they can annoy you. Are you more irritated in the morning or the afternoon? Many good lawyers are watching in the deposition to see, "Ah, this person drinks a lot of coffee, good. When he goes to lunch, he'll probably drink coffee, so I should get him right after he comes back." Or, "Hey, for whatever reason, he seems to go to sleep, and maybe I can catch him asleep at the wheel."

Temper in a courtroom is rarely a positive. People don't like hotheads. Your lawyer can be passionate and outspoken. You can be passionate about your case, but to lose your temper is a bad idea.

Witness preparation should help you and your witnesses understand what the process is like and provide suggestions for rephrasing answers, but the lawyer shouldn't give you an actual script and tell you to memorize it. I prefer to have my own script, where I write questions with proposed answers, but then I let the client or the witness formulate their own answer. I know my proposed answer and their answer, and we may go over it few times, but ultimately I want witnesses to give their own free and natural answer within the guidelines of what's relevant and what might be helpful to the case. That kind of preparation is helpful, but the overbearing preparation that causes a witness to come off as unnatural is silly. The witness looks like someone who's been programmed.

The Longest Day

Trials require great stamina for the attorney, but ask anybody who's ever testified as a witness in a case, and he'll tell you it's one of the single most exhausting processes he has ever endured. If you can recall the most difficult exam you ever took, being a witness in a trial is twenty times more exhausting than that.

If you're on the stand for even an hour, it's exhausting. Some witnesses can be on the stand for half a day, a day, or even more. And they're constantly being peppered with questions, aren't allowed to take frequent breaks; they're just sitting there, answering, maybe drinking a glass of water. First thing in the morning, a witness may be crisp, alert, adrenaline flowing. He'll give good testimony. He gets a little relaxed that the courthouse experience isn't as bad as he thought, and he goes to lunch across the street at an expensive restaurant. He loads himself up with heavy food, gets back in the courtroom—and some courtrooms don't have windows or good circulation—now he's fighting to stay awake. He's on the stand and feels exhausted; there's been a letdown. A lot of courts have a lunch break of an hour or an hour and a half. That's a long time to go if your adrenaline was high for three hours in the morning, and you ate a heavy lunch and didn't walk around to get some fresh air, but went right back into that stuffy courtroom.

Eat light when it's your day in court. Don't be famished, because that can work against you. Sometimes I think a trial lawyer actually needs to know a little about blood sugar levels and stamina! If somebody on the stand is diabetic, your lawyer should know that. Or if somebody has a hard time concentrating after a few hours, your lawyer should know that. If someone gets migraines, you should know that, and make sure he brings his medication.

I tell my clients to bring an apple or some fruit to court. You can go outside and eat it. Know how your body works, and put it in a position where you can be focused, sharp, and crisp. Keep your blood circulating by running in the morning, doing sit-ups at night, or walking around the courthouse during lunch a few times.

See the Sausage Being Made

When a presidential candidate is going to give an important speech at a convention, often he'll visit the podium the day before, look around, and give a dry run. One of the ways you and every witness can learn quickly about this process is to go down to your local courthouse where the case is going to be tried. Ask one of the bailiffs or courtroom personnel where a jury is being picked on that particular day. Go watch how it's done. Ask where a trial is occurring, and watch some opening arguments and see a few witnesses take the stand.

You should not be learning about the trial process the very first time you walk up to the stand. Get a feel for the court. Think about and prepare for the process.

If you're testifying in court, you're going to be worried and intimidated. You'll be in a big government building; you'll walk in and get up on that stand. Maybe the courtroom has windows, or maybe it doesn't, and it's hot and there's no air-conditioning. Maybe the nearest water is a drinking fountain several courtrooms down. Maybe you'll see that the judge is in a bad mood or the bailiff is cross. Maybe there's a very narrow passageway between counsel table and the witness stand, which you'll need to walk through. You don't want to trip over anything on your long walk to the stand.

I urge each of my witnesses, especially those who I think have the time or are near the courthouse, to go down, walk into the courtroom, see the judge, and watch the courtroom in action. Get a feel for the physical layout and see how close or far away from the jury you are. Is there a microphone?

Also, a good trial lawyer will call in each of your witnesses and draw a picture for him: this is where you will be, this is where the jury will be, this is where the judge sits, and I'll be standing here when I ask the questions. This may sound pretty basic, but it's important because it affects people's comfort level when they're in court.

Trial Prep Costs

If your lawyer is working on an hourly basis and you have a budget, trial preparation needs to be regulated. If you have a simple case, maybe you can meet with the witnesses as a group with your attorney. Go over the basic fact pattern with each, and tell them to call your attorney if they have any questions. Then just go in and try your case. By the way, you shouldn't be afraid of doing that.

Watch out if the trial lawyer is on an hourly basis and when the trial nears, you start getting huge bills. At this point you've probably become somewhat used to the litigation process, and you understand how to assess the cost of a deposition or a document request. But now you're seeing items like "Pretrial preparation . . . 8 hours," "Pretrial preparation . . . 10 hours," and "Pretrial preparation . . . 14 hours." Your lawyer may actually be spending those full eight to fourteen hours a day on your case, or he may actually be spending a very soft eight to fourteen hours a day.

Just watch those bills carefully right before trial. Sometimes overbilling arises from overpreparation. Again, witnesses testifying as though they were reading from a script aren't useful.

The Trial

A jury consists of twelve persons chosen to decide who has
the better lawyer.

—Robert Frost, American poet

A trial is unlike any other part of the litigation process. Up to this
point, when you've sought rulings from the court on motions, you've
been dealing exclusively with a judge and maybe a discovery referee,
educated individuals with legal backgrounds trained to look at your
case objectively. In theory, they have been dispassionately analyzing
and making legal rulings on your case.

In a jury trial, however, the focus changes dramatically. The
emphasis shifts to the presentation itself, and to how a group of individuals culled from the community view your case. They're not law-
school-educated; they don't have a legal background. They're going
to look at your case in a much more fundamental way: Who's good?
Who's bad? Who did something right? Who did something wrong?
Who's likable? Who's credible? And they'll fit the decisions they

make along these lines into the legal issues presented when they return the verdict.

A trial is technically a fact-finding expedition where the jurors don't determine what the law is—that's predetermined—they determine facts that are in dispute. Was the light green or red? Did the doctor operate on the right patient or the wrong patient? Did the book fairly cite or improperly borrow from the other book? Those are all factual issues.

The jury doesn't decide what the elements of a particular claim are. The judge instructs them as to what the law is. In a breach of contract action, for example, the plaintiff has to prove there was a duty. Well, proving that may require the jury to read a contract and decide whether somebody in fact assumed a duty. And that might require deciding what somebody meant in a particular closure or paragraph, and what the person's intentions were at the time he signed the document.

Juries make factual decisions about liability and damages, then report those factual findings in a general or special verdict. To do this, they watch the two sides present their case by presenting live testimony, reading depositions, and introducing exhibits into evidence. All of the testimony and exhibits must be "admissible," according to rules that regulate the type of evidence a party can submit to the jury. Submitting admissible testimony and exhibits to the jury in some kind of orderly, effective fashion is the basis of a trial.

The Courtroom as Theater

Law professor Steven Goldberg, in his penetrating book, *The First Trial: Where Do I Sit? What Do I Say?* suggests it's useful to think of a trial as a theatrical production. Some people are uncomfortable with this analogy because theater is fiction; if a trial is theater, then it's not getting at "the truth." In fact, the height of naïveté is thinking that a jury can magically discern which of two people on the stand is telling the truth and which is lying, so that justice prevails. A trial is theater in that information must be presented to the jury in a way that interests and impresses the audience, emphasizing and driving home the important facts that will help ensure that the jury understands what is occurring and makes the right decision. Like it or not, *how* something is said can become just as important as *what* is said.

If a trial is a play, then the trial lawyer is the director. It is his job to rehearse the players, advise them how best to deliver their lines, decide who gets more stage time, and keep the show moving toward its goal. He shapes the drama by cutting unneeded or unhelpful scenes and by spotlighting and adding importance where necessary. The good director must be aware that he is moving toward his goal, because trial theater is competitive, and there are in fact two directors—the plaintiff's lawyer and the defendant's lawyer—who are vying to have their client's story understood and accepted.

Your trial lawyer is using your script, since you are the client. It's your story; you are author as well as primary actor. The trial lawyer must take his actors (the witnesses) as they come, but he will try to bring out their best performances. He must also keep his eyes and ears open at all times, watching the judge, the jury, the witnesses, his opponent, and making hundreds of quick decisions. He constantly evaluates how the show is playing and makes cuts, additions, and revisions on the fly. He is also a key actor as well as a director, so he must have a strong presence that the jury responds to and will focus on.

It's important to have a trial lawyer you're comfortable with, because each one has different views on what's important in a trial. Each has his own style, techniques, and even antics for how to pull off a trial.

Chronology of a Trial

A typical jury trial begins with the arrival of a group of jurors (a jury panel), from which you, your opponent, and the judge select the people who will compose the jury. Some alternates also are usually chosen, in case a juror is unable to complete the case. The jury is then put in the box, and the judge reads some opening instructions on the jurors' duties. The plaintiff and then the defendant deliver opening statements. If there are multiple plaintiffs and/or defendants, they'll go in order: plaintiffs first, defendants last.

The plaintiff then puts on his case. The plaintiff's lawyer calls his first witness and asks questions (the direct examination). When he finishes with a witness, the defense attorney has an opportunity to question that witness (the cross-examination). The plaintiff's lawyer is permitted to ask any follow-up questions he may have, as is the defense attorney, until each has no more questions.

The plaintiff goes through the presentation of his case this way, calling witnesses (who are cross-examined by the defense), presenting exhibits, and reading testimony from depositions of witnesses who are not present in court. When he's finished putting on his case, the plaintiff rests.

The defendant usually then files what's called a Motion for Directed Verdict, arguing to the judge that the case need go no further, because the plaintiff has not put into evidence sufficient facts for the jury to make a finding of fact in the plaintiff's favor. This motion is usually (but not always) overruled, and then the defense puts on its case in much the same way the plaintiff does—calling and examining witnesses (whom the plaintiff's lawyer can cross-examine), presenting exhibits, and reading deposition testimony. The defense rests its case at some point, and then the plaintiff can put on a rebuttal case, if he chooses. This means the plaintiff can actually respond to the defendant's case, but he has to stay within the bounds of what the defendant's witnesses say. He can't just go back to square one and start his case all over again or introduce new, unrelated evidence.

The plaintiff and defendant may each put on expert testimony, usually toward the middle or end of their "case." Experts are not typically the first witnesses out of the box.

After the defendant has rested and any rebuttal case has been made, the plaintiff's attorney makes a closing argument to the jury, summing up and interpreting the evidence and asking the jury to bring back a verdict in favor of his client. The defense attorney then does the same. The plaintiff's attorney is allowed to address the jury again, and has the last word.

The judge decides what jury instructions apply and what the verdict form will look like, and he reads those instructions to the jury. The jurors are dismissed into a jury room, where they confer and render a decision. Once they have, they come back into the court, and the verdict is read aloud by either the foreman or the judge. One of the lawyers may request that the jury be "polled," which means the judge will ask each juror what his individual vote was on each issue, to make certain the count was correct and the required number of votes were actually made. Some jurisdictions require unanimous verdicts; others require nine out of twelve, six out of nine, and so on.

After the verdict comes in, the judge makes a formal record of the jury's verdict, which triggers some time periods by which the loser must make certain filings if he wishes to challenge the verdict (see Chapter 18).

A Jury or a Bench Trial?

As I explained earlier, the difference between a jury and a bench trial is that in a jury trial, a group of jurors hears the case, while in a bench trial the judge (acting without a jury) decides liability and damages. A bench trial can be advantageous for certain types of cases and less desirable for others. For example, let's say you have a case where the focus is on what we would call general or direct damages. You buy my car, pay me $3,000, and give me a note for $6,000; the note is due and payable in a year. A year comes and goes, and you don't pay me, so I sue you for breach of contract. Maybe you allege that I misrepresented to you that the car was in top condition, but you found the engine had some problems and had to have some work done, so you want to offset the cost of the work. That's why you're withholding payment.

If I decide that this appears to be an honest disagreement, and I just need someone to decide who's right and how much I should get paid, why would I have a jury trial? I'm willing to submit this case to a judge for several reasons: First, I'm not looking for a passionate verdict; I'm looking for someone who can just be a good arbiter and make an honest and fair decision. Second—and what everyone should know—if I ask for a jury trial, my case is going to be significantly more expensive, probably by a factor of at least 20 percent.

There are several reasons why a jury trial is more expensive. When preparing for a bench trial, you don't need to prepare jury instructions, so you don't have to pay your lawyer to draft them. Also, the judge usually loosens the rules of evidence and requires that the parties agree to the admissibility of certain documents. The rules of evidence are less of an issue. Let's say you want to prevent the other side from introducing some evidence you feel would be unduly prejudicial against you. You could file a motion telling the judge what evidence you don't want to have presented at trial, and the judge might grant your motion. But in just making the motion you're showing the evidence to the judge, the finder of fact, the person you don't want to hear the evidence in the first place. The motion becomes almost pointless. Thus, there are fewer trial motions. The judge also moves the case along a lot faster if there's no jury. Plus, you're not going to pay for your lawyers to sit there while the jury is out waiting for the verdict; the judge will usually take the case under submission and then report the decision back to you some other time, unless he issues a decision right at the end of the bench trial.

Another advantage of bench trials is that in court systems with too many cases and not enough courtrooms or jurors, a bench trial will generally take place much sooner than a jury trial. I've had cases where the wait for a jury trial would have been at least a year and maybe two or more, but we were able to schedule a bench trial within five to eight months from when we filed our complaint.

So, if you want a case to conclude sooner, if you're paying hourly and want to save money, and if your case is not one of high drama and passion where you could hit a home run with a jury but are willing to live with an intelligent person's decision, then a bench trial might be for you. The cases I tend to take before judges are strong on merits, and they don't have elements of emotional distress, pain and suffering, or punitive damages.

If you're a plaintiff and are hoping for a runaway verdict, you don't want a bench trial. If you know a jury will react favorably to you and unfavorably to the big, bad defendant, then of course you're going to want a jury trial. Unlike juries, judges rarely enter judgments on the basis of passion.

Selecting Your Jury

Lawyers spend years learning how to pick a jury, and there are probably as many different ideas about how to do it as there are lawyers who pick juries. What you should remember is that you're pulling a certain group of people out of society. Unfortunately, a lot of professionals and people who are gainfully employed come up with excuses for why they shouldn't have to be on a jury. As a result, you often have a disproportionate number of retired or unemployed individuals, although not exclusively and not in every community. You generally need to factor this into your thinking about your case. From among the available group, your lawyer will be trying to select people who are most likely to be sympathetic to you or your position.

In fact, your lawyer is not as much selecting a jury as unselecting people you do not want to have on your jury. During a process called *voir dire* (literally, "tell the truth"), the judge and/or the lawyers ask questions of prospective jurors to find out information about them. In some jurisdictions you might get printouts about where each person lives, what his job is, and other basic information. If you own a small business, for example, and are being sued because of wrongful termination, then you probably want a bunch of other small-business owners on that jury. (Of course, the question becomes, How many are you really going to find who were willing to leave their businesses and actually serve on a jury?) What you probably *don't* want are a group of people who were fired from a job.

You have a certain number of peremptory challenges, where you can exercise an automatic right to get rid of certain jurors you don't want (the number of peremptory challenges varies from jurisdiction to jurisdiction). You can also challenge jurors for cause. For example, your attorney or the judge might ask the jurors questions like these:

- Do any of you know the defendant?
- Have any of you worked for the defendant?
- Have any of you had stock in the defendant?
- Are you Republican or Democrat?
- Do you think that all doctors commit malpractice?
- If I were to ask you your reaction to . . . what would it be?

In some jurisdictions judges allow the lawyers to ask few of those questions; in others, judges allow a great deal of latitude.

You should ask your lawyer what type of a juror he's looking to pick and why, and discuss this with him. Some of what your attorney relies on is intuition, and your own intuition may be just as good as the lawyer's. You might even want to sit with your attorney at counsel's table in the courtroom while *voir dire* is happening.

There should be a method to the madness, and you should understand what that is. Selecting a jury is not a scientific process, and no matter how much money you spend trying to figure out what the best jury is, an effective presentation and good facts are crucial. Many people believe that juries drive verdicts, and I've seen that in some cases. The truth is you could try the same case to two different juries and have two different outcomes. You don't ever want to underestimate the importance of jury selection. (When assessing settlement, you want to be thinking about what kind of jury you would be likely to get if you don't settle.) A lot of it depends on where your case is filed and what the potential jury pool is for that jurisdiction.

You could work with jury consultants if you have a big bankroll. Some outstanding firms do this, and the consultants usually have professionals who have studied psychology and understand jury dynamics and demographics. Many such companies have information about the average juror that they can pull out as soon as they know what the jury pool is. Some of them even shadow prospective jurors to find out things like where they work, what time they get home, and how they vote. Those firms can become elaborate in their analysis, which is why they're used primarily in cases where a significant amount of money is involved and the party can afford an expensive lawsuit. And while some lawyers may tell you to forget jury consultants because intuition works just as well, others will tell you that they offer tremendous benefits.

Jury Costs

Each jurisdiction has different rules on paying for the cost of a jury. In most jurisdictions, if you want to have your case heard by a jury, there are rules for when you have to post (deposit) jury fees with the court. In some jurisdictions, if you don't post those fees a certain number of days before trial, you waive your right to a jury. So if a jury is important to you, you should ask your lawyer months before trial what the last day is for filing those fees. Put it on your calendar, and ten days ahead of time, ask your lawyer if he has done it yet.

If you're really worried about the possibility of missing the deadline, tell your lawyer *you'll* pay the jury fees directly; ask him who to write the check to, and send it in. A lot of law firms have computer software to calendar important events or their own internal calendars. These usually contain all the deadlines for various tasks that have to be done on your case. If your lawyer's firm has such a system, you should ask for a copy of the calendar and know what those dates are. Law firms are just made up of people, and sometimes people forget to do things. You don't want your lawyer to forget to post jury fees and end up waiving your right to a jury.

Pretrial Motions

A whole assorted series of trial motions can be filed before trial, and these can affect the evidence and witnesses put on at trial. For example, your lawyer might file to exclude certain evidence. Let's say you're suing on breach of a contract. Somebody ordered fifteen cases of soda from your warehouse and didn't pay you. It turns out that you, the plaintiff and owner of the business, were pulled over the other night for driving under the influence, or maybe your brother who works in the business happens to have been a defendant in another lawsuit for not paying a bill. Those facts aren't relevant to this particular breach of contract case, but people on the other side might decide to play dirty pool. They want to try to distract the jury and pull a completely different issue into play, and your lawyer may decide to file a motion to preclude that evidence from coming in during the trial because it's not relevant.

This is called a Motion *in Limine*, and it's made either a few days or a week or so before the trial, or even on the first day of trial. The court rules on it either before trial or just as the issue comes up. In making such a motion, you might argue that an issue is not relevant to the case: "Your honor, please don't admit it"; or you might argue that although it *is* relevant, it's so highly prejudicial that the jury shouldn't consider it.

It's just about impossible for you, as a layperson, to determine what's relevant or not at trial. It's a hazy legal standard. Basically, anything is relevant if it bears on or is directly—or sometimes indirectly—related to the issues in the case. Relevance is a question for the judge to decide, and he may be ruling on this before or during the trial. What it comes down to is this: Is this evidence helpful to the jury in deciding the question of fact? Does it bear on the issue of credibility? Sometimes, as the case moves forward, a judge's opinion of what's relevant may change. If the trial is taking longer than expected, he may have another case or two or three backed up. If he feels that you've gone far beyond the time that he had allotted for the case, he may suddenly decide that relevance is a very strict standard. He may use relevance as a way of limiting testimony and moving the case along.

You might also file a Motion to Preclude an expert because the expert wasn't properly designated, or a Motion to Preclude a witness because the witness wasn't identified by the other side. Those are issues that your lawyer would identify in determining whether a pretrial motion should be filed. Remember to have your lawyer go over with you any pretrial motions that are going to be filed, and make sure you know why they are being filed. (Remember, if you are paying hourly, these can be expensive.)

Decisions About Witnesses

Who should testify in your case? What should the order of presentation be? Who should be your first witness? Who should be your last witness? Where does your expert witness fit in the presentation? What will have the most impact and make the case easiest to understand?

Decisions about who your witnesses will be are important. If your attorney picks a witness who is discretionary and not really necessary to the case, and the witness turns out to be a horrible liar who brings a lot of baggage, that could be a disaster. The fallout from that one witness could taint an otherwise very good case. Jurors have emotional reactions to people and to evidence. If a witness leaves a bad taste in their mouths, they may get hung up on that. They may talk about it at lunch and at dinner with their wives or husbands when they go home, and again the next morning. They may not really be listening to the important testimony that follows.

What Your Lawyer Should Consider

So your lawyer has to be considering who will be a good witness. Who's really necessary? How can he best help present the story? In the end, you're presenting a story, one that you've lived; it's your life.

You and your lawyer have been sorting through this and talking about it for a year, maybe two or three years, but the jurors are walking into the courtroom from their jobs and lives and don't know who you are. They don't know anything about this case, and it's going to be coming at them in bits and pieces. In truth, a jury trial is told in a very awkward start-and-stop fashion. In a perfect world, one individual would take the stand and dispense a summary of all the testimony in chronological order, and that, along with an organized notebook of exhibits, would be the presentation to the jury. In practice, the jury may only follow bits and pieces of the lawyer's opening statement, where a verbose attorney stands before them and talks about the totality of this case. Following this opening statement is the opening statement by the other side's attorney, who will dispute the first attorney. He'll wander all over the place, and his recitation of events may be entirely different. Then the witnesses testify.

The order of witnesses may be based purely on their availability. So one witness talks about one part of the case, and the next witness gets on the stand and begins talking about an entirely different part of the case. It could be several days into the trial before the jurors actually figure out what the heck those two or three people testifying have to do with any part of the case.

As in a theater production, a lot of thought has to go into who should testify, when those people should testify, what exhibits should be used, and how those exhibits should be presented. Should they be handed to the jurors? Some jurisdictions allow you to "publish a document," i.e., hand it to a jury.

Libraries of books could be written about the order of presentation in a trial, and this book is only a general overview of issues facing litigants. Some lawyers feel that the first witness you put on should be an innocuous witness who's not going to be subjected to too difficult a cross-examination, who may actually paint the general story line of your case. At the start of the trial, everyone, including the lawyer, is a little nervous, so the idea is to avoid drawing blood right away. Other lawyers will say, "The start of a trial is when the jurors are paying the most attention, and with every hour their attention's going to wane. Let's put on our best and most effective witnesses right away, before the jury gets tired and bored."

So there are different schools of thought, and I don't think one is necessarily correct. One trial lawyer I worked for used to talk about witnesses and their testimony as being the equivalent of people carrying buckets of water up a hill. You don't want to give one person too many buckets. He was trying to explain that if you asked an individual to testify to too much information, the witness would eventually burn out on the stand, get confused, or become overwhelmed and have a hard time keeping all the facts straight. This could disrupt the presentation or confuse the jury.

Once, an expert witness was covering a vast amount of territory in his testimony, and the issues were intricate. At one point he got so nervous about mixing things up that he just drew a blank and had to take a time-out right in front of the judge and jury. He was horribly embarrassed, and although it was a light moment, I think it undercut the expert. If your lawyer overburdens any one witness, just like people carrying buckets of water up a hill, they may actually spill some.

Your lawyer should look at what evidence he needs to get in. Is it evidence that the light was green and that the person driving was sober? Which witnesses can best testify to this? Maybe the person on the street corner will testify to what time of day it was and whether the light was red or green, and somebody who was a passenger in the car will testify as to the activity of the driver. Had the driver just gone to a tavern? Was he sober? Was he driving above or below the speed limit? Finally, the police officer who arrived on the scene can testify to the traffic ticket he gave and what he saw. We could try to have the police officer testify about everything, but then there may be questions about admissibility. Maybe he would have to go beyond firsthand knowledge and begin to speculate.

Your lawyer needs to take the story and break it up as if serving a pie. Maybe he'll give a different piece to each witness. Do you give the biggest piece to the person with the most firsthand knowledge of the story? Can different people tell the same part of the story? Which ones can tell it best? And who has too much baggage, so your lawyer wants to unload some or all of what that person can say onto another witness?

Your lawyer should have been thinking about these things when he prepped the witnesses. He should have gauged whether each witness cares about the case, will make a good witness, is alert, and might have a problem in cross-examination. Your lawyer should evaluate how he did in the mock cross-examination.

The Verdict Form

When the jurors adjourn to the jury room to decide the case, they will work with a verdict form. As they arrive at a verdict, they have to check a certain number of Yeses and Nos in order to formally render their verdict. Criminal cases are very simple: do you find the defendant guilty or not guilty? But civil cases are different; the jury may have to answer a complex array of questions to arrive at a verdict. For example, in a breach of contract case, they'll have to answer these questions: Do you find that there was a duty? Do you find that there was a breach? Do you find that the breach was material? Do you find that the breach was the proximate and actual cause of damages? Do you find that there were damages? Do you find that the defendant had mitigated damages? Do you find that the defendant acted with malice? What do you find are the damages?

An amazing number of jurors don't really understand how all these questions correspond to each other. They're used to the high drama of a single yes or no, guilty or not guilty, but they may have eight questions plus instructions that say, ". . . If you answer Yes to Number 2, go down to Part 5 and answer the three final questions. Do not answer Numbers 3 or 4 unless you answered No to Number 1 . . ." It can be enormously helpful for your lawyer to go through the verdict form with the jury.

I often blow up the verdict form into a very large size and walk the jury through it. The judge gives the jury detailed, often bland, legalistic instructions about how to evaluate the evidence. Interpreting those instructions can be like reading a phone book. Therefore, I often use a significant part of my closing argument to say, in effect, "This is what we believe we proved, but now let me interpret the judge's instructions in plain English to explain how you should do your job." Then I show the blowup of the verdict form and tell the jury in simple terms, "If you don't check these five boxes right here on the form, we don't win." I show the judge's wording of the jury instructions, because a lot of judges object to a lawyer recasting or recharacterizing them. In my experience, jurors appreciate the help in understanding what they need to do, what boxes they need to check for you to win or, if you're a defendant, for the other side not to prevail.

Conducting Yourself at Trial

The jury will watch every move you make. The jurors are not allowed to interact with you or, in most jurisdictions, to ask questions. They just sit and take in the evidence. They have no place to go, so they watch everybody. They see what you wear and hear what you say. When they get dismissed, they'll be near you in the cafeteria or on the elevators.

The best behavior in the courthouse is what I like to call "church behavior." That means you wear a good suit, look nice, and act pleasant and polite, even where your opponent is concerned—especially where your opponent is concerned. If you and the other party are walking up to the front of the court at the same time, hold the door open for him.

Now, when I say wear a good suit, I do not mean that you shouldn't be yourself. It would look disingenuous for a rock star to wear a Brooks Brothers suit and cut his hair short. You need to be who you are but mindful that the courtroom is a place of respect, that you're before a judge, and that the system should be held in esteem.

Some clients forget the jury is evaluating their behavior. Some are so anxious about their lawsuit that they berate their attorney about judgment calls he makes during the trial. Or maybe someone is testifying, and the client gets all worked up and starts talking loud enough for the jury to hear. Those types of actions bother jurors. If you're rude to your attorney, the judge, or the people in the courtroom in general, the jurors won't like you. That enters into the equation of how they vote. Sometimes jurors return a verdict in favor of people they don't care for, but if it's a close call and they dislike you, they probably won't find for you.

When you're on the stand, face the jury as much as possible, but not so much so that it looks unnatural. You don't want to be staring at the floor, looking away from the jury constantly, or focusing only on your attorney.

When you're under direct examination, you're probably fairly relaxed and make eye contact with the judge and the jury. When you're being cross-examined, the jury will scrutinize everything: Are you fidgeting? Are you looking away? If you can't look the examiner straight in the eye when he asks a tough question, a lot of people may think that's because you feel uncomfortable about the question. Jurors pick up on a lot of things. If you're sitting with your arms crossed, they may think that you're uptight and defensive.

When you're in the courtroom, the cafeteria, or even a restaurant close by, don't talk with your lawyer about the case unless he knows that no one else is around and that you have privacy. And when you're in court and think, "Wow! My lawyer just asked a great question! I think we destroyed their case! What an admission!" or, "Oh, that was an embarrassing remark!" resist the temptation, as you're leaving the courtroom, to remark about it to your lawyer. You may think that no one else will hear you, but three jurors and opposing counsel could be behind you. Also, if you attempt to unduly influence jurors by talking about your case in front of them, the case can be declared a mistrial, and you might have to start all over again. That could be very expensive.

In a trial, everyone's senses are acute, and everyone is listening closely. Just talk about the weather and keep things to yourself, even facial expressions, until you're somewhere where you're certain you can have a private moment to share what you want with your attorney.

Who's in Charge of Your Case?

Your lawyer—and not this book—will decide how best to present your case. Therefore, what *you* need to be assured of if you're going to trial is that you have a *trial* lawyer. Well before you get close to a trial and probably before you retain anyone, it's very appropriate to ask a lawyer who advertises himself as a trial lawyer how many trials he's been involved in. If he says, "Oh, ten, twelve . . ." say, "Could you do me a favor and send me a list of the case names?" Maybe the lawyer has actually tried only three cases before a jury. This doesn't mean you shouldn't hire him, because he could be a civil litigator who tried three very complex cases and won them all. But you want to know you have a trial lawyer, someone who knows the judges and the way around a courtroom. That way, you can place your trust in him.

If you like to micromanage your attorney, the trial can be a disaster for you. The time to let go, if you haven't already, is at the trial.

Your lawyer has a huge, stressful stage production to worry about, and he has to make, if not dozens, then hundreds of instant judgment calls during the trial. When is the right time to ask a question? When shouldn't he ask a question? When shouldn't he admit an exhibit he thought was going to be helpful? When should he challenge the judge? When shouldn't he? When should he approach the jury? When should he raise his voice? When should he put you on the stand? When shouldn't he?

Once you've gotten to the trial, once you've gone that far with your attorney, he's your lawyer. He's driving your car. If you try to yank the wheel away from him, you're both going to crash. The lawyer will start to tense up even more. Remember, a sharp lawyer generally has sound intuition. If you make your lawyer uptight, if he's crippled because you're hovering over him every second, his intuition may go haywire. Trial lawyers are sometimes like athletes, and athletes who are uptight and self-conscious don't have a free range of movement. They might strike out (or miss the basket or double-fault or throw an interception—pick your own sports metaphor). There's a lot of pressure in the courtroom already, even for lawyers with nerves of steel. Don't be self-destructive and drive your lawyer crazy during trial.

By the time you get to trial, you've usually worked with your lawyer for at least ten or twelve months. You might decide at this late point that your lawyer isn't the most eloquent speaker or as charismatic as you'd like. Even so, you're probably going to do a heck of a lot better if you support him and let him do the best job he can. He may surprise you. Being a trial lawyer is one of the most draining processes you can imagine. You don't want to be in the background whispering at him constantly, distracting him, shoving little notes under his nose.

You and your lawyer should probably agree on a protocol for how to discuss issues during the trial. Perhaps your lawyer will take breaks, and at the breaks you and he can go over your notes. Or maybe you'll write on a pad in front of you, and if your lawyer has the time, he'll look down at your notes. But don't scribble furiously and shove your notes emphatically in front of his face. Neither he nor the jury is going to appreciate that. You need a protocol your lawyer is comfortable with. He is the one who has to perform.

What if You Win?

Suppose you get a good judgment. Can you collect? As I mentioned earlier, investigative services can do financial searches and report the financial holdings of a company before you even file your suit. They may charge a few hundred or even a few thousand dollars, but getting some basic information may be useful.

The defendant may appeal and may post a bond and secure a "stay" to prevent your collecting before the appeal is heard (see Chapter 18). If there is no appeal, do not assume that your law firm, which specializes in trials, also specializes in collections. Nine times out of ten it does not. You might want to hire a law firm that specializes in collection or a collection agency.

In most jurisdictions, if the judgment is entered but not paid, you can take what's called a Debtor's Exam of the non-paying defendant. This is a deposition you can take at the courthouse from someone who owes you on a judgment. In fact, with certain exceptions, you can probably even take personal assets from the person when he shows up that day. In some jurisdictions, you can take the very car he drove up in. There are also generally processes where you can file certain paperwork, often called a Writ of Execution, and then use local law enforcement officials to go out and seize assets.

Some people are totally undone as soon as they realize the losing party isn't going to whip out a check and pay at the end of trial. Sometimes they just give up, figuring the judgment is worthless. But a good collection firm can often collect very quickly and effectively. Such a firm knows how to put leverage on the other side by garnishing wages or putting liens on bank accounts or other property.

Remember, though, if you push too hard, the defendant may file for bankruptcy. If that happens, you'll need to consult with a bankruptcy specialist, because some claims are discharged in bankruptcy and others are not.

How many times do I have to win this case?

APPEALS

The Appeals Process

A defendant is entitled to a fair trial but not a
perfect one.

—U.S. Supreme Court

An appeal is a formal request to have a "higher" court review a ruling
of a "lower" court. You can also appeal rulings made by an administrative body and, in some cases, ask a court to set aside the decision
of an arbitrator.

An appeal is heard by the next higher court in a given court
system. After a trial in state court, for example, you would take an
appeal to the state's court of appeal. If you were on the losing side
of that appeal, then you might be able to appeal in your state
supreme court. The term *state supreme court* refers to your state's
highest court. Different states may have different terms to refer
to their intermediate (appeals) court and their highest (supreme)
court.

Your Right to an Appeal

Any party to a lawsuit who is dissatisfied in part or in whole with the outcome may file an appeal. The party filing the appeal is called the appellant, and the party opposing the appeal becomes the respondent. Typically, appeals are filed by a defendant who loses and wants to get the judgment reversed. However, a plaintiff who lost the case or didn't win everything he felt he should have can appeal to have most any part of the matter reconsidered. It's possible for both sides to appeal different aspects of the same case; one side would appeal, and then the other side would cross-appeal.

You have the right to one appeal to the court of appeal. To appeal a decision by the appeals court (that is, to appeal an appeal), in some states you have to first petition the state supreme court to see if the state supreme court will hear that appeal.

For matters of state law, your state's supreme court is generally the final word, and you can appeal no higher. In the federal court system, you can automatically make an appeal in federal district court. The losing side in that appeal may attempt to have the U.S. Supreme Court hear an appeal.

Basis for Appeal

You can't appeal every issue under the sun. Generally, appeals are made on technical grounds. The primary grounds for appeal are that the verdict in the trial was against the weight of the evidence or that a serious error of law was made in the lower court.

When looking to appeal, you examine the material rulings by the trial judge and look for mistakes. However, not every questionable remark or flawed evidentiary ruling from the trial judge forms the basis for an appeal. Unless you can show that an error was substantial, material, and affected the outcome of the case, it's considered a "harmless error" and carries no weight for the purposes of an appeal. If you argue on appeal that the judge below applied the law incorrectly on substantial matters in the trial, the court of appeal may agree with you and overturn the lower court's decision.

Determining whether the verdict was against the weight of the evidence—and should therefore be reversed—gets into an analysis of judgment calls made by the jury or the judge. In general, when it comes to issues like the credibility of a given witness, the court of appeal usually feels that the trial judge and the jury were uniquely situated to assess credibility. In few instances will a court of appeal revisit the issue of a witness's credibility based on a bland transcript.

The primary issues in an appeal generally involve questions like these: Did the trial judge fail to correctly apply the rules of evidence? Did he approve the wrong verdict form? Was a law not properly applied? Were there other significant irregularities in the trial? Did these mistakes affect the outcome of the case? Is there a legal issue about which the law isn't clear and that the court of appeal needs to clarify?

It's important to understand that the dynamic of an appeal is very different from the dynamic of a trial setting. Most people can relate to a trial because they know its purpose is to present a set of facts and circumstances, and the jury may have an emotional reaction to the evidence. In trial, the parties have a chance to pour out the story of what happened, and if they connect with the jury on an emotional level, they may get the verdict they want. Often, though, clients have a hard time understanding how this relates to the law specifically. For example, in a breach of contract suit, a lawyer knows that to prevail from a legal standpoint, he has to show a duty, a material breach, causation, and damages caused by the breach, and then he has to show that the damages were foreseeable within the contemplation of the parties. Very few individual litigants understand these essential elements; they just know that the other side breached the contract, and they feel it was wrong.

On appeal, however, the emotion is discarded, and the court views the case from a dispassionate, clinical standpoint. Maybe the court of appeal will find, based on its interpretation of the law, that the breach wasn't "material." Maybe there's some legal standard, a presumption, a burden of proof, or some slant in the law that completely changes the analysis of your case. Many clients have a hard time grasping such technical arguments and even more difficulty understanding how the court could reverse the case on this highly technical basis.

In most cases that are fairly straightforward, if the judge didn't make any egregious errors in admitting evidence or expert testimony, and if he used a standard court-approved instruction, one party may appeal, but the appeals court will probably just stamp "Affirmed" (meaning the verdict stands and will not be reversed) on a card and mail it back to the parties. Nothing further can happen. The appeal is over, and there's not even a published opinion. For the court of appeal to become interested and active on an appeal, the case must present unique, interesting legal issues, the judge below really must have failed to apply the law correctly, or something out of the ordinary, like juror misconduct, must have occurred.

Motion for a New Trial

Instead of filing an appeal with a higher court, a party may file certain motions with the trial court to try to nullify the verdict. Generally, the court allows a short time period, such as within ten days of the entry of judgment, for a party to file a Motion to Have the Judgment Set Aside Notwithstanding the Verdict. In this motion you ask the trial judge to reverse the jury's verdict and grant judgment in your favor. Usually, for a judge to decide to throw out the jury's findings, a flagrant or outrageous miscarriage of justice must have occurred.

Normally within the same ten-day time period after entry of judgment, the losing side can file a Motion for New Trial. A Motion for New Trial is almost a preview of the appeal, and argues errors in the court's application of the law to your trial. These kinds of motions are generally long shots, but some defendants are willing to pay their attorney to give one or both a try.

Filing a Notice of Appeal

To set an appeal in motion, a party taking an appeal must file a Notice of Appeal within a given time period. In most jurisdictions, the time period is thirty days after entry of judgment, but it varies by jurisdiction and may be as much as sixty days in some courts. If you fail to file a Notice of Appeal before the deadline, you lose your right to appeal, and it's extremely difficult to have the court grant an exception.

The Notice of Appeal itself is a short document, often only two or three pages long. It alerts the court and the respondent that the verdict is being appealed and puts them on notice in brief of the issues that are being appealed. The Notice of Appeal also divests the lower court of jurisdiction over your case. Therefore, once the Notice of Appeal is filed, the case is before the court of appeal.

Stay of Judgment

If you lost the case and were ordered to pay a judgment, filing a Notice of Appeal does not stay (delay payment of) the judgment. If you owe money, you will need to secure a Stay of Judgment Pending Appeal, which is a separate motion. To obtain a stay, you generally must file a bond that guarantees payment of the money award and indemnifies the party that won. Whether or not you succeed in obtaining a stay, your appeal will continue.

Posting a bond can be expensive. You have to go to a bonding company, which usually requires that you post cash or collateral in the amount of money totaling one and one-half times the judgment. Some people who lose a lawsuit and are required to put up cash are faced with the grim reality of a cash flow problem. Posting bond could be impossible. The cost is in addition to paying the other side's costs on appeal. (When you take an appeal, the losing side pays the winner's costs, just as at trial.) That could be another five or ten thousand dollars on top of everything else.

If you lose and opt to seek a stay and post a bond, your lawyer has to work with a bonding company, and you will most likely be required to make certain financial disclosures to the bonding company. Some parties don't want to do this and will abandon their appeal because they do not want their finances exposed.

If a bond is properly posted and a stay is entered, the winner can't collect the money or do anything toward collecting the judgment until the appeal is decided. The winner can sleep at night knowing that if the loser's appeal is denied and the loser has gone bankrupt, he has the bond. Once all remedies are exhausted on appeal, if any payment is due, it will generally follow in a short time—either from the loser or from the bonding company.

Many people decide to appeal and not post a bond. To keep the winner from collecting, they declare bankruptcy. Just because they declare bankruptcy, however, that doesn't necessarily mean the process of collecting is over. Things then shift to the bankruptcy court. (Consult a bankruptcy attorney.) Also, a declaration of bankruptcy by the defendant does not mean he won't proceed with his appeal.

Designating the Record

A set number of days after the Notice of Appeal is filed, both sides will get a notice from the court of appeal. The court is notifying the appellant that he has a certain number of days in which to "designate the record," that is, provide the court with a list (and eventually copies) of every pleading or transcript that bears on the appeal. Once the appellant has designated the record, the respondent gets to counterdesignate. If a given pleading or some testimony or other evidence is not designated at this stage, it cannot be brought up later to support or oppose the appeal.

A lot of clients who are paying hourly are somewhat mystified by the whole process of designating the record. It can be expensive, because your lawyer will have to spend hours and hours poring over the trial transcript and the pleadings, deciding exactly what should be a part of the record for purposes of the appeal. The appeal will be decided on the basis of the designated record only. You can't present new evidence, only that which was at issue in the lower court.

If you have a short record to designate, it might not be too costly for your lawyer to designate it. For example, let's say you filed a complaint, the judge dismissed it, and you decided to appeal. You would have a limited record: your complaint, the Motion to Dismiss that the other side filed, your opposition, their reply, and the judge's decision. The costs of designating the record in this kind of situation would be much less than if the appeal follows a full trial.

The big costs for designating the record come when a case has gone to trial and there are weeks or months of testimony to study. Then you'll pay a large sum of money to have one or more lawyers review all this material and designate the record. The issue of how expensive designating the record may be has everything to do with how much record exists and must be reviewed. Are there boxes of pleadings? Volumes of trial transcripts and other hearings that were transcribed and were important? Or is there just a very small file?

Once the appellant has designated the record, it's the respondent's turn. His lawyer will go through the same costly review and designate any additional parts of the record that he feels are important to his client's position.

Exchange of Briefs

Once both sides have designated the record, the appeals court issues a briefing schedule informing the parties of the dates when briefs must be filed in the appeal. This can vary greatly depending on what court and state you're in. The appellant may be ordered to file his brief within a month or five, six, or seven months later.

On the date specified in the briefing schedule, the appellant files what's called the Appellant's Opening Brief. Thereafter, the respondent has a set period of time—perhaps twenty or thirty days or longer, depending on jurisdiction—to file the Respondent's Brief and Opposition on Appeal. Thereafter, the appellant will file an Appellant's Reply Brief.

The court of appeal often agrees to give a longer period of time on the briefing schedule, if requested. The parties have a good deal of time to write these briefs, and the page limits are usually much greater than the page limits for motions below in a trial court. While a motion in the trial court may be limited to ten or twenty pages, the court of appeals may permit your lawyer to use twenty, forty, or even fifty pages to present his arguments.

Most jurisdictions have a formal requirement for a special format of an appeals brief. Often, you have to have a specific cover prepared by a professional print shop, use a specific kind of paper and a specific type font, and usually a specified number of copies must be filed at the court of appeal. Decisions at the appeals level are made by a panel of judges, so you must have the requisite number of copies to include all those judges, as well as the other side and, often, a copy for the court below.

Oral Arguments and Ruling

Once the three briefs just described have been exchanged between the parties and filed with the appeals court, there will be a hearing. During the hearing lawyers for the appellant and the respondent will make oral arguments and answer questions posed by the judges.

In my experience, oral arguments before the court of appeal generally have marginal impact on how a case will be decided. Appeals courts probably rule 90 percent on the papers filed and 10 percent on oral argument. Appeals judges want to know in a very black-and-white, bland way the material facts that underlie the issue, your view of the law, and what cases you can cite, and then they'll take it from there. They may limit oral argument to as little as five or fifteen minutes, so you can't bank on some great orator getting your whole story out. It's got to be written, and the judges don't respond to adjectives and rhetoric at all; they just disregard it. Some courts of appeal even deny oral argument in some cases.

Some appeals court judges will have made up their mind before any oral arguments. The court of appeal probably has resources that many lower-court judges do not have—the best clerks, the best libraries. The judge probably has a clerk work up a proposed decision with all the supporting memoranda and case law.

Most of the time the questions the judges ask the attorneys during oral argument signal whether they're following and considering the oral argument, or whether they have no interest because the appeal is just another run-of-the-mill case they're going to stamp "Affirmed" (i.e., appeal denied). Often, by the end of the oral argument, your lawyer will know whether you've succeeded with your appeal.

After oral argument, you wait to get the ruling. The period you may wait varies widely. In California state court, you have to wait up to ninety days to get a decision. The appellate process can move very slowly.

The overall timing for an appeal varies, but you're generally talking about three to six months from the Notice of Appeal until briefs are submitted—sometimes much longer—then another couple of months before the hearing, and then another few months before decision is required. It's not unusual to be up on appeal for a year or a year and a half. In some jurisdictions, the court of appeal has no deadline for issuing its ruling, and your case can sit there indefinitely. If the court of appeal overturns a case, the judges will issue a written judgment detailing their reasons for doing so.

While you usually have one automatic right of appeal to some court, after that it's not necessarily automatic. If you are dissatisfied with the appeals court's decision, you may have to ask the next highest court if it's even willing to get involved. The higher court isn't obligated to take every further appeal, and you may have to spend a lot of time and money just asking whether it will even consider your matter. Usually, your state supreme court will be interested only if it's an issue of "first impression" or an issue of a conflict in rulings between the courts.

Why You May Need an Appellate Specialist

It is unwise to assume that your trial lawyer is the best lawyer to handle your appeal. From an economic standpoint it may be beneficial to have your trial lawyer handle the appeal—after all, he's already up to speed and knows your case—but the appellate process is special. Some lawyers are appellate experts; that's all they do. And for good reason.

The rules of an appeal are distinct from the rules that relate to civil procedure before trial, and the goals are very different. The forum is also dissimilar. In most courts of appeal, you have three judges who sit on a panel. In some jurisdictions you may have five or six judges; the U.S. Supreme Court has twelve. The judges sit together in an elevated area at the front of the court, and the dynamics are unlike a trial court, where you have to deal with just one trial judge. Three or more judges are asking pointed questions, and they have different personalities—Republicans, Democrats, disparate appointees. Your lawyer must quickly figure out how to deal with this mix of personalities and effectively present your position.

Nearly every trial with a substantial dollar amount awarded has appealable issues. Sometimes small firms or contingency lawyers win a huge amount of money at trial on a personal injury or product liability case, only to be outmaneuvered on appeal by the large law firm. Large law firms are very well designed, positioned, and staffed to handle appeals. Often a large law firm will bring in a whole new set of lawyers to write and argue an appeal. In contrast, while many small and midsized firms do well with trials, they rarely have depth in appellate work, too. Therefore, I've seen a lot of trial lawyers from smaller firms do a great job and win $4 million at trial—then lose that $4 million on appeal. So as much as you may love your trial lawyer—because he tells great fireside stories, is passionate, and can make a spontaneous argument in front of the jury that can carry the day—he isn't necessarily the person you want writing your appellate brief.

Appeals panels are usually made up of judges who have esteemed academic backgrounds. Their background is in the law, and they know the law very well. The real issues on appeal are twofold: Was the law improperly applied? And is this an area where the law isn't clear, so we need to clarify it?

Appeals involve a careful academic study of the record below and the evidence admitted, then a detailed analysis of the governing cases. A good trial lawyer, who can take a good deposition on the run and be strong and dramatic in trial, may not have the resources or be suited to do this kind of sophisticated legal analysis. Appeals require a patient lawyer who reads cases upon cases upon cases, and who can make subtle distinctions between two or three cases. The trial lawyer may or may not have that aptitude.

The brief-writing process is one where you can be as involved as you'd like as a client, but unless you've gone to law school or otherwise been trained, it's very hard to tell whether the appellate brief is good. Again, you have to research and consider your options.

Because of the deadlines that you begin reaching soon after judgment is entered, you might plan, when hiring your lawyer at the start, for him to associate with another firm that has experience in dealing with appellate issues, if necessary. You won't have a lot of time after the judgment to quickly get up to speed on these time frames, and if you blow one of these deadlines, you're in big trouble.

How Much Will It Cost?

Many fee agreements are unclear as to what happens at the appellate stage. If you have limited funds and are going with a contingency fee lawyer, you'll want to resolve this up front when you negotiate the fee agreement. Some contingency fee lawyers will write their agreement so it gives them a loophole; if they don't want to handle an appeal, they can get out. Many plaintiff contingency fee lawyers will not accept the obligation to take an appeal if the case is lost at trial.

If you're working with a small firm, the perfect situation is for your lawyer to work with a firm in town that handles appeals, and to bring the firm in when needed. If you're a client on a contingency fee basis, the appellate boutique firms usually don't want to come in for a percentage. They want to work for a flat fee. Many cases are handled through trial on a contingency fee basis, but the appellate lawyers are paid a flat fee. Sometimes the costs of appeal are shared by the client and the lawyer, who are trying to preserve their victory below. Sometimes they'll be paid entirely by the client. In a lawsuit I handled through trial on a contingency fee basis, the plaintiffs won over $5 million. The other side, represented by a huge New York law firm with an entire appellate division, filed the expected appeal. My client decided to bring in a firm that specializes in appeals, paying that firm $50,000 to handle it.

From a budget standpoint, it won't cost much to have your lawyer file a Notice of Appeal. If you have a significant judgment against you, however, there is the related bond issue. Depending on the size of the judgment, that could be very significant.

It's not unusual for a significant appeal to cost—lock, stock, and barrel—anywhere from $15,000 to $30,000. (It can go as high as $50,000 to $100,000 in an extreme case.) These costs usually include, if you're the appellant, writing your opening brief on appeal and your reply brief. Your lawyer will probably spend hours and days preparing for the argument.

The Easiest Way to Blow a Winnable Case

One of the easiest ways to get your case reversed is through bad jury instructions. Some lawyers argue for jury instructions that are very favorable to their camp. The lawyer may know that the law doesn't really support those jury instructions, but he hopes the judge won't realize it. Or maybe the judge is so much in one side's camp that he's essentially going to read the jury *anything* that side gives.

This is a huge mistake. If you have a case you believe you're going to win, and you've picked the jury, don't do something that could come back to haunt you in a big way.

The reality is that very few jurors actually apply in detailed, rigorous fashion the law in those jury instructions. It's often too demanding; it becomes information overload. Jury instructions can sometimes go on and on for hours, and then the jury is told to take those instructions and apply the facts of a trial that may have gone two days or two months. The jury usually understands the general sense of the instructions, and some points will have been hammered home, but it's probably impossible for anyone to absorb complex jury instructions in one sitting.

Never have your lawyer submit to the judge a set of jury instructions that are not firmly founded upon the law and are not well accepted. If you do, you're setting yourself up for a reversal on appeal. It's the simplest way to lose, and it's the most common reason for reversing a trial verdict.

A production company sued actress Kim Basinger for breach of contract and won several million dollars. Basinger was able to get a reversal of the verdict on appeal, though, because the instructions and the verdict form were wrong. The instructions failed to distinguish between Basinger's loan-out company and Basinger herself, the owner of the loan-out company. As a result, the case was remanded (sent back to be tried over again).

Before your trial, ask your lawyer point-blank, "Are you taking an overly aggressive position in this verdict form or in these special interrogatories to go to the jury?" Similarly, if your lawyer knows that certain evidence should not come in at trial because it's highly prejudicial or the case law is clear that it shouldn't be admitted into evidence, don't let your lawyer introduce it, even as an apparent slip of the tongue. It may sway the jury heavily in your favor, but why impregnate a case with issues that are automatic reversals on appeal when you think you can otherwise win?

"Appealing" an Arbitration Decision

Technically, you can't "appeal" an arbitration decision. Unless the arbitration rules provide otherwise, in most cases the arbitrator's decision (the award) is final and binding on the parties. In practice, however, there are ways to attempt to have an arbitrator's award set aside.

In some cases the award must be presented to a court to be "confirmed" so it can be entered as a lawful judgment. Once that happens, the award becomes a legally enforceable court order. You can oppose confirmation of the arbitration award. Generally the winning party in an arbitration will file in court for the confirmation of the award. At this point, the losing party can file an opposition to the winner's petition for confirmation. He may also or instead bring an action to vacate the award (set it aside), although this is usually a long shot.

In general, to get an award tossed out, the loser must show that there was some form of fraud involved in securing the award or that the "neutral" arbitrator had a serious conflict of interest. If the loser can show that the award went beyond the arbitration agreement in some way, he may get the award vacated.

Appealing Decisions of Administrative Agencies

Most federal administrative agencies have appeals boards that hear appeals. Sometimes the agency itself hears appeals. The appropriate U.S. Court of Appeals will generally hear an appeal once the agency has made its "final action." Some appeals must be made in U.S. District Court. Your lawyer will need to research statutes for your particular situation. In general, though, it's hard to reverse decisions by administrative agencies.

You May Only Appeal "Final" Decisions

There are complicated rules about what you can appeal before the whole case is over, and what you can appeal earlier, before your case is over. Appellate courts generally require "finality" before an appeal. In some limited circumstances, you can go to the court of appeal and essentially say, "If you don't rule on this now, by the time we get to the end of the trial, it will be pointless for me to ask." If you lose a motion or ruling before trial and it appears to have a huge, potentially irreversible impact on your case, talk to your lawyer about what appeal options you may have, and when they're available to you.

19

Your Legal Bills

A man may as well open an oyster without a knife, as a lawyer's mouth without a fee.

—Barten Holyday, 17th-century English translator

Unless your attorney is working on a pure contingency basis, you'll receive a monthly bill from your lawyer for the legal costs and fees incurred in your case. (Often, you will receive a billing statement even when your case is being handled on a contingent fee basis.) You want to ensure that you're only paying for what's reasonable, fair, and required according to the fee agreement you signed, and you need to be satisfied that the time billed was actually expended on your matter and was necessary. It's important to understand how your lawyer generates your bill, what stages in a lawsuit are busiest (and therefore most expensive), and how your lawyer's various costs, staffing decisions, and travel expenses might impact your wallet. You want to understand as many of these issues as early as you can—in some cases, before you sign your retainer agreement.

How the Law Firm Generates Your Bill

A lawyer who charges by the hour must, of course, keep records of how he spends his time. Each day, an hourly lawyer records any time he spends on your matter, whether it's noting time on the phone, doing research, writing letters, or anything else. Some lawyers use software on their computers to record their time; they enter time information as soon as they finish a task, and the program keeps tallies. Others use a pad or dictating device to keep track of how they spend their time. Still others wait until just before they leave the office to reconstruct their day and estimate the time they spent on various tasks for various clients.

These systems have potential advantages and drawbacks. For example, a lawyer who estimates his time at the end of the day may forget a task or exactly how long it took and be forced to guesstimate. This can work for or against you. The computer programs, which automatically clock how long a lawyer spends drafting a given letter, do not distinguish between the time the attorney is actually working on the letter versus the time he was talking on the phone or down at the snack bar getting lunch. These programs can only measure how long a file concerning your case was sitting open on the lawyer's computer screen.

At the end of the month, the lawyer's time sheets are tallied up and a preliminary invoice sent back to the attorney or, in larger firms, to a billing partner (a partner responsible for overseeing billing issues). If the lawyer is busy, he may simply wink at the preliminary invoice, say it's OK, and send it out to you. On the other hand, if that partner is concerned with making sure the bill is fair and appropriate, he'll look at it carefully. A conscientious billing partner often "writes down" (reduces) certain portions of the billed time, effectively reducing the invoice. If there is an entry of nine hours to do something on the bill, the lawyer might think, "Well, I delegated that task to an associate, but that associate is still learning. In fairness to the client, that should have taken only six hours, so I'm going to strike out three and write this down to six hours." Or the lawyer may look at the preliminary invoice and say, "I know that task took nine hours, and I would have taken nine hours if I'd done it myself. but I know that this client is having some cash flow problems and we're trying to stay within basic budgetary guidelines, so I'm going to strike out some time here."

Lawyers' (or billing partners') decisions on whether to write off time are usually subjective. Some lawyers feel that, even if the lawyer put in twelve hours on a given day, that just doesn't look right. They're never going to allow a time entry of more than nine hours for any lawyer on a time sheet; they don't want that double digit to show up, so they'll reduce that entry. Some lawyers may think back to an estimate they gave the client for a certain task, and adjust the hours down to fit that estimate. Maybe the client was referred by another firm that sends a lot of business to this lawyer, and the referring firm asked the lawyer to keep the billings down. So the lawyer may routinely take a haircut on the time he's putting in for that client, as a courtesy to the referring firm.

At an appropriate point early on, it may not be a bad idea to ask your lawyer how and when he decides to write down time. Different lawyers have different policies. Some lawyers feel that if they write down even a minute of their time, they're undervaluing their service. Others routinely give their clients write-downs.

Before the lawyer sends the bill to you, he'll also see any costs being charged, the total bill, and any amount past due. Most lawyers will quickly assess whether that whole package seems fair and whether it can be sent to you without your getting too upset. Some, on the other hand, might simply pass their time on through, no matter how much.

Examining Your Legal Bills

When you receive that first bill from your lawyer, it's important to pull out your retainer agreement and make sure that the bill is consistent in terms of the agreement. Are the rates correct? If you have negotiated a special fee or arrangement, the law firm's accounting department will sometimes miss this and put in the lawyer's default rate structure. Make sure your bill is consistent with your agreement.

There's no real standard for how a lawyer's invoice will look. In general, you get a breakdown on your invoice so that you know what the lawyer did on any given day in which there is an entry. Some lawyers will give you short summary statements that simply tell how many hours they or their associates spent on your case that month, and they won't provide much description beyond that. Don't allow your lawyer to provide you an invoice of that type, because it doesn't give you any realistic basis for seeing what each lawyer did and how much time he spent doing it. Without this degree of detail in your invoice, you can't assess whether the lawyer is staying within the budget that you and he discussed, and you're unable to see which lawyers are more efficient.

You'll also be largely unable to learn much about how the law firm is handling your case. Sometimes, through no fault of their own, the lawyers may be spinning their wheels on things in your case that are not that important to you. But you'll only know this if you can identify each specific task the firm is working on. Also, a lack of detail on your bill can make it a lot harder down the road to get your reasonable legal fees reimbursed by the other side after trial if a contract or statute provides for you to recover these fees. The opposing parties could argue that they don't know what specific tasks you're asking to be reimbursed for, so they have no way to evaluate whether they're reasonable.

I would not accept an invoice that simply says, "John Smith . . . 10 hours," and, "Ann Smith . . . 4 hours." You want to see daily time entries by lawyer, what each lawyer was working on that particular day, and how much time he spent on it: "John Smith . . . conducted legal research in connection with Motion for Summary Judgment . . . 1.5 hours." I would even hesitate to accept an invoice that says simply, "John Smith . . . conducted legal research . . . 1.5 hours." If you get your first bill and see general entries like "conducted research," "telephone call," or "draft letter," you should meet with your lawyer right away and explain that you can't accept it. You need to see whom the calls were with, whom the letters went to, what they were generally about, and what the legal research generally concerned.

There's a fine line between asking for this and asking for too much detail. It's reasonable to expect a general explanation for each task a lawyer is billing, but it's unreasonable to expect a busy lawyer to spend eons of time creating, as a separate work product, his bill for the day.

If you have an active case and get a bill with lots of different entries for all sorts of different tasks, it is useful to reorganize that bill on paper and see the total for each given task during a month. You may be looking at a bill that shows preparation of a complaint, meetings with you, interoffice conferences about the preparation of the complaint, legal research, phone calls with you and with the messenger service that's serving the complaint, and so on. A day-by-day breakdown of what's going on can seem very fragmented. But when you put together the picture of what the lawyers are doing and how they're spending their time, you can start to evaluate where there may be areas you need to discuss.

If you just react that the total dollar amount of the bill is too high and demand a reduction, you're making a mistake. If a lawyer senses that your program is to always negotiate his invoice with him, regardless of the merits of the bill, he's going to resent this. The next time he goes through your bill for the first cut, he may be less likely to trim the fat off your bill. Why should he give you a break and write down a bill to start with, if you're always going to try to negotiate down every invoice no matter what?

If you go to a lawyer to talk about the bill, you really want to be prepared. Know what your retainer agreement says, what the budget was for the tasks at issue, and how much time was actually spent on those tasks. In addition to breaking down the bill by task (e.g., how much time was spent on drafting the complaint, how much on legal research, filing, and letters), you might want to analyze how much time was spent on telephone calls, interoffice conferences, and communications with opposing counsel.

This analysis might remind you about what the lawyer said about how much some of these tasks would cost, which would be relevant to discussing your bill. Now you can place the bill into some context. If the lawyer's interoffice conferences about the drafting of the complaint took as much time as the drafting itself, then maybe you want to ask some questions, in a way that doesn't put your lawyer on the defensive: "What was the purpose of those conferences? What did you accomplish during those conferences?" You don't want to discourage lawyer conferences, but you want to make sure that they don't get excessive or out of control.

After you get your bill and have a general reaction, you want to try to move toward a more specific analysis. When you get a handle on how much time is being spent on one type of task versus another, you position yourself to have a more intelligent discussion with the lawyer about whether he is within a budget or within your expectations. Now you're not just talking about the bottom-line dollar amount on the bill, but about how much time the firm spent to get a given task done.

You also don't want to get a bill for any time you spend discussing your bill with your attorney. If you have a question or spot a problem, it isn't fair that you should have to pay to get it resolved. Some firms actually have the audacity to charge you for the time the billing partner spends reviewing your bill. You should never under any circumstances pay for the time the firm spends totaling the lawyer's time sheets and putting your bill in the mail.

Learning the Law

Lawyers do not generally discount their bills to write off time spent learning about an unfamiliar legal issue, but they may if the area is new to them and they really feel that it would be unjustified to ask the client to pay for that kind of an educational process. The problem is that in just about any litigation, you're inevitably going to pay your lawyer to become a student in some way. The key is to pay for no more education than you have to.

One way to do that is to select a lawyer with a lot of experience with your type of claim, if your claim is specialized. A lawyer who specializes in bad-faith insurance claims will be able to prepare a complaint for bad-faith denial of insurance much faster than a lawyer who may deal with a broad array of litigation matters but hasn't handled many bad-faith claims. A lawyer who specializes in the defense insurance field can probably do your case in his sleep. Because of his experience, he's already done most all the necessary research in insurance law, is aware of all the pertinent case law, and stays on top of developments in the law. He doesn't have to charge you for any of that, and you get to ride the coattails of all his other experiences.

In reality, a client typically chooses a litigator based on the fact that he was referred to a lawyer by a friend, the friend said the lawyer was very good and really tough, and the client is impressed by and likes the lawyer. Clients don't often spend much time evaluating the lawyer's depth of knowledge with respect to their particular problem. Also, many clients feel that a litigator is already a specialist—specializing in litigation—so if this lawyer has had a couple of victories and is impressive and reassuring in the first meeting, that's good enough.

Most litigators do specialize in certain types of litigation. They may specialize in antitrust cases, copyright cases, real estate cases, rent cases, cases involving defamation or breach of contract, and so on. And a client often may decide to hire a general litigator he senses is a strong trial lawyer over a defamation specialist who has handled many defamation cases but may not have the same trial track record.

The consequences of the decisions you make when you hire a lawyer will become evident in the bill, at different stages of the case. For example, if you hire a general litigator who is very well versed in trial work but maybe not an expert in defamation law, early on in the case you'll pay that lawyer more to get up to speed on defamation than you would have paid the defamation specialist. But when that general litigator gets closer to trial, he may prepare for trial very quickly, because he's very experienced at preparing for and presenting cases at trial.

If you hire a lawyer who is a specialist in defamation but is a less experienced trial lawyer, he might bill very little time in the beginning of your case because he knows how to prepare these complaints and get the ball rolling in defamation cases. But later, when it's time to prepare for trial, he may spend thousands of dollars in billable hours getting his opening argument ready, getting his exhibit notebooks ready, and so on. He's not as confident and experienced in the trial itself, so you're going to pay as he works and perfects his trial preparation.

In the first interview with a lawyer, it's pretty daunting to find out whether he has a good reputation as a trial lawyer, whether he's adequately experienced in your type of matter, whether you can afford him, whether you have chemistry with him, and whether you think you can work with him. But whatever decision you've made, you'll see the results of the decisions on the invoices.

Learning Your Business

Perhaps as part of the case your lawyer needs to learn how your business—say, the sneaker business—works, and you realize in your first or second bill that he's billing a lot of time for doing this. Before too long you may want to have a conversation with the lawyer and say, "I've noticed that you guys are spending a lot of time over at my offices, interviewing my employees and reading a few of our manuals, and one of your associates charged time for reading a book called *The Sneaker Business.* Can we reach a compromise where I'm not being billed for some of this time? When this case is over, your firm will be able to market yourself to others in the sneaker business, and by the way, it's further entrenching you in your position with our company. I also know that you're not selling widgets, and the only way you guys make money is by selling your time. But I'd like to reach an agreement, because it is costing a lot of money to bring you up to speed on the sneaker business." In situations where a client and I have agreed that my learning the client's business will benefit both of us, I've arranged to share the cost of learning it by affording some write-off or reduction in our hourly rate.

Even if you have a medical malpractice case and your lawyer is the specialist of specialists in medical malpractice cases, he might have to learn something new. He has to learn the facts of your case, examine your x-rays, and talk to your treating physician, and a lawyer will perceive a fresh twist or angle in every case. You can't be resentful that you're paying for him to get an education, because he's going to use that education to effectively represent you. But there's no rule of thumb to say how much of the time your lawyer spends learning should be billed to you, versus how much he should absorb himself. If your lawyer is going to learn your business, talk to him about this and try to save yourself some money.

The Importance of the Estimate

As you go along on your case, it's crucial to have your lawyer give you estimates of how much time it will take to get certain things done. A lawyer won't be able to provide you a quote the way a contractor building something in your house would; litigation is too unpredictable. A lawyer can't anticipate how many nasty letters from opposing counsel he will have to read, consider, and respond to. He can't know how many times opposing counsel will call him, and a lot of time in litigation is spent with lawyers conferring about discovery requests, document requests, settlement, and so on. It's difficult for a lawyer to predict the volume and potential length of those calls. The other side may raise issues that are completely without merit, but your lawyer must still respond. There's no way of getting a computer printout from a lawyer estimating exactly how many hours an unknown task will take.

What you can expect and should ask for, though, are general estimates for any major tasks on your case. If you keep abreast of developments on your lawsuit, and discuss in advance what things are likely to cost, you should never be stunned by a legal bill. Surprised, sure. Unhappy, maybe. But if a client is shocked and dismayed by a lawyer's bill, there has been a communication problem. You must be observant and ask your lawyer questions: What are you working on? What do we plan on getting done this month? How much time do you think it will take? Who will be working on it? How much will this next motion or deposition cost?

Asking these questions gives you the parameters and a sense of what's happening. And if a rough estimate from your lawyer turns out to be low on any given task, you can remind the attorney of his estimate and find out why there is such a disparity. If the discrepancy between estimate and actual cost creates a financial hardship for you, you might be in a good position to get a write-down on that basis. After all, you might not have approved the task had you been given a more accurate estimate.

Ask Questions and Keep a Loose Leash

Feel free to ask your lawyer about his invoices. A lot of clients are shy about their bill. They may be happy to have their lawyer representing them and naively feel it would be presumptuous to ask the lawyer, "There's that one phone call on a Tuesday where you billed an hour and a half. Was that call *really* an hour and a half long? Why did you feel compelled to be on the phone for an hour and a half?"

Question items that are unexpected, ask for reductions if appropriate, and set limits for areas where there may be more expense than you want, but do not micromanage your lawyer. When you hire a professional, whether it's a plumber or a doctor or a lawyer, you have to respect the fact that he is a professional. Professionals—whether they are lawyers or surgeons or baseball players—can't perform at their best if they feel they're under a magnifying glass.

It's a delicate balance. There's a lot of distrust in society, and there are lawyers who gouge their clients. You don't want to be asleep at the wheel, but you don't want to be a backseat driver either. You don't want your lawyer to become so antagonized by your overscrutinizing the bills that he doesn't want to represent you anymore. Maybe the senior partner who should be handling your matter concludes that you're going to be a real pain to work with, so he passes it off to the junior associate. Or, perhaps, your lawyer starts cutting corners because he believes that the only way to make you happy is to deliver a bargain bill: "The heck with spending twenty minutes on the phone on that issue; we're just going to spend five."

Be open to the idea that in some situations, a lawyer may have to be on the phone for an hour and a half. For example, suppose you served the other side with a request for production of documents. Local laws may require that before your lawyer files a motion to compel a more complete production, he must go over each request with the opposing counsel and ascertain what opposing counsel's position is on each one. If you served forty requests, it could take an hour and a half on the phone to talk about them one at a time, make legal arguments on each point, and make notes about the other side's position. Your lawyer might need to go down the hallway and question the associate who drafted the document request and who spoke to you most recently, to ascertain your position on some requests, find out what the law might be, or determine what a request is actually asking for.

You may later want to know why your lawyer was on the phone all that time, but don't lose your temper. If you do, maybe the next time there's a discovery dispute, your lawyer will simply go through the bare minimum: "Look, we disagree, so let's agree to disagree, and I'll file my Motion to Compel." Maybe you will save an hour and a half on a phone call but incur fifteen hours of lawyer time to file a Motion to Compel instead of resolving the issue over the phone. The danger of putting your lawyer in a straitjacket could be that he might not put in the time to save you money in the long run, because he doesn't want to put up with your grief in the short run.

Asking your attorney about your bill can serve a couple of purposes. You can learn more about your case, and you can ask for and receive a reduction for charges you don't believe you should pay. It can help to clarify some reasonable guidelines to help save you money in the future. Asking questions also puts your attorney on notice that you're not just getting your bill, pulling out your checkbook, and paying. He knows he should think twice before he sends out the next bill.

Phone Calls with You and Opposing Counsel

One billing area that catches some clients by surprise is the lawyer's telephone calls with them. If your bill includes a lot of long telephone conferences with you, you may at first think, "I couldn't have possibly spent that much time on the phone with the attorney!" In reality, though, you may have spent exactly that much time. You're excited about your case, the lawyer's now your friend, and maybe you're going to call him up and talk whenever a new thought occurs to you. You like having a colleague on your team, and you may not realize early in the case that every time you get that attorney on the phone, the clock's running.

This is another reason why it's important to separate out items in your bills and analyze them by task and activity. If you see that 30 percent of your bill is for telephone calls between you and your attorney, then you might want to ask yourself, "For my lawyer to be doing his job correctly, do we really need to be spending this much time on the phone? Or have I turned my attorney into a psychiatrist? Am I paying for someone to be a good listener when I could just as well be venting to my aunt, uncle, or wife or putting it in a diary?" People who are emotional about their case will turn their lawyer into a sounding board for hours a week. Expect to pay for that, dearly.

If you think you're being charged for calls that didn't occur or that were much shorter than billed, that's another matter. You might start keeping notes on your calendar when you communicate with your attorney. Each time you speak with someone at your lawyer's office, write it down on your calendar, and write down how long the conversation lasted. When you get your bill, you can check it against your own records and see whether there might be some mistake or other problem. Bear in mind that lawyers sometimes make notes before or after phone conversations, so the time billed may not equal precisely the duration of the call itself. But if you find your twelve-minute conversations are being billed as forty-five minutes, you might have a problem.

Another type of entry that adds up is phone calls with opposing counsel. There's no way of really confirming how much time your attorney spends on the phone with the other side's attorney. You need an element of trust. An attorney who isn't trustworthy may bill a fifteen-minute conversation as a thirty-minute conversation, and so on.

Keep your eye on those calls. If they seem too long or too many, it may be a signal that you need to be a little more focused. You may want to talk about it with your attorney at a certain point. There's nothing wrong with saying, "I'd like to keep a limit on the number of hours we spend talking to opposing counsel. Let's try to communicate with them more in short letters. If you're going to make a call and it's more than just a courtesy call or a perfunctory call, could you please call me first, so we can talk about whether we really want to invest an hour in talking about something? I'd like to participate in that decision."

Staffing

When you hire a law firm, you're usually going there because you know of a particular lawyer and his victory in court, his success, his reputation. But lawyers often use associates, paralegals, and secretaries to work on your case. There's nothing wrong with your attorney delegating work to associates. In fact, if you insisted that your attorney do all the work on your case and make all appearances himself, your bill would probably go up significantly. However, it's important for you to know at the start of your case which attorneys will be working on it and what their background is.

Delegation

If a lawyer hands off a substantial part of your case to an associate, even though there is an assumption the law firm will produce a certain caliber of work product, you want to know who this person is. He is an entirely different individual with an entirely different set of experiences, and he may be either more or less efficient than the attorney you retained. In some cases, a lawyer who's using the delegation process correctly will delegate in a way that causes your bill to be less. However, a lawyer will sometimes delegate for his own convenience, because of another client's demands, or because he wants to train an associate. In these cases, the delegation may cost you more.

If an associate spent eight hours drafting a motion that your lawyer himself could have drafted in four, in fairness the lawyer should only charge you the four hours. That delegation didn't save you money but had something to do with the firm's workload or political considerations. You have to take into account the associate's billable rate, which might be less, but the rule of thumb is that delegation from the partner to the associate should either be a wash or save you money. It should never cost you more. If it costs you significantly more, then you have a right to tell the lawyer that you may not mind that he's delegated, and the quality may have been pretty good, but you don't want to pay extra because of the delegation.

Staffing Changes

When large firms get busy, they sometimes decide to redeploy associates working on one matter to work on other matters. As a result, an associate working with your attorney may become too busy to do all the work on your case, or maybe he's yanked off your case, and another associate is assigned to come in and help. You might see on your bill big chunks of time for the new associate to read through your file in order to get up to speed before starting the work delegated to him. You should never pay for the learning curve of an associate who's brought on due to the firm's staffing rearrangements. The firm should pay for 100 percent of the additional time incurred by its decision to bring in someone else. If a seventh-year associate is replaced with a new lawyer who just passed the bar, take a close look at the hours the new associate bills on your case. You should not pay extra to help educate the firm's junior associates.

If your bill shows a change in staffing on your case, you might want to send your attorney a letter asking that he tell you of any future changes in staffing. I don't mean you should demand to be consulted if a secretary or receptionist is replaced, but if a lawyer or paralegal who potentially will be billing many hours is coming on, you probably want to know about that change. You may not know the person's experience level and whether he's senior or junior. There's nothing wrong with calling up the partner and saying, "I'd like to come in. I've seen Jane Smith's name on this invoice; I don't know who she is. Can we have lunch? Can I meet her?"

As long as you approach your attorney without putting him on the defensive, it's OK to make just about any request. And it's not unreasonable to want to be certain you like the people working on your case, have good rapport with them, and feel comfortable with their expertise. These people are working for you. There's nothing wrong with meeting the paralegal who billed forty hours on your case or the associate who billed sixty.

Red Flags

Be careful if a bill lists multiple lawyers reading the same document. Suppose your bill shows that a pleading came in on your case; the associate, the paralegal, and the partner read it, and they all bill for reading the pleading. Do all these people need to take the time to read that pleading? This can be a tough call. Some lawyers work as a team, so they may all need to read it. At other times, you don't need every lawyer on the team to read a document. Maybe the partner should skim something that comes in, but the junior associate who's going to draft the response should take time to thoroughly read it, mark it up, and outline it. Watch for situations where two lawyers on the same team work on exactly the same task.

Another area to scrutinize is interoffice conferences. In fairness, if you were to sit in a law office during a day, you would sometimes see two attorneys meeting and sharing information on your case. Maybe one lawyer went to one deposition, the other lawyer went to another, and they're going to cooperatively draft an opposition to some other motion. Sharing experience in this instance can be very important, and you would gladly pay for it. Two people on your team are sharing information to help prepare important papers on your case. However, even a discussion that began as a productive conversation may fade into lawyers just shooting the breeze on the case. You can envision it: at the end of the day, one attorney walks into another's office and says, "Hey, when are our interrogatories due? You know, if we're going to answer them, I was thinking that number 15—now, that was an interesting question . . ."

Since you're not there on the spot, how do you police against the lawyer billing you for just shooting the breeze about your case? This is where communication with your lawyer comes in handy. If you see that 20 percent of your bill is interoffice conferences among the lawyers, it's appropriate to call your lawyer and say, "I'd like to cut this down. I don't want to prohibit you guys from doing your job, but when we talked about that Motion to Compel, you told me it would cost around $5,000. My bill is for $6,000. Can you explain to me why 25 percent of the bill is interoffice conferences? What can we do without handicapping you to reduce that?"

If your lawyer provided you with a budget for your case at the start, and then month after month you're seeing lots of interoffice conferences and calls to opposing counsel, that can add up. In a case that has a ten- to eighteen-month lifetime or more, you could pay the lawyers an amazing amount of money to talk to each other and to opposing counsel, or to read the same document. That kind of activity can be regulated without causing the lawyers to feel they're being so policed that they don't want you as a client.

Billing for Costs

Your lawyer will incur and pass along costs in filing fees, deposition transcripts, court reporters, messengers, and perhaps experts. These are pretty easy to verify because your lawyer will pay invoices from third parties for each. Other costs, like charges for phone calls, faxes, photocopying, and word processing, are more difficult to verify. Some law firms also charge for meals, parking, and mileage.

Law firms have different approaches to costs. Some work very hard to charge you precisely what they paid out of pocket; other firms feel this takes too long, so they make assumptions on which they base their billing. Still others try to turn costs into a profit center for the firm, and they'll add in a profit margin (sometimes a large one).

Photocopying

In terms of photocopying, a law firm has costs for toner, paper, and machine maintenance, and it has to pay its secretaries to stand over the machine when they're making copies in-house. How much of these costs should be charged to the client, and how much should the firm carry as a cost of doing business? Every firm has a different formula. You may want to ask, during your retainer agreement discussion, how the firm assesses copying charges. You could talk to other law firms or go to a local copying service and see how that compares. If a firm's photocopying rate seems excessive, it's all right to say that for any big copying jobs, you'd like to arrange to have the copying done outside the firm.

Copying is an area you particularly have to watch out for, because lawyers are pack rats. If two associates are working on your case, both of them may copy every document for their own personal files. When the case is over, they have the pleadings to look at as a model for some future case. If you see large numbers for copying on your bill, it might be worthwhile to try to ascertain why so many copies are being made.

Faxes

Many firms attempt to make a profit from faxes they send out and receive. Ask what your firm bills for these and why it's that price.

Also, consider whether your lawyer needs to fax you copies of everything. Our society has become fax crazy; some things clearly do not require your immediate attention but can be mailed to you. Most documents are just being sent to you so that you can look at them, understand them, ask a few questions maybe, and then stick them in your file. Make it clear that you don't require that everything be faxed. If you get a fax from the law firm and realize you don't need it faxed, call up the lawyer's assistant and ask that things like that be put in the mail. Over the life of your case, you'll save yourself some money.

When you send a fax to a lawyer, it sends an implied message that the lawyer should drop everything he's doing and read it right now. You'll pay for that. Consider whether what you are sending is really that important. Maybe you should just put it in the mail, and the lawyer can read it later.

Phone Charges

Some firms charge for phone calls, and the lawyers and staff dial in your account code whenever they make a phone call on your case. Again, you want to understand their formula for phone charges. Remember that when you're on the phone with your lawyer, you're not just paying for the lawyer's time, but also for the cost of that call. If the firm has a profit built into its phone charges, the calls can get to be very expensive.

Word Processing

Some firms charge for word processing, especially for overtime in their word-processing department. Large firms have a staff of word processors going twenty-four hours a day, churning out the firm's paper. In most instances I would advise you not to pay any charges for word processing without very good reason. When you hire a lawyer and pay a sizable hourly rate, the lawyer's computer and secretary should be included in that rate. Your dentist doesn't ask you to pay for the filling and then to pay extra for the assistant who stood by and sprayed water into your mouth. Neither should you be asked to pay for your lawyer's secretary if she's transcribing dictation.

In large firms your work may not get done until the evening. Typically, the lawyers are working late—not because they worked all day on your case, but because they worked on someone else's case—and at 5:00 P.M., they finally turn their attention to your matter. They dictate a letter or draft a motion, but their secretary is gone for the day, so they send it to word processing. Unless it's an emergency and your lawyer had no choice but to work late and file the papers the next morning, why should you pay a premium to have something typed simply because your lawyer didn't get around to doing it during normal business hours? You shouldn't.

Meals

Under this same logic, don't pay for meals billed to you by the firm, except, perhaps, when your attorney must travel out of town exclusively on your case, in which case it is fair to pay some average cost of a meal. It's the same as the overtime word-processing charges. The associate is turning his attention to your case for the first time that day, and it's 7:00 P.M. The associate's friends down the hall all want some pizza, and they call up and ask for it to be delivered by a messenger service, and they decide that it's your turn to pay for the pizza that night.

If a law firm is going to charge you for meals for anything other than for travel to another city, a red flag should go up. If your lawyers are working incredibly late hours, and you're there with them, you as the client can certainly say thank you by ordering dinner for them a few times if you wish. But as a general matter, being charged for meals is not something you have to accept. If you get a bill with costs for meals, you're perfectly justified to say, "I don't want to pay that."

Mileage

Law firms shouldn't charge for mileage, although some do. Part of the lawyer's job is getting to work and getting to the courthouse. This is a touchy area for some lawyers. Many will charge you for the time they spend traveling from their office to the court hearing.

Travel

If your lawyer travels out of town to take a deposition, review documents, or take other discovery on your case, you need to discuss how travel costs will be handled. Are you paying the lawyer for his time in traveling? Different firms have different policies, and you'll need to decide whether you're comfortable with the firm's policy. If you're on a tight budget and the law firm knows it, this may be an area where you request concessions.

Let your lawyer know early on how you want travel arrangements handled. If your lawyer travels out of town, I recommend that you use your own travel agent so you can ensure you get the best prices possible. Mind you, if you say to your lawyer, "I'd like you to fly on the red-eye to New York and stay at the YMCA," your lawyer may just tell you to go jump off the Brooklyn Bridge. Still, lawyers don't have to fly first-class, unless you're a huge corporate client and that's the message you want to send your lawyer. They should travel coach, and you should be able to shop around for a cheap fare.

If there's going to be travel on your case, tell your lawyer that you'd rather not have decisions about air travel made at the last minute. Lawyers like to ask their secretary to call up two days before they know they're going to another city, and order a ticket that costs $1,500. If the lawyer plans correctly, you should be able to give your travel agent three weeks' notice and get yourself the cheaper airfare. Sometimes it's possible to plan depositions with the kind of planning that goes into a family vacation.

What kind of out-of-town accommodations are reasonable for your lawyer to stay in? Consider the impact on your case. I was recently in a case where I and two other attorneys representing different clients traveled out of town for mediation. One of the clients was stingy and had put his lawyer up in a fleabag motel in a crummy part of town. The other lawyer and I were staying in nice hotels—not hotels with suites and Jacuzzis, but comfortable places. When we made our presentations at the mediation the next morning, the lawyer who had stayed at the horrendous motel had bags under his eyes and just couldn't wait to get out of the city. The third lawyer and I were well rested, in good moods, and gave great presentations. There's a time and a place to pamper your lawyer.

If your lawyer submits a bill for a hotel, you want to see it. If the lawyer visited a friend in that town, and they both ate out of the snack bar or ordered room service, took towels and robes from the hotel, ordered pay-per-view movies until three in the morning, and made $200 worth of long-distance phone calls, you shouldn't get stuck with that. Suppose you get a bill with a listing under costs of "Hotel charge . . . $459." You should stop to think, "Now, wait a second, the room cost $175. What happened to the other $284?" Well, $200 is phone calls—the five minute call to you and all the calls he made to his other clients. Whoa! You shouldn't have to pay for that! I know of lawyers who've charged the client for theater tickets because they were bought through the concierge and rolled into their hotel bill. If you have a cost item that's over $20 or $30, you have a right to see the actual invoice that was paid and the backup. Some firms include it as a matter of course; you may have to ask for it at others.

If your lawyer is going to take an out-of-town trip on your behalf, have a frank discussion and set ground rules. Maybe *you* want to give him tickets to a play or some other perk as a token of appreciation. However, you don't want him riding around in limos, eating at four-star restaurants, flying first-class, and taking advantage of you.

Some people might feel uncomfortable discussing these types of issues. They don't know how to tell their hotshot trial lawyer that he really shouldn't be traveling first-class. Well, you and your spouse don't travel first-class, so you're just going to have to get comfortable having those kinds of discussions with your lawyer. He isn't spending his own money; he's spending yours.

Review of Backup

A few months into your case, when there are some sizable costs on your invoice, you might want to ask nicely if you may go into the office and look at the full backup for the cost bill. I'm not suggesting you audit your costs, but doing it once to ensure that everything checks out can have a powerful impact. You may find some inadvertent errors. Maybe something has been added up incorrectly, or another client's cost was put on your bill. Or maybe when you see what kinds of tasks the law firm is charging for, you realize that you and the firm aren't thinking on the same page about costs.

If you do that once and find any irregularity, believe me, the partner in charge of billing on your case will send a note down to accounting saying, "Let's make sure we double-check these figures in the future." Or he may say quietly to others in the firm, "Let's be careful not to have any fat in the cost section of this bill."

You want to be careful about how you do it. Remember, you probably have a group of people at the law firm working extremely hard for you, and the firm may already be writing down your bills to help stay within your budget. It's a dance, and you want a healthy relationship with your lawyer. You don't want your lawyer feeling that you're auditing him. You want to be team oriented; you and your lawyer are both on the same team. You don't want your lawyer thinking, "My God, this client wants to fight it out with everybody—including me!" Litigators do not perform well in that environment. By the same token, there's a subtle way to send a message to the lawyer that you're not putting your billing on autopilot.

The Client Must Be Honest, Too

While you naturally want to make sure your lawyer is being fair and honest with you, you also have a responsibility to be honest with him. One of the most important things to be honest about as the client is your cash flow. A lawsuit is extremely expensive. It can be as expensive as building a house or buying a car or two or three. Don't buy one if you can't afford it.

I have seen situations where a client decides to hire a lawyer to write a demand letter. The client expects that the letter will get a response and he'll get some cash. The lawyer tells the client that could happen, but it might not. It doesn't happen and the client orders the lawyer to file the complaint and start taking depositions. At every step the client knows he doesn't have the money to fund a lawsuit, but he just doesn't want to walk away from the fight. He's decided that at some point, he's going to break it to the lawyer that he really doesn't have the cash.

I've made many statements in this book about how lawyers can make mistakes or need to be watched so they don't take advantage of you, but there are two sides to every coin. Some people take legal invoices and do what in the restaurant business is called "chew and screw." As much as I might despise a lawyer who overbills, I equally despise a client who basically steals a lawyer's time. If you have a cash flow issue, I strongly recommend that you disclose it before using up your lawyer's time.

Remember that a lawyer is a trained professional. He's not cheap; he's expensive. And if he's very good, he's very expensive. If a lawsuit doesn't unfold as quickly as you hope, it's going to be expensive. If the lawyer was fair with you and gave you an estimate of how much this case will cost, and you knew that you couldn't afford it, then you made a gross error in proceeding.

When you hire a lawyer, you have bought a lawsuit in the same way that you might buy a car or house. And just as you wouldn't buy a house knowing that you're going to default on the mortgage three months into the purchase, you shouldn't hire a law firm and buy a lawsuit if you know you're going to default on paying three months into the lawsuit. You could conceivably end up in two lawsuits: one with the original party and one with your lawyer over his legal fees. Lawyers can be formidable opponents. This is what they do morning, noon, and night.

When clients have told me they have a cash flow problem, I've sometimes been able to help them work through the problem. I may put them on a payment schedule or work out some other arrangement. If a client says, "Look, I love your work. I think you do a great job, but this month I really only can spend $2,000 on the case, even though I may have to make some tough decisions and not pursue certain avenues," I respect that. I'll get that client the best bang for his 2,000 bucks, and I'll do it without his needing to look over my shoulder. I'll try to make cost-effective decisions for him. If the client gets the $2,000 bill, pays it within a few days, and doesn't squeak and try to trim me down to $1,700, then I'm going to be even more likely the next month to try to stay within whatever his budget is.

There are a lot of different approaches to regulating your legal fees. If you're watching your legal bills closely, communicating about them, and communicating about your case, and if you make an effort to understand the billing process, you will end up feeling comfortable about the bills being sent to you.

"Oh, we're just like best friends."

You and Your Lawyer: A Special Relationship

> In the strange heat all litigation brings to bear on things,
> the very process of litigation fosters the most profound
> misunderstandings in the world.
>
> **—Renata Adler, Italian-born American writer,
> film critic, and philosopher**

Without strong facts, compelling evidence, and believable witnesses, the best lawyer can have trouble winning your case. But even with the most powerful facts, evidence, and witnesses, if you and your lawyer don't reach and maintain a healthy relationship, you can still lose. In other words, learn how to get along with your lawyer while protecting your interests. At times the two objectives may seem at odds with one another, and in some instances there may be a conflict. The key is to foster an air of openness, to keep an eye on things, and to be direct and candid with your attorney without putting him on the defensive. The amount of time and money you put into your suit will vary over the life of the case, as may your level of stress and frustration, but you need to keep in mind that your relationship with your lawyer can have a direct bearing on the outcome of your case.

Active Periods

You need to have a frank discussion with your attorney to find out when the active periods in your case will be. A lawsuit (except perhaps a huge antitrust suit) isn't continuously active. Every case has a rhythm and beat. Usually a case is very active in the beginning because you must work up and file a complaint, and then there'll be an answer or motion to dismiss from the other side, an initial status conference, and possibly a flurry of discovery. Then a case often sits fallow for a while, because lawyers eventually have to work on other cases that are more pressing. If there isn't a motion that needs to be decided immediately, the case will be put on a back burner with other cases. It is generally up to the lawyers to decide how quickly and fervently they want to conduct discovery.

If you're in a jurisdiction where it takes years to get a trial date, you should know that you're going to spend four, five, or fifteen thousand dollars to work your case up, get the complaint ready, file it, and go through this initial round—and then the case is going to sit for a couple of years while everybody yawns. In Los Angeles, where the courts have "fast track" rules designed to get cases to trial quickly, it's not an expressway either. The first three months are active with the filing of the complaint and then probably a motion to dismiss the complaint. After this initial flurry of activity, you may sit for six months while little happens until you get to the next active period.

People rarely ask their lawyers how long they will be in the complaint stage and in discovery. They rarely ask what the time will involve: Is it two days of showing up in the lawyer's office for a deposition, or something else? But you need to know, because you've got other things happening in your life. You don't want to find out two days before a deposition that suddenly you have to scurry around your basement, find all the documents that relate to the deposition, have them copied for the lawyer, go to his office and get prepped for the deposition, and finally go through the deposition. You don't want to let the lawsuit take any more time from you than absolutely necessary, because you've got a business or a household to run. Talk to your lawyer early on, and figure out when the case will be active and when the lawyer will need your time and assistance.

Being a Good Client

The most productive attorney-client relationships are those with open lines of communication. You really want your lawyer to feel comfortable enough to tell you when he doesn't know something. Too often the client believes his lawyer does or should know everything about every area of the law. But that's impossible. The law is an infinite body, extremely complex, and frequently evolving. Try to remember that many of the concepts your lawyer is dealing with on your case might be complex, and he might not understand them totally, even though he's spent several years of schooling to learn them.

It can be difficult for your lawyer to express to you the nuances of what may happen in an off-the-record conference with a judge. Maybe during this conference the judge chastised your lawyer for work he did on someone else's case, and now your lawyer is concerned about how the judge's anger might affect your case. Your lawyer is worried that the judge might be biased against him, but he doesn't know how to tell you, because he's afraid of your reaction. You *definitely* don't want this happening on your case.

Once you've chosen your champion and feel he's right for you, honest, and trustworthy, do what you can to make sure your lawyer is never scared to tell you about something unfamiliar, uncertain, or unfavorable. These kinds of situations arise at some point in most cases, and your lawyer should feel comfortable enough with you to give you bad news right away. If he doesn't readily deliver both good and bad tidings, you may be in for a nasty surprise later. There may be an important aspect of your case that you don't even know about.

A lawyer is human (even if some say otherwise). He's sometimes going to make a mistake. He's not always going to have the answer right away. If he's a good lawyer, he's out there doing his best. Understand that, and try to encourage your lawyer to speak frankly to you.

Your lawyer may run into an area of the law on your case where he is totally unfamiliar. If he admits this, you and he can have a discussion where you could ask, "Should we bring in somebody else who has worked on this issue?" Your lawyer may answer that he has always wanted to accrue some experience in that area, and you might get him to agree that while he's spending a gazillion hours getting up to speed on something another lawyer in town might know very well, he won't charge you for some of that time.

Walk a Fine Line

This kind of open dialogue will never happen if your lawyer feels uncomfortable. You absolutely want to watch your lawsuit, shepherd and be involved in it, and know everything about it at all times. To do this, you may sometimes have to walk a fine line. Some lawyers will be uneasy with a client who is overly involved. Some are not used to it. You may want to say, "I'm going to be very involved here; this case means everything to me. But I also want to respect your jurisdiction as the lawyer, and I don't want to get in your way in doing the job. So we're going to have to figure out how to work this out so that I'm not getting in your way and making things more expensive, but by the same token you're not denying my right of knowing and making decisions."

I advocate strongly your telling your lawyer, "This is my budget. I don't want a penny of my money spent that I don't approve. I want to have a say over everything that's going to cost me money or affect my case." At the same time, you have to understand that law firms are businesses and have other customers; you don't want your lawyer to be turned off to you. You don't want your lawyer to get to a point where he says, "What a headache!" and runs from you.

If you're on an hourly rate and are getting a monthly bill, it may be a good idea to meet or talk monthly, not just about the case, but about the bill and any questions you have. It's not always a comfortable process, but you may have to do it. Then talk openly about your relationship: How are we getting along? Are we communicating? Are we not communicating?

If you hire a small or new law firm, the lawyer may be afraid of too much communication: "I'm going to get fired if I'm very up-front about this issue." Remember, there is no downside to creating an atmosphere where your lawyer feels he can speak directly to you.

You don't want your attorney to think you're going to fire him just because he was direct with you. You don't want him to be a salesperson. And at some point you have to get over your need as the client to have somebody else stroke you. You want your lawyer to hit you right between the eyes with the truth.

Don't Throw Your Good Sense out the Window

When some people get involved with a lawyer, all the common sense they employ in the workplace gets tossed out the window. Even people who run businesses or maintain other involved projects where they work as part of a team can't seem to deal with their attorney rationally. Maybe it's because they look at their lawyer as some kind of high priest. He's not. In dealing with your lawyer, don't abandon the commonsense modes that you use with people in your work and personal life.

Signal to your lawyer that it's OK if he tells you you've got a lousy case or that an idea you think will advance your case really stinks. Ultimately, there has to be an element of informed trust.

At a certain point in the case, no matter how involved you are, no matter how many books you read, you have to turn yourself and a large degree of control of the case over to the lawyer. It's like having surgery. At some point the surgeon is going to put you to sleep and cut you open, and you won't be able to wake up, peek over, and say, "Do the incision here." Likewise, you have to trust your lawyer and understand that even though you're the client, you're not going to be able to say, "Hey, put that witness on first. That's my decision, and it's final."

You also have to appreciate that your lawyer has other cases and other clients, all of whom feel the same way you do: "My case is most important. I want to be at the head of the line." Some lawyers take on too many cases and don't have enough staffing. If that has happened, you should be aware of it and take appropriate action. By the same token, you have to understand that, while your lawsuit is the only law-suit in *your* life, so you're angry and want immediate action when you get a brief from the other side, your lawyer does have other clients. He is not always able to ask, "How high?" when you say, "Jump." Unless the house (your case) is burning down, your lawyer should be able to take two or three days to respond to you.

Avoid Litigation Burnout

There may come a time when you're sitting in a meeting or at your kids' recital and aren't hearing anything that's going on around you because you're thinking, "Damn it! That person said *x* in her deposition. I can't believe it!" That's when you'll know you're too close to your case and it's time to take a break. Even a good, professional, involved, active litigant needs to take a vacation from his lawsuit at one time or another. And just as taking a vacation from your own business requires you to trust your employees, you're going to have to trust your lawyer. If he understands you, how you want your case handled, how you want to be reported to, and how you want to handle costs, you'll be able to step away with at least some minimal peace of mind.

Your relationship will be most successful if you and your lawyer are working as a team. You don't want him running off and handling the case simply as he sees fit; neither do you want to ignore his training and advice and basically borrow his license to practice law yourself.

If the lawyer is ignorant of your concerns, goals, or objectives, then the relationship will break down. The lawyer will either blow a budget or be insensitive to the emotional aspects of the case. By the same token, if you're unappreciative of how much time, for example, goes into a motion and are essentially making it an antagonistic or not very profitable venture for the lawyer, he's not going to be happy either.

A lawsuit generates tension, anxiety, fear, and all sorts of negative emotions for everyone involved. If you add to this, lawyers who are usually type A, high-octane individuals and clients who are often agi-tated and stressed due to the matter that brought them to a lawyer in the first place, what you may end up with is a pressure-cooker environ-ment where, at some point, you and your lawyer turn on each other. It happens more than it should, and it's probably not surprising, because when two people are under a great deal of pressure, sometimes one or both cracks.

Fortunately, you now have an inkling of what litigation entails and how you can survive it. And if your lawyer starts giving you a hard time? Well, you can always tell him to read this book.

Just don't let him bill you for it.

Appendix A:
Cost-Benefit Analysis

Read through this book for an understanding of the varied components of litigation. Then take the specifics of your potential case and use Table 4 as a form to help you determine a range of costs and fees.

You will need input from any attorney you're considering hiring. Find out what hourly rate to plug in and get specific estimates of the different tasks unique to your situation. I have attempted to give low and high averages for a variety of tasks, but these are loose guidelines at best. You should discuss with any attorney you may hire how much time and expense he envisions for any of these, based on your situation. Your case requires a unique analysis, and the estimates in the table may not apply to your situation.

Once you have filled out the form and totaled a range of expense, weigh those amounts against the potential benefit of suing. Again, a lawyer should help you evaluate the value of your damages, as this hinges on the unique facts and circumstances of your situation.

Ideally, you should ask your lawyer to prepare a budget for your litigation. You can use the information in this book and in Table 4 to evaluate the budget and consider whether the lawyer may have overlooked anything.

Table 4. Potential Legal Fees

POSSIBLE TASKS	ISSUES AFFECTING ESTIMATE	RANGE OF HOURS	ESTIMATED TOTAL HOURS
Demand Letter			
Draft, discuss, and revise letter (plaintiff only)	• Is a demand letter appropriate for your situation? • How detailed must it be?	2–20	
Evaluate, respond to demand letter (defendant only)	• Is early settlement in your best interest? • Would negotiations at this point be potentially productive?	1–10	
Pleadings			
Prepare and file complaint (plaintiff only) • Hold initial client meetings • Organize file/ learn case • Do legal research for complaint • Draft complaint • Review with client • Revise and file complaint, arrange for service	• How complex is your case? • How long will it take your lawyer to learn your case, prepare and file the complaint?	10–80	
Prepare and file answer (defendant only) • Hold initial client meetings • Organize file/ learn case • Do legal research for answer • Draft answer	• How complex is your case? • How long will it take your lawyer to learn your case, prepare and file the answer?	2–15	

- Review with client,
  revise and file
  answer

Pleading Motions

Motion to dismiss complaint ("demurrer") • Research, draft, and file motion or opposition • Draft or evaluate reply, legal research • Appear at court to argue motion	• Do any of the causes of action invite pleading motions? • Will the defendant be in a position to afford to test the pleadings through costly motions?	8–20× each motion
Motion to strike portion(s) of complaint • Research, draft, and file motion or opposition • Draft or evaluate reply, legal research • Appear at court to argue motion		8–20× each motion
Revise and refile complaint		3–20× each time

Written Discovery

Prepare, serve interrogatories, requests for admission or production of documents • Draft or evaluate requests, questions	• How much does your lawyer intend to use written discovery in your case? • Is the defendant going to try to bury you in this kind of discovery?	5–15× each set
Respond to written discovery		5–20× each set

Discovery Motions

Motions to Compel	• How hard-fought is the	5–20×
• Meet and confer with opposing counsel	litigation going to become? • How many discovery motions are likely in your	each motion
• Draft and file Motion to Compel	case? One? Ten?	
• Evaluate opposition, legal research		
• Draft and file reply		
• Travel to court and argue motion		

Motion for Protective Order		5–20×
• Meet and confer with opposing counsel		each motion
• Draft and file Motion for Protective Order		
• Evaluate opposition, legal research		
• Draft and file reply		
• Travel to court and argue motion		

Negotiate and draft stipulations		1–10× each motion

Depositions

Prepare for and depose each witness	• How many witnesses will likely be deposed in your	2–30×
• Interview witnesses and devise strategy	case? Two? Twenty? • How long will these	each deposition
• Draft subpoena and serve deponent	depositions last? An hour? Four or five days?	
• Prepare for and take deposition	• How much preparation will your attorney require	
• Review transcript	in order to handle these depositions in the most productive way?	

Motion for Summary Judgment (MSJ)

Research, draft MSJ or opposition	• Is a large sum in controversy in your case, which would tend to encourage the defendant to file an MSJ?	10–70
• Analyze reply, prepare for oral arguments	• Will the defendant file a costly MSJ simply to test your commitment to your case and see your case on paper?	
• Travel to court to argue motion		

Punitive Damages, Net Worth Motion

Research, draft, and file motion or opposition	• Is the plaintiff seeking punitive or exemplary damages in your case?	10–50
• Draft/analyze reply	• Does your jurisdiction require a net worth motion in order to take discovery of the defendant's net worth?	
• Prepare for oral arguments		
• Travel to court to argue motion		

Experts

Confer with consultants on issues relating to case	• Do any issues in your case require expert testimony?	5–100 per consultant
	• Is more than one expert needed?	
	• Will you use consultants?	
Interview, research and retain expert		8–200 per expert
• Educate expert on issues of case		
• Consult with and evaluate expert's findings		
• Prepare expert for deposition		
• Depose expert		
• Evaluate and prepare to depose opponent's expert		
• Depose opponent's expert		

Experts (cont.)

Consultant's fee		5–200
		(Flat or hourly rate?)
Expert's fee		5–200
		(Flat or hourly rate?)

Trial Preparation

Miscellaneous research and trial preparation	• Oppose continuance motions?	40–200
• Prepare opening statement	• Might the defendant attempt to delay trial?	
• Review file, review case	• How complex is the case?	
• Witness preparation × ___ witnesses	• How many witnesses need to be prepared?	
• Prepare plaintiff		
• Draft jury instructions		
• Complete general preparation		

Pretrial Motions

Draft Motions *in Limine*, to Exclude; prepare replies	• Are there issues and areas that you or your company do not wish to have disclosed at trial? It's possible to file several such motions.	8–20 per motion

Trial

?? days/weeks Night/weekend preparation during trial	• Your attorney may work 12-hour days or longer, 6 or 7 days a week during trial, or 70-plus hours a week on your tab.	Ask lawyer Ask lawyer
Expert fees	• Experts will be paid for the time they spend waiting to testify, too.	Get budget from expert

Consultation between Attorney and Clients re: Litigation

Faxes, phone calls, letters	• In addition to the calls, letters, and faxes you may exchange with your attorney during the drafting of a motion, or in preparation for a deposition or other task, you will probably be communicating with your attorney on a fairly regular basis. • In addition to anticipating the hours spent talking about specific tasks and issues, you need to anticipate communication you'll be having on a monthly basis.	20–100

Miscellaneous Communications with Opposing Counsel

Faxes, phone calls, letters	• There's no way to know for certain how much communication will need to take place between the lawyers, but for any case with more than just a few witnesses, or with complex legal issues, the lawyers may have to communicate a lot. You'll have to pay for this.	20–100

Settlement Discussions

Faxes, phone calls, letters	• Letters, phone calls, and meetings may occur to try to settle your matter at various points	1–20

Mediation Attempts

Mediation costs
  • Select mediator, agree to terms
  • Prepare briefs
  • Attend mediation
  • Follow up
	• Will you attempt to mediate?
	• The specifics of your case will determine how involved and expensive the mediation process will be.
		15–150

Your share of mediator's fee		Ask attorney

Status Conferences

Court meetings on progress of case	20–30
• Prepare status forms for court	
• Appear at court to discuss case before court officer	

Total hours	_____
Attorney's hourly rate	×_____
Total attorney's fees	_____
Fees:	
Experts	+_____
Consultants	+_____
Mediator	+_____
Other: _____	+_____
Total fees	_____
Related costs*	+_____
Total fees and costs	_____

Estimate related costs for each task, such as service of process, deposition transcripts, and filing fees.

Appendix B:
Examples of Retainer Agreements

Here are two sample retainer agreements. Figure 7 is a simple contingency fee agreement. Figure 8 is a highly detailed hourly agreement.

Figure 7. Sample Retainer Agreement: Contingency Fee

Smith & Smith, hereinafter referred to as Attorneys, and
_____, hereinafter referred to as Client(s), hereby enter into
this RETAINER AGREEMENT for injuries and/or damages sustained
by _____ on or about the _____ day of _____, 19__, in the
County of _____ , State of _____. Client(s) agrees that Attorneys have explained that the fee percentages below are not set
by law and have been negotiated between attorney and client.
The terms are:

1. There will be no settlement without Client(s)'s consent;
2. If there is no recovery, Client(s) will not owe any attor-
    ney's fees.
3. Client(s) agrees to pay an Attorney's fee of thirty-three
    and one-third percent (33^1/3%) of the gross recovery if the
    case is settled at or before the first Status Conference
    (State Court) or Pretrial Conference (Federal Court); there-
    after Client(s) agrees to pay a fee of forty percent (40%)
    of the gross recovery. To the extent that there are any
    minor claimants, any fees charged said minor(s) and any set-
    tlement affecting said minor(s) must be approved by the

317

court. The fees sought from the court will not exceed those fees set forth above.

3a. Said fees will include any and all management information systems costs, including but not limited to costs associated with the automation of Client's case in terms of scanning, coding, archiving, and publishing. These services are charged on a per page basis, and can and will be utilized or not utilized solely at the discretion of Smith & Smith.

4. Should Attorneys advance any litigation costs, including investigation charges on behalf of Client(s), it is understood that all said costs and expenses must be returned to Attorneys. Client(s) agrees to immediately repay all litigation costs upon Client's change of attorneys. Cost advanced will be deducted from the net recovery after Attorney's fees are computed.

5. All medical expenses and charges of any nature made by doctors in connection with the above-mentioned claim are the obligation of Client(s) and will be paid by Client(s).

6. Client(s) has the right to insist that the case proceed to trial; however, should Client(s) reject the good-faith recommendation of Attorneys concerning disposition of this case, Client(s) agrees to repay and advance all necessary costs and expenses of litigation within twenty (20) days of request by Attorneys. Attorneys shall not be required to continue to prosecute any action that in Attorneys' opinion is unmeritorious.

7. All Attorney's fees earned and any costs or expenses advanced by Attorneys shall be a lien on any settlement or judgment made or secured on behalf of Client(s).

8. This Agreement does not contemplate any appeal or retrial, and should an appeal or retrial be necessary, a further agreement shall be negotiated at that time.

9. NO REPRESENTATION OF ANY TYPE HAS BEEN MADE AS TO WHAT AMOUNT, IF ANY, CLIENT MAY BE ENTITLED TO RECOVER IN THIS CASE. CLIENT ACKNOWLEDGES RECEIPT OF A COPY OF THIS RETAINER AGREEMENT. PLEASE INITIAL (____)

DATED: _____, 19__
SMITH & SMITH
By: _____

_____
CLIENT

_____
CLIENT

Figure 8.   Sample Retainer Agreement: Hourly Fee

This Agreement ("Agreement") is entered into by and between _____ (collectively, "Clients") and THINK, SMART, BEFORE, & FILING ("Attorney"), as of August 14, 2002 ("Effective Date"). Unless a different Agreement is made in writing, this Agreement alone shall govern the respective rights and responsibilities of Client and Attorney.

1. **Claims Covered by Agreement.** Clients retain Attorney to represent Clients in connection with the following incident or transaction:

   [DESCRIPTION OF CASE]

2. **Responsibilities of Attorney and Clients.** Attorney agrees to perform legal services, including but not limited to the following, as necessary, with respect to the claims described above:
   - investigation of claims;
   - determination of responsible parties;
   - preparation and filing of a lawsuit;
   - settlement procedures and negotiations;
   - prosecution of claim by arbitration or legal action until award or judgment is obtained; and
   - if judgment is obtained in Client's favor, opposing a motion for a new trial.

   Attorney is authorized to associate with or employ other counsel, experts, and consultants to assist in performing the services required by this Agreement, and to appear on Clients' behalf in any proceeding or lawsuit. Clients agree to cooperate fully with Attorney by, among other things, providing Attorney with all relevant information, documents, and appearances as necessary for meetings, depositions, and court hearings.

3. **Services Not Covered by This Agreement.** This Agreement does not cover other related claims that may arise and may require legal services. If additional services are necessary in connection with Clients' claims, and Clients request Attorney to perform such services, additional fee arrangements must be made between Attorney and Clients. Such additional services may be required, for example:
   - in defense of any other lawsuit, cross-complaint or other cross-demand filed against Clients in connection with the above matter or otherwise;
   - in judgment enforcement proceedings.

   Clients agree to make their own independent inquiry as to the existence of and coverage under any insurance policy that may provide them benefits relating to the subject matter of this Agreement.

4. **Retainer.** Clients shall deposit with Attorney the sum of $_____ by ___[date]___ for use as a retainer. The sum will be deposited

in a trust account, to be used to pay costs, expenses, and fees for legal services. Clients hereby authorize Attorney to withdraw sums from the trust account to pay the costs and/or fees Clients incur. Any unused deposit remaining at the conclusion of Attorney's services will be refunded. This Agreement will not take effect, and Attorney will have no obligation to provide legal services, until Clients return a signed copy of this agreement and pay the retainer.

5. **Hourly Fees.** Clients agree to pay hourly fees at Attorneys' rates as set forth in the attached Schedule. Attorney charges in minimum units of 0.25 hour. To the extent that monetary sanctions are awarded to Attorney during the course of this litigation for work actually charged to Clients, the sanctions award, if and to the extent actually paid, shall be credited against Attorneys' bill for that work. To the extent that the sanctions are recovered for work that was either not billed to Clients or not paid by Clients (whether by discount or otherwise), Attorney shall be entitled to retain such sanctions awards. If the sanctions award includes a cost item (such as the filing fee for making a motion), the amount thereof shall be credited to Clients' costs account when received by Attorney.

6. **No Guarantee as to Result.** Clients acknowledge that Attorney has made no guarantee or promise as to the outcome or the amounts recoverable in connection with Clients' claims. Attorney's comments about the outcome of Clients' matter are expressions of opinion only.

7. **Litigation Costs and Expenses.** Attorney is authorized to incur reasonable costs and expenses in performing legal services under this Agreement. Clients agree to pay for such costs and expenses on a monthly basis, and to advance such costs and expenses on request by Attorney.

   (a) *Particular costs and expenses:* The costs and expenses necessary in this case may include any or all of the following items. This list is not exclusive; other items may also be necessary, and the rates shown are subject to change upon prior written notice to Clients.

   - court filing fees;
   - process serving fees;
   - deposition fees (typically $800.00 or more per day);
   - fees to private investigators, photographers, or graphic artists;
   - fees to experts for consultation and/or for appearance at deposition or trial;
   - jury fees;
   - mail, messenger, and other delivery charges;
   - parking and/or other local travel at $.31/mile;
   - transportation, meals, lodging, and all other costs of necessary out-of-town travel;
   - long-distance telephone charges;
   - photocopying (in office) at $.25/page;
   - facsimiles at $1.00/per page;
   - computerized legal research.

(b) *Clients' responsibility for costs:* Clients are responsible for payment of all costs. In the case of multiple Clients, all such Clients are jointly and severally responsible for all costs incurred in representing Clients; *i.e.,* each Client is fully liable for the entire amount of costs, and Attorney has no obligation to apportion such costs among Clients. Attorney may advance additional costs and expenses on Clients' behalf, but is not obligated to do so. Clients agree to reimburse Attorney upon demand for any such advances. Attorney will provide a monthly billing to Clients listing costs, which shall be immediately paid by Clients. Clients are responsible for monthly reimbursement of all costs, regardless of the status or outcome of the litigation or the amount of any recovery.

(c) *Prior Client approval of costs:* Attorney agrees to obtain Clients' prior approval before incurring any costs or expenses as to any single item exceeding $1,000. Subject to this limitation, Clients authorize Attorney to incur all reasonable costs and to hire any investigators, consultants, or expert witnesses reasonably necessary in Attorney's judgment.

8. **Billing Statements.** Attorney shall send Clients periodic statements for fees and costs incurred. Clients shall pay Attorney's statements within 30 days after each statement's date. Clients may request a statement at intervals of no less than 30 days. Upon Clients' request, Attorney will provide a statement within 10 days.

9. **Withdrawal by Attorney.** Attorney may withdraw as counsel by giving written notice to Clients if Attorney deems it appropriate to do so. Among other things, Attorney may withdraw if Attorney or any Client believes there exists a conflict of interest with respect to this representation, if a Client fails to cooperate with Attorney, fails to comply with this Agreement, or requests Attorney to act in a manner that would violate the Rules of Professional Conduct of the State Bar of California. Such withdrawal shall not affect Clients' obligation to reimburse Attorney for costs previously incurred. In addition, Attorney shall be entitled to recover all costs and fees for work performed prior to withdrawal.

10. **Discharge by Clients.** Clients shall have the right to discharge Attorney at any time upon written notice to Attorney. Such discharge shall not affect Clients' obligation to pay Attorney's costs and fees.

11. **Conclusion of Services.** When Attorney's services conclude, whether by trial, settlement, or otherwise, all unpaid fees and costs shall become immediately due and payable.

12. **Acknowledgment of Value of Services and Attorney's Lien.** Clients shall review all billing statements received from Attorney, and promptly advise Attorney as to any charges or disbursements with which any Client disagrees. Clients' failure to dispute a charge or disbursement contained within an Attorney billing statement within 30 days of receipt of such statement shall constitute an acknowledgment by Clients that such fees and disbursements were necessarily and properly incurred in this matter. Attorney's billing rates are as set forth in

the attached schedule. These rates may be modified from time to time, and Attorney shall give Clients written notice of any such modification. To secure payment to Attorney of all sums due under this Agreement for services rendered or costs advanced, Clients hereby grant Attorney a lien on Clients' claim and any cause of action or lawsuit filed thereon, and to any recovery Clients may obtain, whether by settlement, judgment, or otherwise.

13. **Document Retention.** After Attorney's services conclude, Attorney will, upon Clients' request, deliver Clients' files to Clients. Otherwise, Attorney will maintain the files for 3 years. After 3 years, Attorney reserves the right to destroy some or all of such files. If the Clients request in writing that the files be maintained beyond 3 years, Clients agree to pay in advance to Attorney storage and administrative costs for continuing to maintain the files. In the case of multiple Clients, delivery of the files to any one of the Clients shall relieve Attorney of any further obligation to maintain or produce such files.

14. **Dispute Resolution.** Any disputes regarding this agreement shall be governed solely by California law, regardless of whether other laws or locations are involved in the representation. The exclusive forum and venue for any such dispute shall be in Los Angeles, California.

    Attorney and Clients agree to submit all disputes to binding arbitration by a single neutral arbitrator in Los Angeles selected by the parties, to be preceded by mediation with all parties present. The parties shall be entitled to reasonable discovery, and the California Rules of Evidence, Pleading and Procedure shall govern the arbitration. The arbitrator shall determine the dispute based solely on the law governing the claims at issue, and not on any other basis such as "just cause." Clients are advised that by agreeing to binding arbitration, they are giving up their right to a jury trial and other procedural aspects of a jury trial. Clients are also advised that they have an independent right to request a statutory fee arbitration, pursuant to Business & Professions Code section 6200. Any award in excess of $50,000.00 shall be subject to appeal to a second arbitrator, who shall proceed, as far as practicable, pursuant to the laws and procedure governing civil appeals in California.

15. **Privilege.** Clients acknowledge that they have been advised as to the operation of the Attorney-Client privilege, which protects the confidence of communications between Clients and Attorney, and that the protection afforded by such privilege may be waived should Clients disclose the content of Attorney-Client communications to third parties other than Clients, their independent counsel, or persons reasonably necessary to assist the foregoing. In the case of multiple Clients, they agree to share the privilege with regard to this litigation on a prospective basis, beginning with the execution of this Con-

tract, and Clients have been advised that communications between or among them will be privileged as to third parties but not as against each other. Specifically, in the event of any subsequent dispute between or among Clients, the documents and communications generated pursuant to the joint, shared privilege will not be privileged as between or among such Clients in any such dispute.

16. **Conflict of Interest.**

(a) All Clients wish to engage Attorney to represent them, and Clients agree that all of their interests in this matter are consistent and not in conflict. Based on the agreement between the Clients as to the necessity of undertaking the litigation and as to the allocation of any recovery therein, the interests of the Clients appear to be consistent with regard to this matter. Therefore, at this time, there does not seem to be any conflict of interest between the Clients, and the Clients agree to waive any potential conflict of interest. Each Client agrees to give Attorney written notice if it perceives an actual conflict of interest or a potential conflict to which it objects.

(b) To the extent that damages or settlement obligations or proceeds are clearly severable, each individual Client shall be entitled to receive or obligated to pay such damages or proceeds, as the case may be. Where settlement or damages, such as punitive damages, are awarded in a lump sum without any clear allocation, Clients agree to divide such recovery pro rata among each client.

(c) Attorney cannot represent or advise Clients as to any dispute between or among Clients, and specifically cannot advise Clients as to any allocation of damages or recovery in this matter. Clients specifically agree to waive any actual or potential conflict of interest that may arise because Attorney seeks or negotiates differing amounts for recovery or damages allocable to individual Clients, and they release and indemnify Attorney from any claim for a different share of such recovery or damages.

(d) Upon request or upon Attorney's discovery of an actual conflict of interest with respect to a particular Client, Attorney shall have the right to withdraw as to representing that Client unless Client shall waive such conflict in writing, but Attorney shall not be precluded from continuing to represent the remaining Clients. If a conflict develops between or among Clients with respect to this matter, Attorney shall not represent any Client against any other Client with respect to such dispute; however, Attorney shall be permitted to continue representing the remaining Clients in this litigation. Clients further agree that Attorney shall not be precluded from continuing or undertaking other matters on behalf of any of the Clients.

17. **Errors and Omissions Insurance.** Attorney maintains errors and omissions insurance.

18. **Severability and Enforceability.** It is the intent of the parties hereto that Attorney shall be fully compensated, accord-

ing to the contingency fee schedule, or, in the event of any discharge or termination of Attorney, for the reasonable value of Attorney's services at the rates set forth in the attached schedule. Accordingly, the parties intend that this Agreement shall be interpreted and enforced to carry out this intent, notwithstanding that any particular provision of this Agreement shall be declared unenforceable for any reason.

19. **Clients' Receipt of Agreement and Acknowledgment of Terms.** Clients acknowledge that they have read and fully understand all of the terms and conditions of this Agreement (including the attached Fee Schedule) before signing it. Clients acknowledge that they have had an opportunity to ask any questions and seek any clarification necessary to understand and approve this Agreement. Clients are entitled to and encouraged to seek the advice of independent counsel (at their own expense) if they have any questions or concerns regarding the terms of this Agreement. Clients acknowledge that they have received a copy of this Agreement upon execution thereof.

CLIENT:
_____

CLIENT:
_____

CLIENT:
_____

CLIENT:
_____

CLIENT:
_____

CLIENT:
_____

ATTORNEY:
THINK, SMART, BEFORE & FILING
By: _____

SCHEDULE OF ATTORNEY AND PARALEGAL FEES

Partners	Bill Blue	$300/hour
	Rich Red	$300/hour
	George Green	$300/hour
Associates	Vanessa Violet	$225/hour
	Penelope Pink	$195/hour
	Oscar Orange	$140/hour
	Yolanda Yellow	$140/hour
Legal Assistants	Pete Purple	$70/hour

These rates are subject to change by written notice. Attorney may, without further notice, contract with or employ additional counsel and legal assistants, who shall be billed at rates that are comparable to or in proportion to the rates set forth above.

Glossary

Actionable   Giving rise to an action at law. For example, breaching a contract is actionable; you can be sued for doing so.

Affidavit   A statement made under oath that can be accepted as sworn testimony at court.

Answer   A formal response filed by a defendant to deny the allegations in a complaint and assert defenses.

Appeal   To request that a more senior court or person review a decision of a subordinate court or person.

Arbitration   An alternative dispute resolution method by which an independent, neutral third person (arbitrator) is selected to hear and appraise the merits of a dispute and give a final and binding decision called an award. In contrast to the litigation process, the parties choose their arbitrator and the manner in which the arbitration will proceed.

Arbitrator   A neutral third person who reaches a decision in arbitration.

Attorney-client privilege   A legal principle granting confidentiality to most communications between an attorney and a client.

Award   The final and binding decision of an arbitrator.

Bad faith   Intent to deceive in order to gain some advantage over another person.

Bench trial   A trial with no jury; the finder of fact is instead the judge.

Cause of action   The legal definition of a claim made by one party against another.

Complaint   The initial document filed by a plaintiff to set out the details of his claims against the defendant, his demand for damages, and the nature of the dispute.

Confidentiality agreement   An agreement between parties to treat certain documents and evidence in the litigation in a way that protects privacy.

Contingency fee   A fee paid by a plaintiff and calculated as a percentage of the recovery, if any, arising from the plaintiff's dispute.

Costs   Litigation expenses other than fees for a lawyer's time or for the time of any of the lawyer's associates or office staff.

Cross-examination   At trial, the questioning of a witness by a lawyer whose client's position is adverse to that of the witness.

Debtor's Exam   A deposition taken by the winning side in a lawsuit to determine the financial condition of any party against whom a judgment has been made.

Declaratory relief   An order by the court sought by one party against another.

Defendant   The person, company, or organization who defends a legal action in which a plaintiff has asked the court to order damages or specific corrective action to redress some type of alleged unlawful or improper action.

Demurrer   A motion to strike some or all of the causes of action in a complaint.

Deposition   A formal question-and-answer session where the person being deposed (the deponent) is placed under oath and asked questions that may lead to the discovery of information relevant to the issues in the litigation.

Designation   The formal process of identifying any expert(s) who may be called upon to give expert opinion at trial.

Direct questioning   At trial, the initial questioning of a witness who supports the position of the party who is calling the witness.

Discovery   The formal process by which parties in a lawsuit use depositions, written questions, requests for admission, and requests for the production of documents to find out facts that may lead to the discovery of information relevant to the issues at controversy.

Discovery cutoff   A date set by statute close to the trial date (often thirty days before trial) by which most or all discovery must be taken.

Document   Any tangible thing that may be relevant or lead to the discovery of information relevant to the issues at controversy, including written documents, photographs, videos, recordings, artwork, and x-rays.

Document request   A formal request made by one party to another party—or to a third party—to obtain or copy documents that may lead to discovery of information relevant to the issues at controversy.

Election of remedies   A legal concept that states the plaintiff may choose between different kinds of relief he is seeking, but may not be able to obtain more than one kind of relief for a given controversy; he must elect one relief or another.

Exhibits   Documents to be presented to the jury or the judge (in a bench trial) during trial.

Ex parte   A Latin phrase meaning "for one party only"; refers to a proceeding where one party has not received notice and, therefore, is not present to defend himself.

Expert   An individual with specialized knowledge or experience whose expertise and testimony can help a finder of fact to understand a specialized area.

Fees   Charges, either hourly or contingent, for the work of a law firm's personnel on a matter.

Finder of fact   A person or persons charged with making factual or legal rulings on any legal matter. A judge is the finder of fact for motions and legal issues requiring a ruling; in a jury trial the jury is the finder of fact.

Frivolous lawsuit   A lawsuit lacking sufficient grounds or probable cause to sue the defendant.

Hearsay   Evidence offered by a witness who has no direct knowledge but is only repeating what others have said.

Independent medical exam   An examination of the alleged injuries and medical condition of a plaintiff, conducted by a medical doctor or health provider who is (theoretically) impartial.

Interrogatories   Written questions one party to a lawsuit asks another party.

Jurisdiction   A given court's authority to judge a given situation, as set by (1) the geographic location where acts complained of were committed; (2) the type of case (e.g., bankruptcy actions must be heard in bankruptcy court); and (3) who the person is (military courts have jurisdiction only over military personnel).

Jury instructions   A set of instructions read by a judge to a jury to advise the jurors how to apply the law to the facts in order to return a correct verdict.

Liability   The legal responsibility of one party for the consequences of his actions on another party.

Litigator   An attorney who specializes in representing parties in law suits.

Malicious prosecution   Filing a lawsuit against another party without reasonable cause to do so.

Mediation   A form of alternative dispute resolution that involves appointing a mediator to act as a facilitator, helping the parties communicate to negotiate a settlement. The mediator does not adjudicate the issues in dispute or force a compromise; only the parties, of their own volition, can shift their position in order to achieve a settlement.

Mediator   The independent person who facilitates a mediation process.

Meet and confer   The process, required in most jurisdictions, during which opposing attorneys meet to make a good-faith attempt to resolve disputes during litigation before filing a motion seeking the court's intervention.

Motion A formal, written application to the court during litigation to issue a specific order. After one party files the motion, the other party generally files an opposition to the motion, and the first party then files a reply. Oral arguments are made at court, and the judge issues a ruling.

Motion for Summary Adjudication A motion brought by a party to a lawsuit (usually the defendant) arguing that a portion of the case against him should be dismissed as a matter of law, and without going to a jury.

Motion for Summary Judgment A motion brought by a party to a lawsuit (usually the defendant) arguing that the entire case against him should be dismissed as a matter of law, and without going to a jury.

Motion to Dismiss A motion filed by a defendant to dismiss some or all of the plaintiff's complaint.

Motion to Quash A motion filed by a third party in a lawsuit to void a subpoena that has been issued.

Motion to Strike A motion filed by a defendant to remove some portion of the plaintiff's complaint.

Nonverified complaint A complaint that is not signed by the plaintiff.

Paralegal A nonlawyer who provides a limited number of legal services to a lawyer.

Party (to a lawsuit) A person, business, or government agency that is a plaintiff or defendant in a lawsuit.

Plaintiff An individual, company, or entity bringing a case to court; the party who is suing.

Precedent A case that determines legal principles to a given set of facts, making specific conclusions, and that is to be followed from that point on when comparable or analogous facts are before a court. Precedent gives litigants a reasonable expectation of what legal resolutions will apply in a given situation.

Qualifying Presenting an expert's credentials and experience in order to receive court approval for that expert to testify in his designated area of expertise.

Referee A court-appointed individual who hears discovery disputes and issues recommendations or recommended rulings.

Request for admission A formal written request served by one party upon another party, requesting that the party served admit certain facts as true.

Retainer A sum deposited with an attorney to ensure that the client's final bill will be paid.

Sanctions Monies awarded by the court against one party or his attorney, ordering that party or attorney to pay the opposing party or attorney a sum to compensate for bringing or opposing a motion without substantial justification. Often the sum of money is based on the amount of legal fees and costs the other side incurred regarding the motion.

Settlement   The outcome of a successful mediation; an agreement of the parties to a mediation.

Special interrogatories   A unique set of written questions that one party serves upon another.

Stay of judgment   An order from the court stopping payment of a judgment pending an appeal.

Subpoena   A court document ordering an individual or entity to produce documents and/or appear at a deposition or court matter.

Summons   A court document requiring an individual or entity to appear at court to answer a complaint.

Third Party   An individual who is not a party to a lawsuit but is involved in some other way, such as a witness.

Venue   The specific physical location of a judicial hearing.

Verified complaint   A complaint that the plaintiff has signed under penalty of perjury.

Witness   A person who perceived an event (by seeing, hearing, smelling, or other sensory perception).

Index

Actual damages, 77–78
Administration agencies, appealing
    decisions of, 277
Administrative proceedings, 70–71
Admissible information, 179–80
Affirmative defenses, 116–17
Alternative dispute resolution. See
    Arbitration; Mediation
American Arbitration Association
    (AAA), 234
Appeals
    for administration agencies deci-
        sions, 277
    for arbitration, 276–77
    basis for, 266–68
    costs for, 274–75
    defined, 265
    exchange of briefs for, 271
    filing notice of, 268–69
    finality of, 277
    hiring specialists for, 273–74
    oral arguments, 272
    right to, 266
    rulings, 272–73
Appellant, defined, 266
Appellant's Opening Brief, 271
Arbitration, 231–32. See also Media-
    tion
    appealing decisions, 276–77
Arbitrators, locating, 233–34
Assignment of rights, 66–67
Attorney-client privilege, 146–47
Attorney-client relationships, 301–7
Attorneys
    corporations and, 36–37
    fees for, and damages, 81–82
    finding, 34–35

interview questions for, 39–41
interviewing, 35
selecting, 36, 39
specialized, 42–43
treatment to expect from, 37–39

Bench trials, 69 70. See also Jury tri-
    als; Trials
    advantages of, 251
    experts and, 209
Bills. See Legal bills
Binding mediation, 226. See also
    Arbitration
Blowups, 237
Bond, posting, 269–70
Breach of contract, 56
Briefs, exchange of, 271
Budgets, for lawsuits, 14–16
Burden of proof, 61–62

Captions, 92
Case numbers, 92, 95, 109
Causes of action, defined, 56. See
    also Claims
Charts, 237
Choice of law provisions, 71–72
Citizenship, diversity of, 72
Claims
    appropriate, 57–59
    countering, 57
    defined, 56
    elements of, 57–59
    proving, 60
Clerks, law, 73
Client honesty, 299–300
Client-attorney relationships, 301–7
Common law system, 56

Communication
between attorney-client, 146–47
between husband-wife, 146
Communication protocols, 15
Compensatory damages, 77–78
Complaints, 87–88. *See also* Lawsuits;
Subpoenas
amending, 99–100
body section of, 95–97
captions in, 92
case numbers, 92, 95
countersuits to, 121
defendants' responses to, 113–14
defined, 88–89
Doe defendants in, 94–95
drafting proper, 89–90
exhibits to, 99
filing, 100–104
importance of understanding, 104–5
preliminary motions by defendants,
117–19
procedure for, 92–99
as public documents, 91–92
serving, 109–12
summary of damages section of,
96–97
titles, 95
types of answers to, 116–17
unverified, 97–99
verified, 97–99, 116
Compromise. *See* Arbitration; Mediation
Confidentiality agreements, 142–45
Consequential damages, 78
Consortium, loss of, 76
Constructive eviction, 57
Consultants, 207
Contingency fee arrangements, 21–23,
24–26
appropriateness of, 25–26
modified, 23–24
remaining in control in, 27–28
Continuing damages, 78
Contracts, 71–72
Copying costs, charging for, 294
Corporations
lawsuits and, 64–65

selection of lawyers and, 36–37
Cost-benefit analysis, of litigation,
29–32
Costs. *See* Legal costs; Legal fees
Counterclaims, 121
Countersuits, 121
Court forms, 57
Court reporters, 163
Creative settlements, 232–33
Credibility, of witnesses, 180–81
Cross-complaints, 121
Cross-examinations, preparing for,
240–43

Damages. *See also* Relief
attorney's fees and, 81–82
determining, 76–77, 80–81
discovery and, 82–85
excessive, and defendants, 82
monetary, 77–80
punitive, 84
requests for, 80–81
Debtor's Exam, 263
Declaratory relief, 60–61
Defendants
countersuits and, 121
defined, 55
demurrers by, 119–20
filing answers to complaints, 116–17
preliminary motions and, 117–19
responding to complaints, 113–15
service of complaints and, 112
strategy for summary judgment motion, 196–98
Demand letters, 47–49, 88
defense mentality for, 51–52
determining when to send, 49–50
precautions for, 53–54
successful, 50–51
Demurrers, 119–20
Depositions, 129, 130. *See also* Witnesses
answering questions during, 166,
171–73
arguing during, 170–71
basic rules for, 160–61
bringing notes for, 170

characterization during, 173–74
common objections during, 174
controlling pace of, 168–70
defined, 159
egos and, 162
"I don't recall." response, 166–68
limiting testimony during, 161
listening during, 166
lying and, 162–63
making good impressions during,
    163–64
out-of-state, 189
preparing for, 175–76
remaining focused during, 170
remaining silent during, 164–65
speaking audibly in, 163
speculation and, 165
swearing during, 171
understanding questions during,
    164
videotaping, 189
Designating the experts, 209–10
Designating the record, 270–71
Discoverable information, 179–80
Discovery
    confidentiality agreements and,
        142–45
    damages and, 82–85
    dangers of, 151–52
    defined, 124
    document request form of, 125–31
    as harassment, 152–54
    interrogatory form of, 131–39
    minimizing harassment during,
        155–57
    professional behavior for, 154–55
    request for admission form of, 140
    standard of, 124
Discovery referees, 141–42
Dispute resolution. See Arbitration;
    Mediation
Diversity of citizenship, 72
Documents
    defined, 126
    organizing, 45–47
    requests, 125–31
Doe defendants, 94–95

Elements, of claims, 57–59
Estimates, legal bills and, 286–87
Evidence. See Testimony
Excessive damages, 78
Exemplary damages, 78–79
Exhibits, 236–38
Expenses. See Legal costs; Legal fees
Experts. See also Witnesses
    bench trials and, 209
    budgeting for, 210–12
    common mistakes and problems
        with, 214
    cross-examining, 217–18
    designating, 209–10
    independent medical exams by,
        218–21
    jury trials and, 209
    need for, 208–9
    privilege and, 212–13
    qualifications of good, 214–15
    qualifying, 210
    reports by, 216–17
    rich defendants and, 213
    role of, 206–7
    vs. consultants, 207

Fact witnesses, 179–81
Faxes, charging for, 294
Federal courts, 72–74
Federal question jurisdiction, 72–73
Fee caps, 20–21
Files, orders sealing, 91–92
Filing systems, 15
Flat fees, 19
Form interrogatories, 132–39
Friendly witnesses, 160

General damages, 79

Hall, Charles, 66–67
Hostile witnesses, 161
Hourly fees, 19–20
    estimating, 28–29

IMEs. See Independent medical exams
    (IMEs)
Impeachment, 187

Independent medical exams (IMEs),
     218–21
Information
     admissible, 179–80
     discoverable, 179–80
Insurance coverage, 65–66
Interoffice conferences, 292–93
Interrogatories, 131–39
     form, 132–39
     special, 132–39
*Intex Plastic Sales Co. v. Charles
     Hall*, 66–67
Invoices. *See* Legal bills

Judges
     determining names of, with case
          numbers, 109
     disqualifying, 118
     federal, 73
     state, 73–74
Judgments, collecting, 263
Juries, 11–12, 69–70
     costs of, 254–55
     in federal courts, 74
     instructions for, 275–76
     selecting, 252–54
     in state courts, 74
Jurisdiction
     personal, 67–68
     subject matter, 68
Jury trials, 70, 247–48. *See also* Bench
     trials; Trials
     advantages of, 251–52
     experts and, 209

Law clerks, 73
Lawsuits
     budgets for, 14–16
     as business venture, 3
     cutting losses and, 12–13
     drafting, for federal or state courts,
          72–73
     estimating costs of, 3–4, 8–11
     insurance coverage for, 65–66
     pros and cons of, 5–6
     as stories, 58
     strain of, 4–5

taking inventory of, 12
Lawyer-client relationships, 301–7
Lawyers. *See* Attorneys
Legal advice, 6–8
Legal bills
     estimates and, 286–87
     examining, 281–84
     generating, 280–81
     interoffice conferences and, 292–93
     law firm costs and, 293–98
     lawyer education and, 284–86
     reviewing backup for, 298
     staffing and, 290–93
     telephone calls and, 289–90
     tips for containing, 287–89
Legal costs, 18–19, 293–98
Legal fees
     contingency fee basis, 21–23
     cost-benefit analysis of, 29–32
     fee caps, 20–21
     flat-fee basis, 19
     hourly fee basis, 19–20
     modified contingency basis, 23–24
Legal jargon, 104–5
Liquidated damages, 79
Litigation, typical costs of, 30
Litigation reaction, 2–3
Loss of consortium, 76

Material misrepresentation, 194
Meals, charging for, 295–96
Mediation. *See also* Arbitration
     binding, 226
     nonbinding, 226
     pitfalls of, 228–31
     process of, 224–26
     reasons for entering, 226–28
Mediators, locating, 233–34
Meet and confer requirements, 150–51
Mileage, charging for, 296
Monetary damages, 60
     actual, 77–78
     compensatory, 77–78
     consequential, 78
     continuing, 78
     excessive, 78
     exemplary, 78–79

general, 79
liquidated, 78
nominal, 78
presumed, 78
punitive, 78–79
special, 79–80
statutory, 79
treble, 80
Motions
to Compel, 128, 150, 154
defined, 149
for Directed Verdict, 250
to Have the Judgment Set Aside
    Notwithstanding the Verdict,
    268
in Limine, 255
for New Trial, 268
to Preclude, 256
for Protective Order, 150
to Quash, 145
Section 170.6, 118
to Set Aside Default, 113
for Summary Adjudication, 201–3
for Summary Judgment, 193–201,
    203

Negligence, 56
Net worth, discovery for, 84–85
Nominal damages, 79
Nonbinding mediation, 226
Notice of Appeal, 268–69
Notice pleading, 88

Parties, defined, 55–56
Partnerships, lawsuits and, 64–65
Party affiliate witnesses, 179
Patience, 15
Percipient witnesses, 179
Personal jurisdiction, 67–68
Phone calls, charging for, 295
Photocopying costs, charging for, 294
Plaintiffs
defined, 55
strategy for summary judgment mo-
    tion, 199–201
Pleading, rules for, 119–20
Post bond, 269–70

Prayer for relief, 88
Preliminary motions, 117–19
Preponderance of evidence, 61–62
Presumed damages, 79
Privileges
attorney-client, 146–47
spousal, 146
work product, 147
Process servers, 110–11
Proof, burden of, 61–62
Punitive damages, 78–79
discovery and, 84

Relief, 77
forms of, 60–61
prayer for, 88
Request
for admission, 140
for Identification and Production of
    Documents, 126–28
Respondent, defined, 266

Scorched earth style of litigation, 184
Section 170.6 Motion, 118
Service
of complaints, 109–12, 117
for discovery, 141
Special damages, 79–80
Special interrogatories, 132–39
Spousal privilege, 146
State courts, 72–74
State supreme court, 265
Statementizing, 187–88
Statute of limitations, 62–64
Statutory damages, 79
Stay of Judgment Pending Appeal,
    269–70
Stress, 15
Subject matter jurisdiction, 68
Subpoenas, 145. *See also* Complaints;
    Summons
Suing. *See* Summons
Summary judgment motion, 193–95,
    203
defendant's strategy for, 196–98
plaintiff's strategy for, 199–201
timing for filing, 195

Summons. *See also* Subpoenas
  response time for, 107–8
  rules and regulations for, 108–9
  serving, 109–12

Telephone calls, 289–90
Testimony, 160. *See also* Depositions
Themes, trial, 238–39
Third parties
  defined, 56
  subpoenas for, 145
Third-party witnesses. *See* Percipient
  witnesses
Transcripts, 163, 176
Travel, charging for, 296–98
Treble damages, 80
Trial lawyers, 261–62
Trials. *See also* Bench trials; Jury trials
  chronology of, 249–51
  collecting judgments, 263
  conduct at, 243–45, 260–61
  decisions about witnesses for, 256–59
  jury selection for, 252–54
  preparation costs of, 245
  preparing cross-examinations for,
    240–43
  preparing for, 235–40
  pretrial motions, 255–56
  rehearsing for, 244–45
  staying in peak readiness for, 243–44
  as theater, 248–49
  themes, 238–39
  types of, 69–71
  verdict forms for, 259–60
  witness preparation for, 238–40

Unavailable witnesses, 188–89
Unverified complaints, 97–99

Venue, 68–69, 71–72
Verdict forms, 259–60
Verdicts, reversing, 275–76
Verified complaints, 97–99, 116
Videotaping, 189

WHEREFORE, 96–97
Witnesses. *See also* Depositions;
  Experts
  biased, 181–82
  contacting, 182–84
  credibility of, 180–81
  determining potential, 178–79
  fact, 179–81
  friendly, 160
  hostile, 161
  lawyers representing, 189–90
  naming, 184–85
  obtaining statements from,
    187–88
  order of presentation of,
    257–58
  party affiliate, 179
  percipient, 179
  perspectives of, 185–87
  preparing, for cross-examinations,
    240–43
  preparing for trials, 238–40
  trial decisions about, 256–59
  unavailable, 188–89
Word processing, charging for, 295
Work product privileges, 147

About the Authors

Gerard P. Fox, Esq.

Gerry Fox wins important and challenging civil litigation matters for a wide variety of clients, including many entertainment stars. Fox graduated magna cum laude from Georgetown Law School in 1985 and, upon graduation, was the "number one draft pick" of several leading law firms. He was hired at Covington and Burling in Washington D.C., where he worked on litigation between the NFL and the USFL. Fox left Covington to work for Collier, Shannon, Rill & Scott in Georgetown, and soon found himself as lead counsel defending Cumberland Farms, a large company embroiled in a large lawsuit.

In 1990, Fox moved to Los Angeles to work with Pierce O'Donnell at Kay, Scholer, Firman, Hayes & Handler. At the time, O'Donnell was representing Art Buchwald in what was to be his successful suit against Paramount Studios over the film *Coming to America*. After working with O'Donnell on a variety of cases over three and-a-half years, Fox accepted an offer to work under well-known Hollywood litigators Howard King and Howard Weitzman at Katten Muchen Zavis & Weitzman.

In 1995 Fox opened his own law firm. His practice includes litigation on contract disputes, disputed royalties, copyright infringement, and general litigation. He is also considered an expert in handling "stalker" cases, and his clients have included Madonna and M.C. Hammer. Fox was also trial counsel for the Isley brothers in their successful suit against Michael Bolton, Sony, and Warner Chapel for copyright infringement over the song "Love Is a Wonderful Thing." Fox has six children; lives in Palos Verdes, California; loves baseball; loves to win; and hates to lose.

Jeffrey A. Nelson

Considered (by his wife and children) to be the most brilliant author in the universe, writer/producer Jeff Nelson has written and produced commercials, documentaries, TV movies, an NBC mini-series, and is the coauthor of the bestselling *Handwriting Analysis: Putting It to Work for You* (also published by NTC/Contemporary Publishing Group), with FBI graphologist Andrea McNichol. Nelson is the owner/operator of VegSource Interactive (http://www.vegsource.org), the most popular vegetarian website on the Internet. He lives in Los Angeles, California, with his wife, three children, two cats, and a dog.

Visit http://www.WinYourSuit.com to learn more about how to Sue the Bastards!